BLESSINGS or CURSES

For The Next Generation

BY DR. PETER WYNS

Great Reward Publishing

CONTENTS

DEDICATION

Only one person comes to mind as I think of a dedication for this book: my grandfather Derek Prince. I am named after him; his name is really Peter Derek Prince. I am very grateful to him, for I have benefited from the blessings that this book highlights because of him.

While Derek Prince was a missionary in the Holy Land, my Jewish mother (as a little girl) was adopted into his family. Years later, when I was born, I became a recipient of the generational blessings that he passed on to his descendants. As a young man, he became my spiritual mentor along with my father who was also a minister.

As an international Bible teacher, Grandpa Derek helped restore major truths to the church. He helped recapture powerful New Testament doctrines that many in the church seemed to overlook. In doing so, he often brought controversial themes to the table, and faced significant opposition from those who disagreed with his teaching.

Derek Prince championed such biblical teachings as: changing a nation through prayer and fasting; God's end-time purposes for Israel; the five-fold ministry gifts; deliverance from demons; responsibility and accountability for church workers; foundations for Christian living; caring for widows, orphans, and the poor; and of course, breaking generational curses.

His book on breaking generational curses is his most popular theological writing. I gladly dedicate this book to him, for without his teaching on the subject, I do not think that the church at large would be functioning in this essential ministry today.

With more than 50 books in print, a huge number of teaching tapes and CDs in circulation, thousands of spiritually powerful meetings and a world-wide radio ministry, Grandpa Derek impacted the church around the world. Everywhere I minister, someone inevitably approaches me to tell me of the life-changing encounter they experienced under Grandpa Derek's ministry. He became famous because of his sound doctrine and because of the powerful miracles that followed the preaching of God's word. In my opinion, he was what a five-fold ministry teacher should be. He taught the word of God with authority but also demonstrated God's power with healings and deliverance. In this regard, few modern-day Bible teachers have done what Derek Prince did.

Week after week, as I minister to different groups and churches, I am faced with challenging situations and I often ask the question, "What would Jesus do if He were here in the flesh, ministering to these people?" I also find myself asking, "What would Grandpa Derek do?"

More often than not, I find myself preaching the same themes as he did and praying for the multitudes as he did. Although I am very different from him, I have come to recognize that the supernatural anointing that Grandpa carried is flowing through me. I remember the time that He and Ruth laid their hands on me and blessed me with Grandpa's ministry mantle. I am thankful for the spiritual heritage and the ministry mantle that Derek Prince confirmed and released in me. My aim is to be a man of God who impacts the world and serves my generation as well as he did.

Although at this time I cannot see him, I am sure that from his vantage point in heaven, he can see me. Grandpa Derek, I dedicate *Blessings or Curses for the Next Generation* in honor of you. Thank you for who you are, for the great part you played in the kingdom of God and for the many blessings that you released into my life.

Your Grateful Grandson,
Peter Derek Wyns

ACKNOWLEDGMENTS

I exend special acknowledgments to my wife Joy, who is my partner in the ministry. She prays, prophesies, and brings words of knowledge and wisdom as we minister together. Her counseling skills, especially with women, are amazing and her discernment and other supernatural gifts in the Holy Spirit are essential for the work of the ministry that we do.

And to Mary Greene and Jesse Enns, my son-in-law, who did the re-edits for this second printing. And to my son Matthew Wyns, who organized and procured the design work for the printing of the book.

INTRODUCTION

A GLOBAL RECOGNITION OF CURSES

People, the world over, recognize the existence of curses and their effect on families. Even non-Christians will say, "What goes around – comes around." Some may not believe in a supreme creator, but they still fear curses and instinctively know that extreme wicked behavior will produce a backlash of unsolvable trouble.

MODERN CHURCH THINKING

The opposite is also true; much modern thinking has led to a sanitized spiritual position. It refuses to believe in such phenomena as demons and curses. This oversight has become popular in some quarters of the Church. It is a head-in-the-sand perspective and it is far removed from the true teachings of scripture. Jesus cast out demons, and the Bible describes the trauma of curses from Genesis to Revelation; yet many believers completely ignore these subjects as if they are inconsequential.

CHRISTIAN COUNSELING

When Christians encounter people who have deep problems, many point to the need for counseling. Their reasoning suggests that if a troubled person can vent their struggles and get their thinking

adjusted by a Christian counselor, then their psychosomatic weaknesses will be removed. Some seem to believe that educated profession-
als can heal the wounded hearted through Christian psychotherapy.

In my opinion, modern psychotherapy is not helpful, but good Bible-
based Christian counseling is. It can help a person understand their
spiritual dilemma. It can be instrumental in leading a person to believe in Christ, to assist a person in recognizing and repenting of their
sins and to help them forgive and bless their abusers. These directives
are often given through a Christian counselor and that is a wonderful
ministry. These dynamics are necessary steps for salvation and healing, and those who follow them will find great blessings. Sometimes,
however, there is need for much deeper ministry, and traditional
Christian counseling is not enough. Only the power of the Holy Spirit and the authority of the cross, ministered with power and anointing, can drive away demons and break devastating curses. Unless a
counselor is willing to break generational curses and deliver a person
from demon spirits, their work with many people will be incomplete.

THIS BOOK

Christians who have called out to God for salvation have secured their place in heaven, but many are still living in pain and
turmoil. Millions are spiritually, economically, physically or socially dysfunctional and are demonized. Families are plagued
with unreasonable troubles and catastrophic problems, and to
them, it does not make sense. They need more help than the average church is providing. They are afflicted with harassments and
are frustrated with their lives even though they are Christians.
This book has been written to help restore the biblical truths about
blessings and curses and to help equip God's people to minister to
others more effectively.

The first section of this book is a study on biblical blessings: how to receive them and how to release them to one's family.

The second section of this book is a study of curses. It focuses on the sources, causes and the effects of curses.

The third section of this book is a study of how to minister to people's deeper problems. Salvation moves people from a position of darkness to light but does not immediately remove all of the darkness that is in them. All of God's light is not released to a person at the moment they pray a prayer of dedication. From my study of the scriptures and my personal experience in the ministry, I have gathered insights that will help equip ministers for their work in the ministry. Along with other dynamics, this includes the ministry of breaking generational curses.

I ask all who read this book to do so prayerfully. May the Holy Spirit use *Blessings or Curses for the Next Generation* for the deliverance of many individuals and families. My prayer is that God will use this book to help teach Christians all around the world to partner with Him in setting captives free and releasing the amazing blessings of heaven.

PART ONE

BLESSINGS COME
FROM GOD

Chapter One

THE ULTIMATE BLESSING

REACH MUCH HIGHER

As a Christian, I want to see every person become a believer, every believer become a disciple, and every disciple become a minister for Christ. Once we become ministers, we have two assignments:

1. To shift people from the kingdom of darkness to the kingdom of light.

2. To help people distance themselves from every evil, such as generational curses, and to help them receive more of God's abundant blessings. Blessings from above include everything that is good. God is love; He wants us to be blessed. The Apostle Peter taught us that we are called by God to the purpose of receiving blessings. It is heaven's intention to bless people.

Peter said, *"You were called* [by God] *so that you may inherit a blessing"* (1 Pet 3:9).

Some believers seem to think that they received everything when they became Christians. They act as though they have taken hold of every blessing that was paid for them by Christ's death on the cross. The truth is that nobody on the earth has yet received all that was provided for them on the cross.

Even the amazing Apostle Paul said, *"Not that I have already obtained all this, or have already been made perfect, but I press on to take hold of that for which Christ Jesus took hold of me. Brothers, I do not consider myself yet to have taken hold of it. But… I press on toward the goal to win the prize for which God has called me …"* (Php. 3:12-15).

There are so many more blessings available to us than what any of us have received so far. In the Bible passage that introduces the Ten Commandments, we discover that curses can trouble a family for four generations, but blessings can extend over a family for a thousand generations.

We read, *"…God, punishing the children for the sin of the fathers to the third and fourth generation … but showing love to a thousand generations of those who love me and keep my commandments"* (Ex. 20:5-6).

THE THOUSAND GENERATION BLESSING

At this early stage in our study, I want to focus on the blessings. The Bible says that a "thousand generation blessing" is possible. This is literally out of this world because the human race has only been around for 300 generations. Calculate with me. Let us say that a new generation comes every 20 years. This means that in 100 years there are only 5 generations. At that rate, there are 50 generations in every one thousand years.

If humankind has existed for 6 thousand years since Adam

then the human race contains only 6 X 50 generations. That adds up to 300 generations since Adam. If you receive God's thousand generation blessing, it means that you and all of your generations are blessed for all of this life and for eternity as well.

Besides the length of time involved in the thousand generation blessing, the intensity of the thousand generation blessing is even better. It is extremely powerful; it is accumulative and progressive. If two consecutive generations walk with God, the power of blessings over that family will be great. If three or four generations of a family walk close to God, the blessings over that family will be even more potent

There is a build-up of spiritual strength and a special anointing that every godly grandparent wants to see for their great grandchildren. This is the battle for the glory of God. Great individuals, like Paul, have reached high for this blessing, and it is in the reaching that they touch the heart of God.

THE PROBLEM

The problem is that curse-causing sins bring judgments that undo God's blessings. Man's folly requires restoration, and when humans fall, the next generation must reestablish the power of the thousand generation blessing over a family. This is especially necessary when it has been lost because of curse-causing sins. This requires repentance, intercession, godly living, good works, sacrifice, intimacy with God, and a powerful, active faith.

There is no blessing more powerful than the thousand generation blessing. It is the ultimate blessing, and those who press into God for this blessing can restore entire families to the path of greatness. These people are warriors who fight for the glory of God; they are partners with Jesus in bringing the kingdom of God to their families and to the earth.

A ROYAL FAMILY

Salvation, and even the supernatural gifts of the Holy Spirit, are not earned. God gives them freely to all who will receive Him and exercise faith. Even first generation Christians can have a powerful ministry and a great anointing.

The thousand generation blessing, however, is quite different. It releases a level of peace, joy, godliness and holiness that causes a family to glow with spiritual strength. It is a godly anointing on a family that leaves a blessing on each of its members, on the neighborhood they live in and even on their nation. The children of the thousand-generation blessing shine bright and the parents of that family are admired as patriarchs who walk in the ways of God. The family with the thousand generation blessing becomes full of honor, dignity and strength. They radiate God's peace, express a never-ending joy and possess a righteousness that is refreshing and wholesome. This righteousness can never be found by obeying legalistic rules or heavy handed religion. The thousand generation blessing is a deposit of God's glory, and only He can give it. It comes out of friendship with God. Christians should walk in partnership with God until they receive the thousand generation blessing for their families.

SEEING MANY GENERATIONS

Most of us are not thinking of the thousand generation blessing; we are concerned only for the immediate generations that we can see, for our children and grandchildren. The thousand generation focus, however, embraces the heart of God. It looks as far as the millennial reign of Christ and beyond. It inspires us to reign in this life as though we were already ruling in the millennium. This focus will seat us in heavenly places with our Lord, cause us to be over-comers, and to reign with Christ in this life.

Adam had the thousand generation blessing on his life, but the sin of witchcraft (communicating with and obeying the devil) caused him to lose the fullness of the blessing. He was driven out of the garden.

Even after the Adamic curse was in effect, the early patriarchs lived to be almost a thousand years old. It was easy for them to observe the effects of blessings and curses on the generations because people lived long enough to personally see many generations alive at the same time. They were witnesses of the long-term effects of sowing and reaping on families. They saw terrible judgments caused by accumulated evil, and they saw the powerful intensity of accumulated blessings as well.

For example, Adam lived for 930 years. His son, Seth, knew Enoch. Enoch was the seventh from Adam, and he was Seth's great, great, great, great, great-grandson. Seth was still alive for another 53 years after the great man, Enoch, who walked with God, was taken up into heaven without dying. Seth witnessed the amazing thousand generation blessing that rested on Enoch.

Noah lived for 950 years. Abraham and Sarah were alive, and more than 50 years old, when Noah died. They could have met him. They were related to him even though they were born 11 generations after him. It is no wonder that Abraham had the faith to look for a city that had foundations built by God. God found a man, in Abraham, who earned the right to be called the father of the faithful. Abraham was not born in a vacuum; he received the powerful story of Noah probably from somebody who had met Noah, and it marked him for life.

Shem, the son of Noah, died when he was 600 years old. Jacob and Esau, the grandchildren of Abraham, were 48 years old when Shem died. Like Abraham, they could have met him or talked to people who knew Noah's family personally. Surely they talked about the godly man named Noah, who they were all related to. Noah walked so close to God that he found God's grace to be saved when the rest of humanity was destroyed in the flood. Adam, Enoch, Noah, Abraham and many others witnessed the power of the thousand generation blessing.

GENERATIONS IN THE MILLENIUM

In the new millennium, after the second coming of Christ and the resurrection of the dead, people will live for a thousand years again. At that time, most people will be immortal but some will be mortal. We know that many are mortal because they will die when Satan is released from the Abyss to tempt the nations (see Revelation 20:9). Some of these mortals will have babies and will live for a thousand years. They will see many new generations emerge (see Isaiah 65:20,23). Like with the early patriarchs, people will witness the power of accumulated blessings and see many living under the power of the thousand generation blessing.

We are living in the time period between the ancient patriarchs and the new millennium. In this age, life is much shorter, and we can only see a few generations on the earth at one time. The power of the thousand generation blessing is still in effect though, and it is our task to reach for it.

WALKING WITH GOD

The secret to receiving more of God's blessings lies in walking with God. The Bible tells us of three levels of walking with God.

1. Many godly people have ***walked in the ways of the Lord***. This is hearing and obeying the commandments of God. It brings great blessings

2. Many godly people have ***walked before the Lord***. This is a step up from walking in the ways of the Lord. It is a constant presenting of our lives to God and living in response to the leading of the Holy Spirit. This activity releases even greater blessings into our lives.

3. Only a few people have actually ***walked with God Almighty***. The Bible gives us only three names: Adam; Enoch; and Noah, who walked with God. It is the goal of every disciple to one day walk with the Almighty. One day, in eternity, it will happen (see Revelation 22:3). For now, we reach forward and draw as close to God as we can.

All of these walking steps are wonderful. Each level of intimacy with God releases more of the thousand generation blessing. Because of the thousand generation blessing, Adam was in unified partnership with God, Enoch obtained a special intimacy with God, Noah found an exceptional grace from God, and Abraham saw it and received an extraordinary faith from God.

EXPECT GREAT BLESSINGS

Get ready; great days are ahead of us! Before the return of the Lord, many saints will walk so close to God that the thousand generation blessing will fall on them. Some will gain the power to live through the great tribulation and witness the second coming of Christ. They will witness the greatest miracles, gain unbelievable protection, and be used of God to bring about the greatest revivals in all of history (see my book *Unexpected Fire*). Some will even overcome the devil during the great tribulation.

They will do it by the blood of the Lamb and the power of their testimony, and they will not be afraid to die (see Revelation 12:11).

Press into God as much as you can and reach high. Reach for the thousand generation blessing for your family. As this blessing comes, you will receive the blessings of Adam, Enoch, Noah and Abraham.

PREACH THE IDEAL, HANDLE THE REAL

I felt it was important to begin this book by describing the ultimate blessing. Like Paul, we should reach for it; there is always more of God to receive. We should keep the hope of the thousand generation blessing before us and wrestle with the angel of the Lord, as Jacob did, until we receive it.

We may preach God's thousand generation blessing as our goal, but we must also face the present situation that we find ourselves and our families in, today. That is why we study to understand ancestral curses and biblical blessings. This book is intended to move people from the curses and bring them to the blessings. It is designed to bring change to you and your family. This change is described in the scriptures. The Bible tells us that the path of the just (a godly Christian) is as a bright light that gets brighter until it reaches the full brightness of noon day (see Proverbs 4:18).

As we continue this study, we humble ourselves, open our spiritual ears and listen to the Lord. We pray that the Holy Spirit who is our teacher, our comforter and also the one who releases God's authority and power in our lives, will give us revelation and equip us for change. We open our hearts and minds to the Holy Spirit, and we receive by faith that which comes from Him.

Chapter Two

THE ANCESTRAL SUITCASE

HISTORY HAS CONSEQUENCES

Our family history continues to unfold every day because we are adding to it. No person lives in isolation; we have a legacy behind us and a deposit to give to those who follow us. All of us play a role in a six-thousand year epic story that is filled with so much tragedy and triumph.

Each of us is born with generational baggage. Hidden in our prenatal suitcase is the spiritual DNA of our ancestors. The luggage has been passed down to us from the past and its contents will have a profound effect upon our behavior, status and disposition in life. It is not just biological information, personality traits and physical similarities that we have inherited from our folks. With all of that, we have also received a legacy of blessings and curses.

Some of our own acts and choices, whether good or bad, will be added to the luggage as well. Our family suitcase will get larger as we add our personal contributions. We will pass on to our children what we have received from our ancestors and some of our strengths and weaknesses will be added to it.

GENERATIONAL FLOORBOARDS

The spiritual DNA of parents, provide the first platform that children stand on, giving them their initial foundations. The floorboards that children receive may be strong and beautiful like the marble of a palace. Conversely, the platform may be made of rotten wood. We could pass on to our children a rickety floor that is so nasty it will not hold their weight. It may resemble a condemned floor of an old, abandoned farmhouse. Some children have very little to stand on when they come into this world. Their floor is moldy, bug eaten and falling apart. Only the mercies of God and the compassion of other people can save these disadvantaged children from utter destruction.

Every person in the world passes on a mixture of blessings and curses for the next generation. Most people do not experience the extremes of evil or kindness but live somewhere in the middle. A lot of people, however, will make some major mistakes, like having an abortion for example. They will often carry those mistakes with them, unresolved, to the grave. If their failures were bad enough to produce curses, those curses will not stay in the grave. They will be passed on as judgments that will affect their children.

The choice is before us: some celebrate godliness while others celebrate evil. Some embrace extreme righteousness; they live holy lives and pass blessings on to their children. Other people dive into extreme wickedness; they live like the devil and their evil existence produces a legacy of ruin and disaster for their children. As you consider your own ancestors and their behavior, which category do they fall into?

We cannot know all the details of our grandparents' lives. Even the very best of saints may pass on unknown curses because of their grandparents' folly. Likewise, the worst offenders of righteousness may have had a great-grandmother who walked before the Lord.

Her life and prayers have provided a secret strength and an unknown blessing. One godly grandparent may be the only reason why some people are not living in a totally hellish existence.

Not every action in life becomes part of the ancetral suitcase. Godly activities and vile wickedness, however, will leave their mark. Godly exploits, holy living and outstanding acts of sacrificial kindness will release powerful blessings that will give a head start to our children. Alternately, heinous crimes, perversions, and a lifestyle of evil will produce debilitating curses for those who follow.

It is time to ask the deep, probing questions, "What things are in my ancestral suitcase, and what am I passing on to my children?"

The Bible says, *". . . none of us lives to himself alone and none of us dies to himself alone"* (Rom. 14:7)

BIBLICAL EVIDENCE

Blessings and curses are clearly documented throughout history. Even before the Jews became God's chosen people, the Bible narrative reveals the effects of generational blessings and curses on people. In the scriptures, mothers, fathers, rulers and leaders are shown to be godly heroes or unscrupulous villains. Their behavior had consequences for their children. They set in motion chain reactions that affected the generations that followed.

The pattern begins with the first family; they entertained witchcraft. Eve broke God's law and listened to the devil, and a curse came down upon every woman because they are her daughters. In a similar manner, Adam also broke God's law, and a generational curse came down upon the entire human race. Every person on earth is presently under a generational curse because of Adam's sin. If this were not true, no one would die.

We see the pattern continue after Adam. Ham, one of Noah's sons, dishonored him and a curse passed on to Noah's grandson, Canaan (see Genesis 9:22-25).

Thank goodness it is not just curses that are generational, and God-sent blessings are much more powerful! We see this in the story of Phinehas. Psalms 106 describes a long list of sins that were committed by the people of Israel. Curses fell on Israel because of their sins, but a man named Phinehas stands out as a hero. Because of him, God blessed his descendants forever. In the following scripture, we read of Israel's sin of witchcraft and then of the zeal of this godly man named Phinehas and the generational blessing that was given to him.

"They yoked themselves to the Baal of Peor and ate sacrifices offered to lifeless gods; they provoked the Lord to anger by their wicked deeds, and a plague broke out among them [Numbers 25]. *But Phinehas stood and intervened, and the plague was checked. **This was credited to him as righteousness for endless generations to come"***
(Psalm 106:28-31 - emphasis mine)

Another stand-out verse that describes God's amazing generational blessings can be found in Romans chapter eleven.

"As far as the gospel is concerned, they [the Jews] *are enemies on your account; but as far as election is concerned, they are loved on account of the patriarchs."*   (Rom. 11:28).

Paul says that the Jews, who would not come to Christ, are enemies of the gospel but they are still blessed because of the patriarchs. Abraham, Jacob, Moses and David are some of the patriarchs who became God's friends. They acted valiantly and God blessed their descendants. Even when their generational sons and daughters walked away from God, He continued to love those children because their fathers walked with God. Like the ancient patriarchs, our behavior has a powerful effect upon our children and the generations that follow.

TEN COMMANDMENTS

The truth of generational blessings and curses comes to light in the writings and teachings of the Ten Commandments. Here is a section of the Ten Commandment as recorded in the Bible.

"I, the Lord your God, am a jealous God, punishing the children for the sin of the fathers to the third and fourth generation of those who hate me, but showing love to a thousand generations of those who love me and keep my commandments" (Ex. 20:5-6).

It is not sound doctrine to agree with the parts of the Bible that we like, and discard the parts we do not like. Many Christians will warmly embrace the Ten Commandments yet reject the thought of generational judgments (curses) or blessings. The Ten Commandments teach us that ancestral downloads are a reality. The truth of generational blessings and curses is bound together with the Ten Commandments. In order to be consistent, we must embrace one with the other.

OUR PERSONAL SUITCASE

All of us have a large ancestral suitcase. It is full to the brim with the spiritual DNA of our mothers and fathers. Some things in the suitcase are special gifts, but some things are time bombs that need to be defused and removed. It is for freedom that Christ has set us free. We have not received salvation to remain in a prison built by the sins of our ancestors. Sort it out. Act valiantly, and do what is necessary to prepare your family so that they might receive the blessings of God.

Chapter Three

MY FATHER'S SUITCASE

PERSONAL EXAMPLES HELP

No one likes to uncover their family's dark secrets. Knowing some of them, however, and being brave enough to talk about them with redemptive intentions can give insights of a family's strengths and weaknesses. Hopefully, a bit of our family story, given discretely, will serve others who are in desperate need. I see my parents as heroes. I pray that the example of their healing and restoration will bring hope, instruction and strength to others.

I have included these next two chapters about my mom and dad at the beginning of this book to show the reader that all of us have stuff to work through. My family and I have battled with curses and have overcome. With God's help there is hope for every family.

This chapter reveals some of the stuff my father had to overcome to provide a good platform for the lives of his children. The next chapter uncovers some of the details of my mother's heritage. The details are sketchy, but it is not difficult to read between the lines and see the on-going strengths as well as the setbacks that both of my parents so gallantly faced.

I know that my parents, like many others, overcame extreme

hardships and spiritual obstacles that were common to their generation. Many people reading this book will join with me in giving thanks for their parents and grandparents, for their resilience and strength. Together we lift our voices and thank God for them.

DAD – WHERE DID YOU COME FROM?

Irvine George Wyns, my dad, was born in Ossa Holling, Inner Mongolia, which is actually part of northern China. We will call it Mongolia, for that is how it was referred to in the many stories I heard as I was growing up. Dad spent the first 7 years of his life with his mother, my Grandma Clara. Dad and his older sister were raised on the mission field in a small, dusty out-of-the-way town, called Gashatey. That is where Thomas and Louise Hindle established their mission compound and led, "Mongolia for Messiah Missions". They were the founders of the mission where my grandparents served.

Before going to China, Grandma Clara was a missionary to the Native Indian people of Lethbridge, Alberta, Canada. Her first husband died just after they were married and in time, she married George, the man who would become my grandfather. The two of them boarded an ocean liner and left the shores of Vancouver in May of 1920. They left Canada to begin a new life as missionaries in Mongolia.

Months later they arrived at their destination, and as they had been warned, it was a wild and hostile environment set on the outer fringes of the Gobi Desert. Already Grandma was pregnant and she soon gave birth to my Aunt Maliya, which I have been told, is Mary in Chinese.

The people of Gashatey did not connect well with foreigners. They were closed to outsiders and it was hard to win their trust; nevertheless, they were in desperate need of the gospel. A few examples will help to illustrate the depravity of their lives. They lived under a demonic stronghold of witchcraft, superstition, poverty and unrestrained violence. Curses hung over their lives making their existence miserable.

One demon-inspired act that was popular among the local people was the binding of the feet of baby girls. My dad would hear the screams of innocent children as their tiny feet were twisted and bound tight by their parents every night. A cloth was pulled around their toes forcing them to be bent under the child's feet. The girls wore these restrains all of their lives. As they grew into adulthood, their feet remained the size of a young child's. The women were unable to walk or run properly; they could only hobble. They were kept subservient by their husbands. Years later, the act was outlawed by the government, but it was the tradition for hundreds of years and was very popular during my father's childhood. This barbaric act was just one of a long list of demon inspired superstitions that were instigated to keep the women under their control.

Girls, as a whole, reaped the worst horrors of this society. Another demonic custom was to dispose of newborn baby girls. Some were abandoned and left to die because parents were poor and girls were not as useful as boys. Usually they were discarded like garbage in the dry river bed where they would be eaten by wolves. Before abandoning them, their parents would burn a hole in their backs to ward off evil spirits, and then they would give them over to the afterlife. Grandma Clara was able to find, rescue, and raise some of these children. One of those little girls became a foster sister and a childhood playmate for my dad. They called her Mary.

Every week, gangs of robbers riding horse-back would tear up the desert and descend upon the village to rape and pillage. They were mostly ex-soldiers who had gone AWOL to escape Sun Yat-sen and Chiang Kia-shek's armies. Thousands of these mercenaries, some more vile than others, were on the lam, living like pirates of the desert. They were always on the move, invading vulnerable communities, and it seemed that one of their favorite haunts was Gashatey. The closest police station was 200 miles away, and the police marshals who visited town were few and far between.

There in Gashatey, George and Clara Wyns poured out their lives in love and sacrifice to help a poor group of very needy people. My grandparents were constantly living in harm's way, yet their efforts were rewarded. They helped save thousands of people from starvation, gave hundreds of children an education and saw many converts won for Christ. As that happened, curses were broken, foolish superstitions and acts of witchcraft were halted, and people began to understand the freedoms of Christ. For many years, the missionaries of Gashatey were involved in feeding, praying for and preaching to the robbers. The nomadic raiders were a mission field in their own rite, and most of them were hungry to learn the story of the Christian God and find some hope for their miserable and desperate lives.

TRAGEDY STRUCK

About a year and a half into their tour of ministry, tragedy fell upon my grandparents. My grandfather, George, suddenly left Mongolia and returned to Canada. Grandma Clara stayed behind to continue her missionary work. By this time she had two children. Clara had her precious baby Maliya, and she had just given birth to another child. Irvine, my father, had come into the world.

As a young boy growing up, I heard Dad tell of miracles and many amazing stories that took place on the Mongolian missionfield. We children would probe to find out why grandpa left, and the answer would always be the same. Dad didn't really know the details, but said he was told by Grandma that Grandpa had to leave because of heatstroke. Many questions were left unanswered.

For the rest of his life, my dad was not reunited with his father. He had no contact with him until 1952, when he located him and was able to correspond by letter. Here are a few paragraphs from reply letters that my grandfather sent to Dad.

April 29, 1952

Dear Irvine,

It is with difficulty that I attempt to answer your touching and sympathetic letter. I am indeed grateful son to you and the authorities here and am trying to show my gratitude in the only way I know — that is humility. I did many questionable things before being admitted here thinking they were in God's will, only to discover later on, they were my own rebellious nature.

I am distressed to hear of your dear wife's demise and mourned for her as though she were my own. There are certain questions you asked in your letter which I do not feel at liberty to answer . . . suffice it to say, yes I remember everything that transpired in Mongolia.

November 19th 1952

My Dear Son,

It is with difficulty that I write this letter, but it must be done. First of all dear boy I feel I owe you an apology, or do I ?

received your first letter on May 31st but refrained from answering it thinking I might catch up on my strength sufficient to do myself justice, but adverse conditions proved directly to the contrary. What those conditions are, are best summed up in Burns. On his "Epistle to a Young Friend," he writes:

[Peter Wyns gives his interpretation of Burns, following each line, to help the reader understand]

"Aye free, aff-han', your story tell,

["Yes, free but half-hang back, your story tell,]

When wi' a bosom crony;

[When with a bosom buddy;]

But something to yoursel',

[But still some things you must keep to yourself,]

Ye scarcely tell to ony:"

After receiving your first letter and meditating on suitable words for a reply — I was under constant inspiration of the Holy Ghost.

I read with much regret about your recent bereavements; they are mine too! Perhaps the Lord is allowing such things to happen . . . as a means to draw us still closer to himself. Let's hope so. Have faith in God. I well can remember your birth away back in 1923, as I held you in my arms. With toothless gums you looked up *into my face and laughed — you were just one month old — and bubbling over with confidence. Now at the age of 29, I want you to hold the same faith and confidence in Almighty God to straighten out this tangle. There are a good many things I would like to write about but I must close for now. Wishing you all a Merry Christmas and a Happy New Year..*

Your Loving Father,

George Wyns

HULDA HINDLE

Several years ago, I visited my father's closest childhood friend, Hulda Hindle. She now has a different last name through marriage, but she was one of the daughters of Thomas and Louise Hindle, the founders of Mongolia for Messiah Missions. She grew up playing as a child with Dad on the mission field. She was 5 years older than Dad and knew details of my grandfather's departure from Mongolia that he did not know. Over the years, she was able to put together more pieces of the puzzle. She was able to talk things through with her parents. Although, Grandma Clara would not talk about Grandpa George with my dad, Hulda reluctantly told me what she could.

GRANDPA GEORGE

Hulda said that my grandfather was a godly man but that he had a lot of baggage. Apparently, grandpa had some hidden and some not so hidden problems. He was apprehended by the police marshal and was told that he had to leave China because of his disorderly and violent conduct. Hulda said he was an angry man and he would beat his wife during times of great frustration. She said that his moral conduct was also suspect.

Gashatey, with its isolation, demonic strongholds and warring thieves, was a place that brought both the best and the worst out in people. I do not think that Grandpa George was an evil man, but there are no excuses for beating your wife or being promiscuous. Grandpa had curses on his life that needed to be broken. He also needed an understanding of generational blessings and his responsibility to bless his children. His personal failures, however, added to the negative baggage that he had inherited. Dark curses, most of them unknown, haunted him for most of his life and eventually they affected his family.

GRANDMA CLARA

Over the next 7 and 1/2 years, Grandma Clara served the Lord Jesus like a Mother Teresa in Mongolia. Young Irvine, Maliya and Hulda were shielded from most of the trauma, and despite the hardships, they have only good memories of life in Gashatey. Grandma, however, became so weary that she ended up being burned out. During the last two years of her ministry there, Thomas and Louise Hindle left her in charge of the mission while they returned home to Canada for a much needed furlough.

Replacement missionaries were hard to come by for such a place as Gashatey, so Grandma and Miss Fordam, her assistant, ran the mission. They had help from some men who were Chinese and Mongolian evangelists. They had received Christ at the mission-station and were on fire with the message of the gospel. Often, these bold missionaries were on a mission of their own, visiting other villages to spread the message of Christ's love. Most of the time, Clara and Miss Fordham were leading the cause of Christ in this hostile place without the help of any men.

TRAUMA IN ENGLAND

In 1929, a weary and worn out worker, my grandmother, left for England on furlough. It seemed that she left her heart in China. Although it was her wish, she was never able to return. Further trauma came upon her in London. She and her two children found a place to live in a single room in the home of her poor sister Alice. What follows is a sad story. Grandma received almost no honor or recognition for her outstanding work abroad because no one knew her in England. She had been sent to the mission-field from Canada, and it seems that she had no money or reason to return to Canada. For the rest of her life, she lived in poverty, and the only job she could get was cleaning houses. In those days, that job did not pay well, but she was hard working and it was better than nothing. Dad said she never stopped being a powerful woman of faith, and she lived to the end of her days with the joy of the Lord. When World War II broke out, Maliya died in a bombing raid, and Grandma Clara died a couple of years later from cancer.

Even though Grandma had served the Lord so well, the power of curses seemed to undo all that she worked for - at least in this life. Clara Wyns should have received the Biblical blessings of wealth and honor, and she should have enjoyed a good old age. She was, in fact, robbed of all of these things.

It is not that there was no pleasure during their time in England. Life is always a mixture of things, and they enjoyed many good times, but the special blessings were definitely blocked from reaching them. I have no doubt that these blessings were blocked by curses. The generational curses should have been broken off before she ever went to China. It has taken a couple of generations to put our family back on the blessings track once again.

Despite the weariness and poverty that came upon her in the last years of her life, Grandma Clara is a great hero to me. I am confident that she wears a brilliant crown today and that her heroic life is one of the reasons that I continue to receive God's grace and favor.

MY DAD

By the time Grandma Clara died, Dad was married and was a fine young preacher. He was blessed to sit under the ministry of such anointed men as Smith Wigglesworth and George Jefferies. He and his wife, Doreen, had 5 children when he became an assistant pastor to Derek Prince in a newly formed church in London. Then another great tragedy struck the family. Doreen, Dad's wife, died while giving birth to twins. One of the babies died as well. My dad was so beaten up inside that he even entertained thoughts of suicide. He had seen so much pain. His sister, his mother, and now his beloved wife and newborn had died. Years later, he told me that he wanted to die and it was only because he had other children, whom he loved and needed to care for, that he continued on. Only God's grace and mercies were sufficient to bring him through that season.

In time, Dad married again. Magdalene, one of Derek and Lydia's adopted Jewish daughters became his wife. I am her firstborn. Besides me, another 4 children were born into the family, bringing the total to eleven children. This book does not allow the space to adequately relay the story of our move to Canada or my parents' hardship and poverty in the years that followed, but I must give some details.

I was 3 years old when, in 1957, my dad and mom moved across the Atlantic. By this time, Dad's father had already passed away. My dad flew to Toronto to secure a job, purchase a home and send for the family. Everything happened as planned, and Dad called for the family to come. On the very day we arrived from England, Dad lost his job along with 8,000 other workers who were laid off with him. Soon after, Dad was broke and his newly purchased second-hand car was repossessed. He began digging septic tanks and ditches for minimum wage and mom, who had 11 children, went to work as well. She worked the night shift, leaving her children to be raised, some of the time, by their older siblings and Dad.

The enormous suffering and pain of my father's years in England and the traumas he faced in Canada, ripped at the soul of our family and left some of my siblings with deep scars. I know that heavy generational curses have come down upon our family from distant generations. As mentioned earlier, I do not place the lion share of blame at the feet of Grandpa George, but on the generations before him. On the other hand, I really thank God for a grandmother who paid a great price, and I thank God for a very special father who stood his ground, believed God, and fought for the blessings of heaven to fall upon his children.

DAD'S TRIUMPH

When the family came to Canada, Dad and Mom were determined to start a new life, but it took a couple of decades to really see the blessings of the Lord. Eventually, the blessings proved to be far more powerful than the curses. My parents broke the pattern of curses and catapulted the family into a blessed future.

Even in what seemed to be the worst of times, I never saw Dad lacking in faith. Regardless of his disposition he was always and forever a positive overcomer. I never heard a complaint of financial lack come from his lips, nor did he ever stop praising the Lord. Besides being a mechanical tradesman in the early years, Dad was a powerful preacher. As a pastor, he helped so many people and those of his generation say that his leadership in their lives produced for them the best times they ever had. They tell stories of how Dad brought them through difficulties when they had no strength of their own.

A couple of years ago I was the keynote speaker at the 40 year anniversary of the church that Dad planted in Toronto, Canada. The testimonies about the love given from my dad and mom to those people were absolutely fantastic. It was amazing to realize again, that during the years when my parents were in great financial turmoil, they founded and built this church and rescued and strengthened so many people. Even in a time of great trauma, Dad was a powerful man of God; his sacrifice laid a godly foundation for so many people.

BLESSINGS NOW

As I look at our family today, I realize that of the eleven children, none have suffered from poverty. Five of Dad's sons have become preachers of the gospel, some with international ministries. By the time I became a man, Dad and Mom were already financially stable. They never made a lot of money as pastors, but they invested their savings in their homes and when Dad went to be with the Lord just a couple of years ago, he left more than $350,000 to be shared among his children. Most children in our society do not receive 30 thousand dollars as an inheritance, but my dad, who fought with the shield of faith, gave more than that to each of his children. I know that he turned the corner from curses to blessings for our family.

Dad was the last surviving member of his family. If he had died without children, our Wyns family would be no more. He had very weak floorboards to stand on when he was born. I thank God that he and Mom rebuilt the family floor and laid new planks for me and my children to stand on. Today, Dad and Mom have more than 85 descendants, and what a privilege it is to be a part of this great family. The blessings of God are everywhere, and we are so proud of our children and what they are accomplishing for Christ.

Dad is looking down from heaven upon many grandchildren and great grandchildren who serve the Lord with dignity and grace. Many are ministers, and each generation seems to be stronger than the previous one. After curse-breaking prayers, generations of faith and acts of good works, it is clear that the blessings have overtaken the curses. Our family is flourishing in the goodness of the Lord.

MY BROTHERS AND I

To bring things to the next level, my brothers and I went a step further. Several years ago my 4 preacher brothers and I met in England to pray for each other and break off the generational curses over our family. We had such a powerful experience together. We enjoyed great fellowship, but it was a fabulous time of spiritual breakthrough, as well. I believe that we suffered some backlash from the powers of darkness because of the ground we took during those days, but a battle was fought and a good foundation was laid.. It will serve many generations to come.

Today, we continue to teach our children about the power of blessings and curses. We are thrilled to watch them raise their own families under an open heaven of blessings. Our prayer is that you will press on to win the prize of God's blessings for your family as well. No matter how deep the hole or how dark the path, it can be changed. The Lord Jesus will help all who put their trust in Him.

In the next chapter, I will tell you my mother's story. She was adopted by Lydia and Derek Prince.

Chapter Four

MY MOTHER'S SUITCASE

BEYOND WORDS

Miryam Magdalene Katz was my mother. Her friends called her Magdalene. My precious last minutes with her were very dramatic, for she was prepared for her imminent departure, but I was not. She was lying on a Florida hospital bed with more than 20 family members gathered around. Mom was so full of joy and faith, even though she was well aware that she was dying. I was not thinking that her passing would come so soon and was about to return home to Canada for a few days. I leaned over her bed and said, "Mom, I have to go back to Canada, but I will see you soon."

Her response came without a flicker of hesitation. With contentment and peace radiating from her face, she responded, "No, you won't Peter; you will see me in the resurrection."

I immediately fell apart! I leaned over, hugged her and quickly turned away, as I tried to hide the gush of tears and the painful emotions that overtook me. I cried for most of the next day. Within 24 hours after arriving home, I received the news that Mom had gone to be with Jesus. To my regret, her departure had come much quicker than I had expected. I wish I had stayed.

Our entire family fell into an extended season of mourning. The grieving, in one sense, was not for her because we were well aware of her victory. We knew she was with the Lord, that she was sharing the joys of heaven alongside of Jesus. It may sound unusual, but amid the great mixture of uncontrollable emotions, most of our crying was because we felt such enormous loss; we were missing her so much.

I have heard that most of the family cried, off and on, for at least a year after Mom passed. She was such a source of enthusiasm, laughter and love and now she was not with us. Simply put, she was more special to her family and friends than words can convey.

TROUBLE IN PALESTINE

For the purpose of this book, I want to tell you about her victory over curses. I will have to be brief, for it would be easy for me to write many chapters as I reminisce about her.

Miryam Magdalene Katz was born to Penina Katz in the Jewish town of Tel Aviv on January 1, 1934. History records that the world at that time was very anti-Semitic, and Mom, of course, was a Jewess.

Hatred and persecution against the Jews had been a perpetual event, not for centuries, but for thousands of years. Long before the II World War, racial aggression against God's chosen people had boiled and simmered and erupted with such violence that hundreds of thousands of Jews had been murdered.

In 1933, another holocaust was brewing against the Jews, and this time it would be worse than all of the previous ones combined. One year to the month, after mom was born, Hitler took power as both president and chancellor of Germany. It was not Germany alone, however, that harbored distain toward the Jews. The entire world was set against them, and this hatred was certainly felt throughout the Middle East.

With all of the pressures conspiring against it, Palestine, as it was called, was spinning in a vortex of trouble. The people were caught in a grinding crucible of ethnic strife and frustration. Besides the mountain of daily hardships that burdened the people, the region had been under British occupation since World War I. The locals were past the point of desperation; they wanted their freedom and independence. A problem like cancer was rapidly growing throughout the land because both Jews and Arabs wanted ownership, and the Brits had, on separate occasions, promised Palestine to both parties.

A stronger force than any British occupation was inciting lay in the hearts of the people of Palestine. It was the historical and spiritual conviction that both Jews and Arabs held: each thought they were entitled to rule over Jerusalem and the surrounding country. The region was being squeezed beneath the pending weight of 3 violent fronts:

1. The early stages of civil war between Jews and Arabs
2. The ongoing violence toward their British overseers
3. The dramatic increase of anti-Semitism that would soon find its climax in the devastating holocaust of World War II

Perhaps more immediate than the civic unrest, was the on-going threat of criminal activity, the constant economic strain and the desperate struggle for simple everyday provisions. Poverty, disease and lack of essential amenities were everyday challenges for the local people. The entire region was steaming and getting ready to blow, and Palestine was at the top of the metaphorical Middle East volcano.

LYDIA CHRISTIANSEN

It seems strange that a single, unmarried Danish woman would be called by God to be a missionary to such a place, at such a time as this; nevertheless, God sent Lydia Christiansen to the Holy Land. She arrived in Palestine without financial backing and set herself up in the town of Ramallah just 20 miles north of Jerusalem. In keeping with her call, she began witnessing and sharing the gospel with both Jews and Arabs. Immediately, she came up against a stiff wall of opposition and discovered that her ministry attempts were unsuccessful. No one would listen to her. She was a woman, and more to the point, she was a Christian woman. Lydia was soon battling the discouraging setbacks of starting a new ministry in a foreign and fragile land. Financial lack combined with the heavy shunning was a constant challenge to her faith; but at a time when Lydia felt like a complete failure, something unexpected happened.

It was nothing she anticipated or even wanted, but disadvantaged Jews began bringing their children to her. For one reason or another, they were unable to keep these children, and Lydia took them into her tiny one room home and cared for them. As a result, the local women became friendly. They began to visit her and her tiny brood of orphans. They saw her love for the children and soon opened their hearts, and Lydia was able to share the good news of Christ with them.

RESCUED FROM DEATH'S DOOR

Before long, Lydia was caring for 4 children in her one room apartment. Her toilet was an outhouse in the back and her drinking water came from the communal pump out on the street. One day, amidst the noise of her crying children, a knock was heard at the door. With the youngest child still in her arms, Lydia opened it and there before her stood a weary looking, middle-aged rabbi. He appeared anxious and his clothes were disheveled. He was carrying a newborn child in his arms. He introduced himself and then, right on the doorstep, asked if Lydia would take the baby into her care. Without hesitation, Lydia refused, citing her lack of a proper facility and the 4 children she was already mother-ing. The rabbi was crestfallen; he turned slowly and walked away.

The next day, as the winter rains were falling heavy, Lydia heard a knock and opened the door again. There standing in the torrential downpour was the same rabbi looking even more desperate than he had the day before. He was totally drenched, as if he had walked for miles to arrive at her door. Immediately, without even speaking, he threw the bundle of rags he was carrying into Lydia's arms and ran off down the street.

After closing the door, Lydia laid the tender bundle on her bed. She knew this was the baby who had been presented to her the day before. As she pulled back the soaking wet blanket from the child's body, a birth certificate appeared. It read, "Miryam Katz", and upon seeing it, Lydia discovered that the infant had only been born 5 days earlier. That little bundle was my mom.

As Lydia began undressing the infant, she realized that little Miryam had not been changed or properly fed for a long time. In fact, the child was very ill, and without some immediate attention, this new-born would die. As she undressed her, the baby's skin began to peel off because her clothing was stuck to her body. Her crying was weak. She was in pain. Lydia named her Magdalene Miryam Chris-tiansen - "Magdal", for short. Lydia loved Magdalene and em-braced her with the same care that she gave the other 4 children. She nursed Mom back to health as if this tiny baby was her own. Lydia cared for more than 80 children during her mission years in the

Holy Land and sometime over the years that followed, Magdalene won her heart and became one of the 8 adopted daughters of Lydia and Derek Prince. Years later, one more baby girl, this one from Kenya, would be added to the family to bring the total to 9 adopted girls.

TRUTH AND TRAGEDY

Soon after Lydia took my mother under her care, the neighbors learned of the story, and word came back that the rabbi was indeed the father of the child. Some said they knew who he was and where he lived. Although we cannot be definitive in the telling of the story, it would appear that the rabbi had a secret affair with the young lady, Penina, who conceived out of wedlock. She was taken to the hospital in Tel Aviv, a town on the Mediterranean coast, to deliver her child.

In recent years, as we have tried to trace our heritage, the name Magdalene Miryam has raised more than a few eyebrows among the Jews. A Jewish friend told us that a name like Mom's was usually given to one who was born out of wedlock, and the baby's mother was likely a woman of questionable morality.

The rabbi, although a sinner, was likely a God-fearing man, and, if so, he would have no part in helping to procure an abortion for the baby. Any Jew who believed in the Bible would know that an abortion would result in a far more devastating curse coming upon him and his family. He would avoid that at any cost.

In a land of such poverty and strife, the young mother, Penina, could not care for the child, and the rabbi would not entertain the possibility of bringing his secret offspring into his own home. That could result in the ruin of his family and great disgrace in the Jewish community. His family and, for sure, his traditional Jewish world would come unglued if word of his sinful behavior became public. If that happened, many more people would suffer. So from our vantagepoint, it seems apparent that he tried to keep the entire matter a secret.

The rabbi could have taken the baby to a government orphanage; the British authorities had set up several such institutions throughout the land. If he did that, however, his sin would be known, and the trouble he was trying to avoid would come crashing down upon his family. He probably felt he had no choice but to secretly give the child to a kindhearted foreign missionary. He had heard of this gentile Christian lady - this new, so called, "Mother-in-Zion." Although it would be unconventional to give a Jewish baby to a gentile, the rabbi had thought it through. This was best for the baby and for everyone involved, so he took little Miryam to Ramallah. With unwavering determination, he threw the baby into Lydia's care and when he did, Magdalene landed in the arms of God.

Betrayal, abandonment and rejection created the ancestral floor that my mother was placed on when she was born. The anti-Semitism and the sin of her birth parents are all we know for sure, but much worse horrors could have been hiding in the deep corners of her ancestral suitcase. For certain, there were piles of curses that hung over her when she was born.

WHAT AN AMAZING MOM

You do not know my mom, but if you did, you would never forget her. She was the kindest, most giving person that you could meet. In her youth, she was absolutely gorgeous, but she was also rugged like a tomboy. Village violence in Ramallah forced Derek and Lydia and their 8 children to move to a different home in the relative safety of Jerusalem. Magdal was the rough and tumble girl in the family. As a child, she was always in trouble for climbing the mulberry and pomegranate trees in the front yard of their home.

When Mom was 15, the family was still living in Jerusalem when the blue and white flag was hoisted and Israel became a nation. The very next day, the Jewish war of independence erupted throughout Israel and as soon as possible, the family got out of the country. Derek and Lydia took the girls and boarded the last available plane for London, England.

MAGDALENE GETS MARRIED

Three years later, at the young age of 18, Magdalene married Irvine. He was already the father of 6 children, and one of them was just an infant. No one worked more diligently than Mom as she filled the gap and cared for her new family. It seemed that her love, however, could never be enough for the children of her new family. They, like many grieving children, had a difficult time accepting their father's new wife. With the pain of the loss of their mother, the children often reacted to Mom in their frustration. Those were trying days for the young, beautiful, newly married Jewish girl who had all the pressures of being an adopted child herself.

Within a year, I was born and over the next 10 years, Mom had another 4 children besides me. As I mentioned in the previous chapter, this brought the total number of children in the family to 11. In 1957, when Mom was only 23, she boarded an ocean liner bound for Canada with 8 children at her side. Dad had gone to Canada 3 months earlier to secure a job and find a home for the family. He was a tool and die maker, and soon after arriving in Canada, he secured a good job at an aircraft design and production factory.

Dad was very diligent. He bought an older home and a used station wagon car; then he counted the days, waiting anxiously for his family to arrive. The very day that we arrived in Canada, the A.V. Roe aircraft factory cancelled their production of the famous Avro Arrow airplane and Dad, along with thousands of other workers, was laid off.

Like when Dad's mom left the mission field of Mongolia and moved to England, the family, now in Canada, fell under a cloud of serious poverty. It was a return performance or an apparent generational repeat. During the first 10 years in Canada, dire poverty and teenage strife caused great pains within the family.

Mom was an amazing champion through it all; she held things together with great fortitude. With babies at home, she was forced to go to work late at night on a packaging line. She also worked out of the home as a seamstress, and finally she ran a boarding house with 10 boarders - as if her own family was not large enough! Alongside of Dad, she did what she could to put food on the table and raise a family for God.

APOSTLE OF HOSPITALITY

Within the first year of moving to Canada and for the next 45 years, mom was a pastor's wife. Dad would not allow the struggles of life to stop him from serving the Lord, and Mom was of the same mind. They continued to live in faith, joy and happiness, regardless of the trials they faced. As a boy, I remember the laughter and the fun that filled our home as friends came to visit. Everyone seemed to love the fellowship they had with my mom and dad.

After several years, Mom started and ran a daycare center out of our newly acquired church building. Besides her regular responsibilities, she was also busy leading the women's ministries within the church. She was such an amazing example for so many women, and her unusual gift of hospitality always stood out. Every Sunday, at least half a dozen church people would be invited to our home for lunch. Dad did not force this task on her; on the contrary, she would be telling

Dad who she had invited for the meal. Then we would sit down to, what is still to this day, a regular Sunday tradition (Mom passed it on to Joy). It consists of tender roast beef with rich gravy, roasted potatoes, carrots, corn and delicious Yorkshire pudding. All of this was topped with some fancy dessert like English trifle.

Nobody could visit our home for the first time without my mother giving them a personal gift. She would take a picture off of the wall or bring a knickknack out from a drawer and give it to our guest before they left. It was not anything of great value but something small and beautiful. People around the world have kept the precious treasures that they received from Mom; they have often told me so. Mom's love and care for all who came to our home was so personal and so amazing that I nicknamed her "The Apostle of Hospitality."

Our family calendar seemed to revolve around her. She was the glue that held our family together. Mom and Dad's visit was always the highlight of any season. When she came she would sew something, wallpaper a room or cook a favorite dish. She never came to any of her children's or grandchildren's homes without bringing a suitcase full of gifts for everyone. Her love and service to her family became a powerful expression of God's tenderness and kindness to all of us. No one in the world could be missed more than my mother is by her family and friends. There was just no one like her.

FROM CURSES TO BLESSINGS

As with my dad, my mom displaced the curses of her rough start and her questionable heritage and released an unusual blessing on her children. No doubt, there was a great mixture of blessings and curses that she inherited. Her Jewish heritage included many Biblical blessings, and Mom knew how to fight hard, walk with God and tap into them.

Furthermore, when she was adopted by Lydia and Derek Prince, she received added blessings because they were God's special friends. She honored them and took hold of the marvelous spiritual inheritance that they gained through their ministry unto the Lord. It is no small thing to be descendants of Lydia and Derek Prince, even if the linage has come to us through adoption.

Whatever curses had come from Mom's birth experience or from her ancestor's sins have been overcome and displaced by the power of godly blessings. In place of judgments, she embraced the kindness and faithfulness of God. Her life of heartfelt service to the Lord was an example of righteousness, peace and joy, and God blessed her and enabled her to give a great spiritual foundation to her children.

A BLESSINGS FUNNEL

Looking over my own life, I am taken aback at the thought of the many layered blessings that have come down upon me. In effect, I have had three sets of godly grandparents. Clara and George Wyns, the rabbi and Penina Katz, and Derek and Lydia Prince.

I know that each of my grandparents, in their own way, fought hard against many ungodly forces. Through the tests and many failures of life, they did their best and God has honored them. Then my mom and dad took what they had been given and made it better. I know now that I have had an amazing head-start in the ministry because of their diligence.

I have lived beneath an invisible funnel that has allowed a continuous stream of godly blessings to be poured out upon me and my family. My children and their many cousins have an even better foundation because each generation within the family is shining brighter than the one before. If great volumes were to be written about my family, they would be full of stories of blessings that have overtaken curses.

Our ongoing prayer is for greater godliness and multiplied blessings for our family. May your family, like ours, rise up in partnership with Jesus to break through the heavy prisons and chains and
receive the abundant blessings of God.

Chapter Five

WHAT ARE BIBLICAL BLESSINGS?

KING DAVID'S LIFE

The famous and sometimes infamous life of King David has all the markings of blessings and curses. The focus of this chapter is not to dwell on curses, so we will not spend much time on those details. Still, for our purpose, it is instructive to note that David committed adultery with young Bathsheba. Then he murdered her husband by telling the general of his army to place Uriah in such a situation where he would be killed by the enemy. Later, the prophet, Nathan, came before David and uncovered all he had done.

David was a fallen man. He was cursed (punished) by God and as a result, his and Bathsheba's first child died and 25 thousand people within his kingdom also died. Notice that those under his authority bore the brunt of his actions; they received a generational curse. His fatherhood and national leadership negatively impacted his child and the citizens within his domain.

David's family was later torn apart by his son Absalom who betrayed him and David spent most of his life warding off attacking armies.

His hands became bloody with war, and because of that, David was forbidden to build the temple. He had to forfeit the honor of building the temple, which was his inheritance and destiny, because of the sins he had committed. Without going into the details of these and other aspects of his failure, it is easy to see that a great malaise came over him because of the terrible sins he committed. In the end, those sins were very expensive. He and those around him suffered greatly because of them.

DAVID - THE MAN OF GOD

Even with such negative behavior, the scripture reveals that David was a man after God's own heart. Despite enormous failures, he walked with God. He was not a perverse or evil man; he was a good man who fell into sin. David did not live a lifestyle of wickedness, and after he sinned, he repented. Severe judgments came to David, but God also blessed him greatly because he was a man after God's own heart.

At the end of David's life, the scripture says of him, *"David son of Jesse was king over all Israel. He ruled over Israel forty years – seven in Hebron and thirty-three in Jerusalem. He died at a good old age, having enjoyed long life, wealth and honor. His son Solomon succeeded him as king"* (1 Chr. 29:26-28).

Here are the 3 biblical blessings: long life, wealth and honor.

SOLOMON'S WISDOM

Solomon, David's son, succeeded David on the throne of Israel. Like David, his father, some of Solomon's writings became part of the Bible. Most of the book of Proverbs was written by him. Proverbs is a book that highlights the blessings of wisdom and the curses that come from foolish living. We will look at the 3 biblical blessings as described by King Solomon. It is obvious that he learned much by observing the life of his father.

THREE BIBLICAL BLESSINGS

The Bible reveals many blessings, but there are 3 main blessings that stand out from all others. They include long life, wealth and honor, and the scripture records that God gave all 3 of them to David.

Proverbs chapter 3 is dedicated to the study of these three Biblical blessings. Take special note of the first four verses:

"My son, do not forget my teaching, but keep my commands in your heart, for they will prolong your life many years and bring you prosperity. Let love and faithfulness never leave you; bind them around your neck, write them on the tablet of your heart. Then you will win favor and a good name in the sight of God and man" (Pro. 3:1-4).

This passage reveals that obedience, love and faithfulness will produce the 3 biblical blessings. Godly behavior brings long life, prosperity and a good name (honor).

All blessings and curses are a direct result of human behavior. If we act wickedly, curses follow and affect generations to come. If, however, we walk with God, then blessings come. Godly behavior is called wisdom. Notice that long life, riches and honor are connected to wisdom.

"Long life is in her [wisdom's] *right hand; in her* [wisdom's] *left hand are riches and honor"* (Pro. 3:16).

When we walk in wisdom, our right and left hands will possess long life, riches and honor. Proverbs 3 has much more to say about these blessings.

LONG LIFE

Long life is the first commandment with promise.

The book of Ephesians says, *"'Honor your father and mother'-which is the first commandment with a promise - 'that it may go well with you and that you may enjoy long life on the earth'"* (Eph. 6:2-3).

INCLUDING ENJOYMENT

David not only lived long, he enjoyed a good old age. God's blessing of long life comes with a package of other blessings. This package includes good health, peace of mind and godly purpose. Who wants to extend their life if it is full of extreme misery and suffering? I think that only those who fear death want to stay alive if their quality of life has been reduced to a painful existence sustained only by life support systems.

Most seniors that I know tell me that if they have lived a long life and they find themselves in need of extensive life support systems, then it is time to go. If they are living in great pain, and they are so incapacitated that they are not able to care for themselves or be of benefit to others, and if they are unable to communicate or interact with life, then they want to die. Especially if they are a wearisome drain on the family and they know that their time has come, then they want to leave the planet and make a victorious journey into God's presence.

INCLUDING GOOD HEALTH

Proverbs 3, our blessings chapter, gives us more instruction.

It says, *"Trust in the Lord with all your heart and lean not on your own understanding; in all your ways acknowledge him, and he will make your paths straight. Do not be wise in your own eyes; fear the Lord and shun evil. This will bring health to your body and nourishment to your bones"* (Pro. 3:5-8).

Trusting the Lord explicitly, walking in humility and turning away from evil will result in good health; it will bring nourishment to your bones. Your blood is made in your bones. Good blood and a strong skeletal system are huge components of good health. That is part of God's blessing for long life.

INCLUDING PEACE

The blessing of long life also includes peace. Proverbs 3 reveals more benefits for those who live with wisdom.

We read, *"Her* [wisdom] *ways are pleasant ways, and all her paths are peace ... Then you will go your way in safety, and your foot will not stumble; when you lie down, you will not be afraid; when you lie down, your sleep will be sweet. Have no fear of sudden disaster or of the ruin that overtakes the wicked, for the Lord will be your confidence and will keep your foot from being snared"* (Pro. 3:17,23-25).

Many seniors do not finish their twilight years in peace. They are tormented, fearful and overcome with worry. The long life blessing that God gives is so powerful that it brings safety from enemies, pleasant ways, peace of mind, sweet sleep and strong confidence.

INCLUDING PURPOSE

Meaningful and purposeful existence is part of the godly blessings of long life. Proverbs 3 says that wisdom produces a productive life.

"She [wisdom] *is a tree of life to those who embrace her; those who lay*

hold of her will be blessed" (Pro. 3:18).

Here are some of the purposeful activities that often accompany wise seniors. The long life blessing from God will be fruitful even to the end. Wisdom is a tree of life that continues to grow, producing fruit and shade for others. The productive life of a blessed senior brings help to the next generation.

1. Grandparents may become the most significant example and the most important friend for their grandchildren.

2. They may become pillars in the church. This requires solid leadership; it includes being a spiritual father or mother.

3. Some blessed seniors will rise to national or regional positions in government. This often happens only after they become seniors

4. Others who are blessed with long life find themselves writing their acquired wisdom into books for the next generation.

5. Some go to a mission field because at this time in their lives they have the finances and the freedom to do it.

6. In the latter years of life, many saints have the resources to help finance other ministries. This is an amazing blessing because many missions have been held back because of a lack of financial support. A senior, led by the Holy Spirit, can be used to launch the purposes of God. Their gift is indispensible.

FULFILLING YOUR DESTINY

Many who are blessed of the Lord discover that the most meaningful and productive years of their lives come after they reach the good age of 60. Some will still have 20, 30 or even 40 years of usefulness in front of them and they will learn to relish and savor those dynamic years like a piece of fine Belgian chocolate.

The long life that comes as a blessing from God gives a person the time they need to fulfil their destiny. It affords the peace and safety that is necessary to enjoy those years and be full of purpose. Those who are blessed will enjoy life because their efforts are making a powerful difference in the lives of others.

WEALTH

The second great biblical blessing is wealth, and Proverbs 3, our blessings chapter, has much to say about it.

"Keep my commands in your heart for they will ... bring you prosperity" (Pro. 3:1-2).

"Honor the Lord with your wealth, with the firstfruits of all your crops; then your barns will be filled to overflowing, and your vats will brim over with new wine" (Pro. 3:9-10).

The blessings of godly wealth comes as we honor the Lord with the firstfruits of what we have. This involves giving tithes and offerings to the Lord. The key phrase is "honor the Lord." Let me explain.

If a parent asks a child to stop what he is doing and clean his room, it may be a great challenge for that child. This could be true if his play time is being interrupted. He may argue, complain or even refuse to obey. That child is not honoring their parent. What a wonderful blessing it would be if the child, when asked to clean their room, would jump to his feet with cheerful obedience. The child would be honoring the parent. That would be an amazing, feel good moment for the parent.

God is not just asking us to give a portion of our finances to Him, He is asking us to honor him with our giving. That means we give of our firstfruits. We give a tenth (see Malachi 3:8) of all we make to the Lord as soon as we receive it. We do not wait to see how our budget will work out. Then, on top of that, we add special offerings to our tithe as soon as the Lord prompts us. Our swift actions and eager attitude honor the Lord. Giving cheerfully and promptly without worry or hesitation communicates our trust in God's ability to take care of us. It is a matter of the heart. Like the willing child who promptly cleans his room, we honor the Lord with a cheerful immediate response. *"God loves a cheerful giver"* (2 Cor. 9:7).

Proverbs 3 emphasizes the importance of promptness when we give to others as well.

We read, *"Do not withhold good from those who deserve it, when it is in your power to act. Do not say to your neighbor, 'Come back later; I'll give it tomorrow' – when you now have it with you"* (Pro. 3:27-28).

Some say that King Solomon (the writer of proverbs) was the richest man who ever lived. Today, we have more than a thousand billionaires in the world, so I am not sure if Solomon's boast still holds, nevertheless, he was very rich. He tells us not to be envious of the wicked if they have great wealth. He strongly advises us not to follow their example, for they may have money, but they are not rich. Listen to Solomon's words.

"Do not envy a violent man . . . [because of his great wealth] *or choose any of his ways, for the Lord detests a perverse man but takes the upright into his confidence"* (Pro. 3:31-32).

It is wrong to envy a wicked or perverse man because they have a lot of money. There are many people in the world who have become rich because of evil crimes and ungodly behavior. Solomon warns against following after them; he says that the Lord detests them. No man is wealthy if God detests him.

Wealth is enjoyable when God brings a person into His confidence. The upright become God's friends, and He shares His secrets with them. They enjoy a wealth that the wicked will never know.

Wealth, like long life, must be qualified. Long life must be accompanied with health, peace and purpose to be a real blessing. So also, financial abundance may not be a real blessing if it lacks certain key elements. Godly wealth includes financial abundance, lands, children, family, godly friends, peace of mind and treasures that are waiting for us in heaven.

Some have inherited great wealth because of the blessings of their forefathers. They may have money but then misuse it. This may result in a lack of family peace and unity and end up in a broken home and displaced children. That is not godly wealth no matter how much money is in the bank.

Wealth includes a home filled with love, loyalty and security. If spouses love each other and children gather around and enjoy their parents, and if grandparents are cherished and friends are treated like part of the family, that is a wealthy home. If a family has all that they need materially, and the presence of God is felt, and angels visit and bless their home, then that is a wealthy family.

WEALTH AS A MINISTRY

Financial wealth releases the opportunity and the blessing of helping others. It is a privilege to support ministers, assist the poor and to help build organizations to make this world a better place. Many people give small amounts to these endeavors and wish they could give more; often it is the humble poor who have the biggest hearts. When, however, God blesses someone with great wealth, an extraordinary opportunity arises. A godly person with great wealth is able to give large amounts of money as they partner with God.

They are used by God to release amazing blessings on the earth. God owns everything and He entrusts some folk with the task of distributing it for His glory. The wealth is not in the having alone, but also in the giving, for it is more blessed to give than to receive.

WEALTH IN HEAVEN

Jesus taught, *"Do not store up for yourselves treasures on earth, where moth and rust destroy, and where thieves break in and steal. But store up for yourselves treasures in heaven, where moth and rust do not destroy, and where thieves do not break in and steal"* (Mt. 6:19-20).

Salvation is free for the asking, but treasures in heaven are earned. Good works, kindness, generosity, helping the poor, refreshing the saints and spreading the good news of Christ accumulates treasures in heaven. This is especially true when personal sacrifice is involved.

Curses extend to generations here on earth, but are totally removed when a soul arrives in heaven. It is possible for a person to be poor in this life because of generational curses and yet be rich in heaven because that person has served the Lord.

HONOR

Proverbs 3 has taught us about long life and wealth; it also teaches us about honor. Honor is a blessing that comes from both God and man. Even those who have not yet found salvation may be used by God to bring honor to a person that God is honoring.

Proverbs 3 says, *"Let love and faithfulness never leave you; bind them around your neck, write them on the tablet of your heart. Then you will win favor and a good name in the sight of God and man"* (Pro. 3:3-4).

Sacrificial love and service will yield honor and a good name. Honor is earned by two things: good works and unusual kindness. This was true of Cornelius, the Roman centurion. His good works and kindness went up to heaven as a memorial (see Acts 10:4).

Cornelius grew in favor with God and with man. Angels were sent to bless him. The Apostle Peter was also sent to teach him about the grace of God. Cornelius received salvation for himself and his entire family. He received great honor from God and from man.

JESUS RECEIVED HONOR

As a child, Jesus grew in favor with God and man (see Matthew 3:46). When He was just a boy, Jesus was a kindhearted servant. Scripture says that He loved to help others; He was full of wisdom and the Holy Spirit. He was and is honored here on earth.

His honor also extends throughout the halls of heaven. He is worthy to receive honor and glory and praise because of all that he has done to save the world and destroy the works of darkness (see Revelation 5:12).

In coming to earth and dying on the cross, Jesus humbled Himself and became obedient to His Father. He received favor from God and man and was given a name that is above every other name. He is greatly honored! (see Philippians 2:6-11).

HONOR IN FAMILIES

Honor should be earned within one's own family. If a mother is virtuous and godly, Proverbs 31 tells us that her children will rise up and call her blessed. Her husband will also honor her and he will sit with leaders of the community. An honorable wife is amazing; she even provides a platform for her husband's success.

Honor is not the same as fame. An athlete, for example, might become famous because he accomplishes great physical feats, but at the same time, he might be unfaithful to his spouse. That person may have fame, but he does not have honor. Fame alone is notoriety, but it is inferior to the blessing of honor. A person blessed with honor has favor with God and with man. They have a quality about them that others look up to. To receive honor, a person must possess godly character and wisdom and exercise sacrificial service to help others.

A ROMAN GENERAL

Godly character followed by godly acts will bring honor. Even a Roman Centurion who served the Roman government in their occupation of Israel was a godly man. He and his family were devout, God-fearing people. He gave regular offerings to the poor and prayed continuously. In time, an angel visited him and said, *"Cornelius! ... Your prayers and gifts to the poor have come up as a memorial offering before God"* (Acts 10:3-4).

It was said about Cornelius, *"He is a righteous and God-fearing man, who is respected by all the Jewish people"* (Acts 10:22).

Cornelius cared for the poor and his kindness and good works won him a good name and gave him respect, favor and honor on earth (even from the enemies of his nation) and in the courts of heaven as well. Because of his lifestyle, his whole family received honor.

Proverbs 3 says, *"The Lord's curse is on the house of the wicked, but he blesses the home of the righteous. He mocks proud mockers but gives grace to the humble. The wise inherit honor but fools he* [the Lord] *holds up to shame"* (Pro. 3:33-35).

WISDOM IS CHARACTER

The opposite of honor is shame. God causes the fool to be shamed. That is the work of a curse. God, however, honors those who are wise and extends blessings over their homes for generations to come.

Godly wisdom is not mere intelligence, nor is it an accumulation of factual knowledge; it is the character of Jesus working in someone's life. James describes godly wisdom for us.

" . . . the wisdom that comes from heaven is first of all pure; then peace loving, considerate, submissive, full of mercy and good fruit, impartial and sincere" (Jas 3:17).

Godly wisdom is a right attitude that leads someone to help others and God rewards wisdom with 3 biblical blessings: long life, riches and honor. This is generational; whoever earns these blessings will pass them on to their children, and they will prove to be much more powerful than any curse.

Chapter Six

YOUR FAMILY
AND THE NATIONS

THE TEN COMMANDMENTS

*T*he Ten Commandments reveal the power of blessings and curses. Although we have already referred to the Ten Commandments, we will do so again for emphasis and further instruction.

We read, *"You shall not make for yourself an idol ... You shall not bow down to them or worship them; for I, the Lord your God, am a jealous God, punishing the children for the sin of the fathers to the third and fourth generation ... but showing love to a thousand generations of those who love me and keep my commandmnets"* (Ex. 20:4,5-6).

These verses highlight one of the Ten Commandments. It tells us that making and worshipping an idol is forbidden by God. Worshipping an idol is witchcraft, and it produces a curse. Curses bring judgments or punishments from God, and those judgments will adversely affect 3 or 4 subsequent generations.

Three or four generations are specific numbers; God has given us a couple of numbers to work with. If an evil pattern looms over your family, you only need to look back into your history for 4 generations to find the culprit. It is possible that witchcraft may have been in your lineage for thousands of years, but it will only affect you if someone within the last 4 generations has participated in it.

The demons of witchcraft may have enticed your great, great grand-parents, drawing them into their deceptive web. It would have taken significant spiritual power and godly fortitude to resist their seduc-tions, especially if their parents allowed a stronghold of darkness to work within the family. If your recent relatives have entertained the activity of witchcraft, then the dark judgments of ancient curses came on them, and it has been passed down to you and your family. This is a perpetual pattern for many families, and it must be broken.

COUNT YOUR BLESSINGS

Besides curses, the Ten Commandments teach generational bless-ings. Those who keep the Ten Commandments will receive godly blessings, and they may be passed on for a thousand generations. Blessings are far more powerful than curses. If God assigned a spe-cific number to show us the limits of generational curses, (3 or 4 generations) then it is logical that His value for blessings is also a real number. In the same teaching of the Ten Commandments the scripture records that godly blessings extend for a thousand genera-tions. In other words, one of the reasons that you are blessed today is due to the godly behavior of your ancient ancestors. Some of them may have lived a hundred generations before you were born. They kept God's commandments and the Lord blessed their descendents.

"... but showing love to a thousand generations of those who love me and keep my commandments" (Ex. 20:6).

Here are the Ten Commandments. Look at them in the context of blessings and curses.

1. Have no other Gods before you.
2. Do not make an idol to worship it.

3. Do not misuse God's name.
4. Remember the Sabbath to keep it holy.
5. Honor your father and mother.
6. Do not commit murder.
7. Do not commit adultery.
8. Do not steal.
9. Do not give false testimony against another.
10. Do not covet anything that belongs to your neighbor.

THE POWER OF BLESSINGS

Blessings are far more powerful than curses. If we take God at His word and do the math, our findings are amazing. Blessings are 250 times more powerful than curses because curses go for 4 generations and blessings go for a thousand generations.

Let us look then at the power of curses. Given that a new generation comes approximately every 20 years and curses come down from 4 generations, then you may have trouble because of the behavior of your ancestors who lived between now and the last 80 to 100 years.

We have already discovered that godly blessings go for a thousand generations; they are so powerful that they can extend the full length of the history of the human race. This means that what we do for good today, may affect all of our generations until Jesus returns.

A BETTER WORLD TODAY

Despite popular opinion, the world is a much better place than it was 2,000 years ago, or 500 years ago or even 100 years ago. I am confident that godly generations have been responsible for this great improvement. God has rewarded them by blessing their families. Did I get ahead of myself and present an idea too quickly? Let me explain. In fact, I will let my good friend, Harold Eberle, explain. Hedoes a great job of communicating this idea in one of his books.

And I quote: "Start by taking a snapshot of what life was like in the United States 200 years ago. In the early 1800's there was about 5000 immigrants in the United States, but 20 percent of them were slaves. The age of sexual consent in many states was 9 or 10 years old. Abortion was legal throughout most of the nineteenth century, and records tell us that more than one fifth of all pregnancies were aborted, … Alcoholism was much higher than it is today. Prostitution was also higher, … the mayor of Savannah estimated that his city had one for every 39 [men]. … Native Americans were being forced off of their lands and in some cases murdered. Tens of thousands of Chinese people were being brought into the West … to serve as forced laborers. … Many people in the West carried guns for protection because murder was common place. ... women could not vote, and men could beat their wives as long as they did not maim or kill them. Things in the United States were not better morally, ethically or spiritually. …

Let's go back further in time and take a snapshot of the whole world around the time Jesus came as a baby. … In Italy approximately 40 percent of the population consisted of slaves. Throughout the empire [Roman] homosexuality was commonplace … Most of the Roman and Greek people worshipped many gods such as Jupiter, Juno, and Neptune. … people in Africa, Asia and Australia worshipped nature, demons and their own dead ancestors. … In South America, millions worshipped a bloodthirsty god, and they offered human sacrifices, often numbering in the thousands in one ceremony. When Jesus came to earth, there was only one tiny nation located in the Middle East that had a revelation of the one true God. All the rest of the world was in darkness."

("Victorious Eschatology" by Harold R. Eberle & Martin Trench, Worldcast Publishing, Yakima, Washington, 2007)

Earnest Hampton Cook wrote, "The fact is that bad as the world still is, yet morally it is vastly better than it was when Jesus was born in Bethlehem of Judea. ... Few people in these days have an adequate conception of the misery and degradation which were then the common lot of almost all mankind, owing to the monstrous wickedness of the times, to continual war, to cruelties of political despotism, and of everywhere-prevailing slavery." Cited on: (http//www.preteristarchive.com/StudyArchive/h/hampden-cook-preterist.html)

These authors have painted for us a dismal picture of world history, but to that we could add the evil dark-ages in Europe and the barbarism of ancient tribes and civilizations. The entire world faced much greater suffering in the past. Calamity came because there were no hospitals, medicines, orphanages and other humanitarian institutions. Poverty was commonplace in many more nations of the past than today. It is evident that, really, there were no "good old days" unless you go back to Adam walking in the Garden of Eden before he sinned.

Today is the best time in all of history to be alive for most people. Wickedness still abounds and lack and suffering are still prevalent in the world, but it is not nearly as bad as it was. The blessings of God are accumulative and they have been overtaking curses.

YOUR FAMILY

Most families have it better today than their own ancestors did even 80 years ago. I have heard so many stories of the terrible hardships that grandparents faced. Some tell of slavery, of relatives fleeing from oppression, of people breaking their backs to clear the land or struggling through the great depression. Some remember the hundreds of thousands who died due to flu epidemics or the ravages of war. Most families can say that they have a better life than their parents or grandparents had.

TWO DIFFERENT DYNAMICS

The blessings of those who have walked with God have made the world a better place, but sin continues to rule the hearts of many, and darkness is growing rapidly. Two dynamics are emerging at the same time: one of extreme darkness and one of extreme light. Materialism, success and advanced exposure to sexual perversion through modern technology has produced a generation that has turned their backs away from God. Most of the world is now swimming in a sea of gross spiritual darkness, and a whirlwind of judgment and wrath is coming like a hurricane on the horizon. The Bible teaches us that gross darkness will cover the earth, but at the same time, God's amazing glory will rise upon His people (see Isaiah 60:1-2).

As the end of this age closes in on us, God's people will become more passionate for Him. They will shine as salt and light in the world. Kingdom-of-God families will glow brighter as the world grows darker.

We, in this generation, have the opportunity, through our God, to realize blessings more powerful than any generation before us. Our children can receive extensive blessings if we learn the power of walking with God and the importance of leaving a blessing for the next generation.

The blessings of God are 250 times more powerful than curses. With all of the evil that men have perpetuated, with all of the wickedness that is growing in the world, the blessings of God will prevail for the families that walk with Him.

You may recognize the external advantages that you and your children have compared to your forefathers, yet today, you may see great weakness and troubles brewing in your family. It is time to press forward. Think of what you can do with the blessings that God will give you. Think of the great blessings you can leave for your children.

Godly families are destined for blessings and we have the opportunity of catapulting our children forward into greatness. In the next few chapters, we will look at the importance of teaching our children about generational blessings. We will also study the power of God's prophetic words over our lives and what we must do to take hold of our family's spiritual inheritance.

Chapter Seven

TEACH YOUR CHILDREN ABOUT BLESSINGS AND CURSES

TEACHING THE NEXT GENERATION

Someone once said, "We must begin teaching our children 25 years before they are born." In other words, the best teacher is one who has first learned through their own experiences.

I am not referring to math or literature but that which is taught in the school of the Holy Spirit. The Holy Spirit is the greatest teacher, and He brings to His students the wisdom from above (see James 3:15). The wisdom from above is about character and behavior. Math and spelling are important, but learning how to live and act in a godly fashion far exceeds all other learning.

Later in this chapter, we will look at the biblical model (the Hebrew model) for teaching, but first, we will discover what is the most important thing to teach our children and what hinders us from teaching it.

GOD INSTRUCTS HUMANITY

God tells us what we need and what we should teach our children.

The most important teaching for anyone, at any time, is summed up by the words of Jesus; God's instruction for humanity hinges on these words.

We read, *"'Love the Lord your God with all your heart and with all your soul and with all your mind.' This is the first and greatest commandment. And the second is like it: 'Love your neighbor as yourself.' All the Law and the Prophets hang on these two commandments (Mt.22:37-40).*

Everything that God wants us to learn hangs on these two themes. If we learn what they mean and do them, we will have the wisdom from above. These themes keep us from selfish behavior, keep us walking in the purposes of God and keep us caring for others. Any person who is addicted to loving God and loving people has discovered how to receive God's amazing blessings. This is what we must teach our children.

THE FAMILY LINEAGE REVELATION

As parents, it falls on us to give the next generation a family lineage revelation. Without this understanding, it may be difficult for them to think consequentially. How will young people know the full importance of their behavior unless they know that their actions will have a powerful affect on the generations that follow?

Speaking about Abraham, God said, *"For I have chosen him, so that he will direct his children and his household after him to keep the way of the Lord by doing what is right and just, so that the Lord will bring about for Abraham what he has promised him* (Gen18:19).

God chose Abraham with the understanding that Abraham would

teach his children well. Teaching the children about blessings and curses (the importance of doing what is right and just) was the only way that God's blessings would fall into place for Abraham's future.

Our challenge is to teach our children; but sometimes it seems they are not listening. It is not that they want to hurt the next generation, but often they do not understand. They do not realize that their actions, even when they are teens, can affect those around them with such far-reaching consequences. Many children who were not taught at home may reach the age of 45 and still not realize that their behavior has powerful generational repercussions.

Most parents live for their children, but some focus on their own lives and put their children's wellbeing at a distance. They take care of themselves, plan their future and get out of life what they can. Some ignore the pitfalls or nasty side effects that come with personal pleasure seeking. They think that if they get hurt, they are only hurting themselves. They feel that it is their life to waste if they want to.

Most are not intentionally trying to ruin the next generation; they are just ego-centric. They are focused on themselves and do not have an "FLR" - a family lineage revelation.

MIDLIFE CRISIS

For most young people, the spotlight shifts from themselves to the family once they get married and have children. Then they are not so self-focused because they have the responsibilities associated with loving a spouse and raising children.

The revelation that their lives will affect the generations that follow, however, is often still weak. That is why mid-life crisis affects so many people. Once the children are grown up and their immediate responsibilities are over, some people return to pleasing themselves.

They face midlife crisis because they realize they are getting older, life is flying by and they have not collected all that they wanted to get for themselves in this life. Some will try to relive the wild adventures of the self-seeking teen years and that is often destructive.

A NOBLE PERSON

A noble person will always serve the best interests of the family. They understand that godly behavior is the only way to live. A wise parent will leave their children much more than money because money is not always a blessing. An individual may receive great amounts of money because of criminal activity, but if it comes through ill-gotten gain, money is no blessing at all. It will likely produce a family curse.

A noble person has a better revelation; they want to leave godly blessings for the generations that follow. Passing on one's financial wealth is part of a godly heritage, but there are more important riches that one should pass on as an inheritance to their children.

I have been in many homes where there was no righteousness, peace or joy. The parents did not walk with God and they had nothing of depth to pass on to their children. Over the years, I have also visited the homes of the righteous. Those homes were overflowing with godly blessings. The man or woman who really succeeds in receiving God's blessings will have a house full of riches and wealth to pass on to their children, and they will have a lot of fun passing it on. Where there is true righteousness, there will be peace, and if there is peace, there will be joy.

Life, for the family of righteousness, peace and joy, is usually a fun-filled adventure. Those families:

1. Build a strong financial base through godly financial gain and that is very satisfying.

2. Build a strong moral home and that is a fountain of life and a haven of peace.

3. Build lasting memories for they enjoy wholesome fun and fellowship together.

4. Build treasures in heaven because their family will minister and serve others.

5. Build a base of wisdom because they worship God and explore the earth. In that context they discover the diversity of the nations and the glories of the natural world.

Life is not boring for one who is focused on establishing godly blessings; it is the very best life possible. While doing the things that bless the next generation, an individual will be blessing themselves with the most rewarding lifestyle. This is what we must teach our children.

THE HEBREW MODEL

God taught the Jews how to teach and train their children, and we should follow that example. Here is the model:

"Hear, O Israel: The Lord our God, the Lord is one. Love the Lord your God with all your heart and with all your soul and with all your strength. These commandments that I give you today are to be upon your hearts. Impress them on your children. Talk about them when you sit at home and when you walk along the road, when you lie down and when you get up. Tie them as symbols on your hands and bind them on your foreheads.

Write them on the doorframes of your houses and on your gates"
(Dt. 6:4-9).

Teaching the ways of the Lord should always be a very natural experience. Passing on the wisdom that comes from above is as normal as breathing if people love God with all of their hearts. It is
not legalistic or heavy-handed but loaded with love, gentleness and
patience. If the Holy Spirit lives and moves in the parents, He will
manifest His glory through them to the children. The process becomes more than teaching; it naturally turns into training. Teaching
is giving instruction, but training adds the personal touch; it involves taking children by the hand and leading them through life.

EXAMPLES FROM OUR HOME

As my wife and I look at our 4 grown children, we give thanks
to God, for they are all walking in the faith and blessings that we
have passed on to them. It is not that they have had a perfect journey to bring them to this place; in fact, some stages of their walk
were very challenging for them and for us as parents. The results of
our focused efforts, however, have ultimately proven effective by
God's grace we see His glory unfolding in their lives. All of them
love the Lord and they love people. We see that they are doing as Jesus commanded; they love the Lord with all of their hearts and they
love their neighbors as themselves. They are all serving the Lord in
different avenues of ministry. We are very proud of them!

We followed the Hebrew model of teaching and training. The key
is to live God-centered lives focused on loving other people. That
was the example we gave our children.

I think of the practice I have of thanking my wife with a kiss after
every meal. Even if, on the rare occasion, the meal did not turn out

great, I would still walk to the other end of the table and kiss my wife and thank her for the food. My children saw this every day.

A short while ago, my son Andrew, now married with two children, told me a cute story. He decided to cook the evening meal for his family. At the end of the meal he walked to the other side of the table and kissed his wife. He said to me, amid some laughing, "Dad, I was so used to kissing my wife and thanking her after every meal, just like you always did with Mom, that I walked to the other side of the table and kissed her like always. This time I cooked the meal, but it didn't seem complete to leave the table without thanking her with a kiss."

The Hebrew model requires demonstrations like the thank you kiss; it involves teaching during the flow of everyday life. In this way, my wife and I were always giving our children godly instruction. Parents who pass on the task of having someone else train their children have missed the mark. Parenting can be even worse than that, if children are left on their own to be taught by their friends or by the television. When that happens, parents have sidestepped their responsibility.

The Hebrew model is to teach your children as, *"you sit at home and when you walk along the road, when you lie down and when you get up"* (Dt. 6:7).

This is very different from the Greek, classroom model of teaching, which is often used for traditional, family devotions. They are tedious and usually boring. With the Greek model, children are brought together, sat down, and forced to listen to a Bible reading. They are instructed as if they were at school. This is usually a painful experience for children, especially as they get older. They will often rebel against it. The Hebrew model is much more fun, and we still use it in our home today, even though the children are now adults.

Here are some practical examples of how the Hebrew model worked in our home. When the children were young we made learning a game. We often played the Bible game around the table, following the supper meal. I would tell a short but exciting story from the Bible. Then I would go around the room and ask each child an age appropriate question. They would get points for a correct answer. Even when they were young teens they enjoyed these challenging quizzes.

Sometimes, for a change, we played the fast moving, but very educational, animal game. I would begin by saying something like, "I am thinking of an animal that is black and white."

The children would randomly call out "Penguin, Zebra, Panda Bear, or Holstein Cow." I would continue to give clues until one called out, "A Dalmatian dog." It was so much fun that our children would ask if we could play even when their friends were visiting. Their friends were over at least a couple of times every week, but we played the Bible or animal game almost every night. Sometimes we would sit for an hour around the table and I would have to bring the family time to a close so we could move on to other things. Our kids became so skillful with their knowledge of the Bible and of animals that they could tell you the name of David's oldest brother or what was the fastest living creature on the planet (By the way, it's not the cheetah, it's the peregrine falcon).

Throughout the game, I would be slipping in interesting facts and godly instruction, and often following the Bible or animal game, the children would ask amazing questions. Some would be quite deep and we would end up in theological discussions for another half an hour or so. Our children became experts in the study of scripture and doctrine, and they accumulated truckloads of wisdom that comes from above.

THE GREAT OUTDOORS

Besides our daily teaching games, every Saturday was family day and we would do something together. Sometimes they brought a friend but our time together was a priority and our children had to attend. We would often pack a lunch, stuff it into backpacks and go on a great bike ride adventure. We had a 35-mile paved bike trail and our family used it well.

Every year we went wilderness camping, took hikes through the woods, and vacationed in adventurous places. Wherever we went we talked about life, about the Jewish people, about God or angels or how to minister to needy people. The conversations never lacked depth or scope and the opportunities to teach and train our children were endless. Our times together were always full of fun.

OUR BEST FRIENDS

Our oldest daughter was the valedictorian of her graduating school class. As she gave her speech to students and staff she said, "I want you all to know that my parents are my best friends."

When our oldest son graduated from his very secular and rather rough, city High School, he, like all the other students, was given 30 seconds to tell, in a sentence or two, what his goals and ambitions were. To our shock, in front of hundreds of people, he said, "I will go on to college, but my ambition is to be just like my dad." A hush came over the room, then the crowd cheered enthusiastically. I was proud, if not a bit choked up, as I saw a young 18-year old man of God speak before a secular non-Christian crowd in such a tender, yet bold, manner.

When our firstborn was just 5 years old she was so smart that she kept me on my toes. I remember going for a walk with her in the forest near our home. On that occasion we saw a family of raccoons, a mother with babies walking along an old log in single file. A few minutes later, while holding my hand, she said, "Dad, I just don't get it."

She repeated the phrase again and again, "Dad I don't get it." Finally, I stopped and sat down with her on an old tree branch and said, "What is it Rachel? Tell me honey, what don't you get?"

Then, seemingly out of the blue, she said, "Dad, how could God be in the beginning before anything else? I just don't get it."

I responded, "I don't understand it either, Rachel. I just know that everything has a beginning and in the beginning of all things, there was only God."

I am glad she didn't push the question further, but how I loved watching the Holy Spirit bring revelation and a sense of awe to such a young child.

A FOUNTAIN OF LIFE

Right from the start, I instigated the spiritual lessons in our home, and I would do it in a fun and an enjoyable manner and often at unexpected times. Soon, I did not need to start up the conversations because our children started them. They were fascinated with the greatness of God and they became hungry for knowledge and understanding. Through it all, we taught our children how to love God and how to love other people, and we did it using the Bible/Hebrew model. In my opinion, I think they have become champions.

EVEN TODAY

Two of our grown children are presently living in our home - not out of necessity, but because it is just right for this season. Every day in our home, we have discussions or debates, and we share revelations with each other about the scriptures, about God, about life and about the spiritual needs of the world around us.

I receive phone calls every week from one of our other children or from one of their spouses. Usually it involves a question or a revelation that they wish to bounce off me. All of us continue to learn about the God we love. If we talk about other people in a ministry or church setting, even if those people are in sinful failure or struggling with difficult matters, the answer will always end up on the same track. What is the best way to love these people so they will be encouraged and strengthened? This direction is especially important if people have hurt or misused us personally. The focus remains the same: how can we forgive and love them?

THE CHILDREN ARE TEACHERS

These days, I find my children teaching me almost as much as I teach them. Some of it is a reminder of things that I have taught them, and some is just fresh revelation that comes as a precious gift from God. I am constantly blown away as I discover the wisdom that God releases through my children and their spouses. They are still best friends to my wife Joy and I.

TRAINING IN BLESSINGS AND CURSES

Blessings and curses are intricately connected to our understanding of loving or not loving God and people. If we love God and people, it will ultimately produce blessings. If we rebel against God and hurt people, it will eventually result in some kind of curse coming to us and our families.

My on-going task is to remind my grown children to keep themselves in the love of God. That will always involve loving people, especially the unlovely. It involves living a life free from reaction and offense. It involves forgiving, praying for, blessing and loving even our enemies. We refuse to let the garbage of unforgiveness find a place in our family.

Peter said, *"Do not repay evil with evil or insult with insult, but with blessing, because to this you were called so that you may inherit a blessing"* (1 Pe. 3:9).

We live to love God with all of our hearts and minds, and we love people. This brings blessings, and we will pass this teaching on to our grandchildren so that, by God's grace, the family lineage revelation, "FLR," will continue.

Chapter Eight

PROPHETIC WORDS - A DOORWAY FOR BLESSINGS

EVERYONE'S GIFT

I ask the reader to bear with me as I offer some explanation about the prophetic gift. Heaven's release of this gift is absolutely amazing. Understanding the prophetic gift will help connect us with our families' future.

The Bible speaks of true prophecies and false prophecies. A false prophecy is one that does not come from God. In this study, I am only focusing on true prophecies.

Every individual has many spoken or unspoken prophecies intended for them and all true prophecies begin with God's kindness. When God creates a human being, His intention for that person is always good. The prophetic words over one's life are always conditional, but all of them point to blessings and greatness.

Peter said, *"to this you were called, so that you may inherit a blessing"*
(1 Pe. 3:9).

We have been called to receive blessings, and those blessings must be spoken in a prophetic word. When the church was birthed on the day of Pentecost, 120 disciples spoke in a language that was different from their native tongue. Each one received a special Holy Spirit anointing that came to them because of a prophetic word.

The disciples preached, revival fell, and three thousand people were added to the church on that day. During the revival, Peter gave an explanation. He said that this outpouring of the Holy Spirit was the fulfillment of a prophecy spoken by Joel, hundreds of years before. Then, using Joel's prophecy as an example, he explained how the gift of prophecy should be exercised by all believers.

He said, *"this is what was spoken by the prophet Joel: 'In the last days, God says, I will pour out my Spirit on all people. Your sons and daughters will prophesy, your young men will see visions, your old men will dream dreams. Even on my servants, both men and women, I will pour out my Spirit . . . and they will prophesy'"* (Acts 2:16-18).

Under the Old Covenant, prophecies were rare, but a new day emerged as the New Covenant came, and since then, all believers may prophesy. Even today, every Christian can hear from God directly and speak forth His word. Sons and daughters, old men, young men and even servants may participate. According to the Apostle Peter, the prophetic gift is given to every person who receives the infilling of the Holy Spirit.

If every believer can prophesy, then it stands to reason that God will be doing a lot of speaking through a massive number of people. What would one billion Christians say if they were all prophesying?

It is fantastic; God is using multitudes to share prophetic words with other members of His family. Even though every believer is able to hear God personally, God has determined that some instructions will not come to us directly, but though someone else. The Holy

Spirit chooses who will have a prophetic word for whom, and without those words, people will be incomplete.

Can you picture the prophecy assigning administrative system in heaven? Because God is omnipresent, omniscient and omnipotent, I am sure it is a smooth operation. Through His Holy Spirit, He can speak to all believers at the same time and give each one a different message. If this administration were organized by human abilities, it would involve a frenzy of activity 1000 times more chaotic than the bidding of stocks and bonds on the floor of the New York Stock Exchange. Think of it: maybe one billion prophetic words are sent from heaven every day! The words come through dreams, visions, revelations, illuminated scripture passages and angelic visitations, and that is only a few of the possible pathways. Some prophetic words come directly from the scriptures; other words come through an angel speaking in our dreams; still others come to us through a prophetic person who has been commissioned to pass the word on.

Despite the mountain of misuse due to false prophecies, presumptuous words, unspoken prophecies or mishandled words used to control or manipulate others, the gift of prophecy is still the communication method of choice that God uses. Regardless of all of the possible mishaps, scripture says, *"Despise not prophesyings"* (1Thes. 5:20 - KJV).

If we want to fulfill our God-given destiny, it is essential that we seek, desire to hear, be open to receive and be willing to walk in the prophetic words that are intended for us. Roadblocks such as unbelief, sarcasm, sin, pride and curses will keep us from fulfilling God's prophetic words for our lives. In many cases, we will not even receive God's word if we have a doubting or cynical spirit.

The gift of prophecy is on the rise. It will only increase and become more commonplace as God unfolds His end-time glory for the Church. All of this points to the magnificent truth that God has great prophetic words for you and your family. The prophecies intended for your family are doorways to blessings.

PROPHECIES ARE CONDITIONAL

Some global prophetic words, such as those recorded in scripture, are unchangeable and irrevocable; they must come to pass. Prophecies for our personal lives, however, are conditional; they are God's good intentions for us. Prophecies are given to individuals as guide posts, encouragements, directional targets, instructions and motivational confirmations. Many prophetic words, however, are never fulfilled because people lack faith or they fail to pursue the directives that God has given them.

When a genuine prophecy is given, it must be received as an instruction from God. The person who received it is not aimless anymore; they have been shown a path or destination that is part of their journey. It is imperative that each person test the word to confirm that it is from God; then, once they are sure that the prophecy is from God, they must press into it with everything they have.

Too many people sit back and wait for God to fulfill His word over their lives when they should be working with God to make it happen. Faith is not idle waiting, but persistent movement in response to what God has said. Faith without works is dead, and prophecies without faith-filled pursuit will never be fulfilled. To be clear, if God tells you that you will one day be a missionary in Africa, then you should get your passport in order, start to save money for the trip and investigate mission organizations that can help you fulfill God's plan for your life. He will guide your steps for the right timing, who you should work with and what part of Africa you should aim for. If, however, you are not pursuing the prophecy, you will probably never see Africa. Here are 7 steps that will help you receive the blessings of the prophetic word that God has given you and your family:

1. After confirming the word, come into agreement with God concerning it.

2. Pray diligently for its fulfillment in your life.

3. Obey God by going to the place or doing that which the prophecy dictates. Too many people sit back and wait for a prophecy to be fulfilled instead of going after it.

4. Walk in righteousness and faith, and do not forfeit God's plan over your life by walking in sin.

5. Allocate your resources and energies to fulfill God's word for your life.

6. Listen to the leadership of the Holy Spirit as He guides you forward, holds you back or redirects your path in a different direction.

7. Network with others, and be willing to go beyond your parochial box to find God's bigger purpose. The path of God will take you from a puddle to an ocean.

ABRAHAM AND HIS DESCENDANTS

The story of Abraham is often used to hold people back from stepping out in faith. Abraham was told that he and Sarah would have a child, but Isaac was a long time coming. Abraham disobeyed God and conceived a child with his servant, Hagar. That child was Ishmael. This was not the child of promise, and generations of untold trouble and strife came to Abraham's descendants because of Ishmael.

Many do not pursue their prophetic words because they do not want to produce an Ishmael. Abraham's problem was not that he pursued the prophecy but that he disobeyed God and did things that God never instructed. Too many people have used the story of Abraham and Ishmael as a reason for inactivity. They become passive and inactive concerning their prophecies. It would be better to look at the story of Abraham's twin grandchildren. Jacob and Esau were sons of Isaac, the son of promise. Esau was born just minutes before Jacob and was in line to receive the best family blessings. He did not pursue his prophetic blessings but treated them casually. Jacob, on the other hand, went after the prophetic call with everything he had. The story reveals that God loved Jacob because he pursued his birthright, but He hated the ways of Esau who ignored the prophetic words of God for his life. We must wrestle like Jacob and take hold of our prophetic blessings. At times, they seem just beyond our reach. Learn this lesson: we will not receive the prophetic blessings unless we reach forward

PROPHECIES ARE FOR FAMILIES

Heaven releases prophecies for only one reason: so they may be fulfilled. The purpose of every fulfilled prophecy is to bring glory to God. While it is a great blessing for the person to whom it is given, its larger purpose is to reflect God's love and power.

Most prophetic words tell us that God is going to do something fantastic with someone. Usually, the prophecy promotes a direction that, in the natural, seems improbable or even impossible. God, however, wants to glorify Himself by using an ordinary, unqualified person to do an extraordinary thing. A prophecy is, therefore, an advanced warning of the amazing thing that God wants for someone.

All positive prophecies involve godly activity, and when they are fulfilled, they always bring blessings. When prophecies are given to an individual, they are given to a family, because the blessings of fulfilled prophecies have generational ramifications. When the individual completes a prophecy, a blessing always comes upon their family. Even though it is the responsibility of the individual to complete the prophecy, they are really working to bless their family. That is another good reason why a person should passionately pursue their prophesies

FAMILIES WHO CHEER EACH OTHER ON

Individuals in a godly family have the responsibility of cheering other family members on. There is no room for jealousy or rivalry; each family member has a different destiny but their success will impact the entire group. One person's blessing spills over to the others. Understanding, confirming and helping each member fulfill their prophetic destiny is the godly challenge for every family. As one encourages, supports and promotes the other, they add strength and increase to the growing basket of generational blessings.

Families must work together to fulfill every prophetic word that has been spoken over their parents, grandparents, brothers, sisters, children and grandchildren. This will result in future generations breaking through to new levels of encouragement and blessings. A godly momentum will emerge that can carry a family to amazing heights in the purposes of God. The blessings of the Lord will overtake them.

A family working together for the completion of their prophetic mandates will become the greatest support system available on the planet. It happens when wives stand by the godly dreams of their husbands and husbands release and support their wives to do their God-given work in the ministry. It happens when parents prepare, provide for, and promote their children toward their God-given destinies and brothers and sisters stand by one another with unfailing commitment and faith. Cousins join in by prompting their fellow cousins to accomplish great things for Christ, and grandparents, along with uncles and aunts, do their part by releasing finances, adding support and bringing wisdom and irreplaceable encouragement to the table. If an entire family takes hold of this vision, the prophecies of God will no longer fall to the ground, but fly forward until they hit the target. The family that works together like this will be unstopple in their godly endeavors, and the blessings of God will fall upon them with overflowing abundance. It is time for each saint to press forward, complete their individual prophecies and encourage their families in the pursuit of their prophecies. The blessings of God are waiting.

Chapter Nine

ACTIVITIES THAT BRING BLESSINGS

SOWING AND REAPING

Whether we are alive today or we lived 3,000 years ago, God's law of sowing and reaping is the same. It can be summed up in a sentence: "Whatsoever a man sows, that he will also reap" (see Galatians 6:7). The Bible teaches that curses come when people behave wickedly, and blessings come when people behave with extraordinary kindness and righteous living. The scriptures focus on blessings far more than curses. These blessings come from 3 directions:

1. The righteous actions of rulers.
2. The righteous actions of our parents and ancestors.
3. Our own acts of righteousness.

We have discovered what biblical blessings are and how important they are for our families. In this part of our study, we focus on the activities that produce blessings. A good example of people who have produced spiritual blessings can be found at Yad Vasham, the Holocaust Museum, in Israel. There you can see that special honor has been given to extraordinary Gentiles for their amazing efforts to save the Jewish people from genocide.

Israel calls these people "Righteous Gentiles." Heaven also honors and blesses these heroes, for any person who sacrifices to help bring liberty and justice for any people, sows seeds that result in blessings.

LEVELS OF BLESSINGS

Blessings come in lesser or greater amounts. All of us need godly blessings arriving at our door. The more blessings we gain, the more we are able to bless others such as our children or people in need. Here are 8 biblical activities that bring blessings:

1. Blessings come to those who fear and obey the Lord.
2. Blessings come to those who shun evil behavior and company.
3. Blessings come to those who endure hardships for righteousness' sake.
4. Blessings come to those who give generously to help the poor.
5. Blessings come to those who help liberate the oppressed.
6. Blessings come to those who preach the gospel.
7. Blessings come to those who serve and support ministers of the gospel.
8. Blessings come to those who work hard and handle business with integrity.

RECIPE FOR CREATING BLESSINGS

Here is a recipe for creating godly blessings: Fear the Lord, Shun evil, Endure hardship for Christ's sake, Give generously to the poor, Liberate the oppressed, Be a minister of the gospel or Help a minister of the gospel, and Be a diligent worker who will not compromise on his integrity.

If a person does all of these things well, godly blessings will come to them in abundance. Even if a person does some of these things well, then some blessings will come to them. We will explore each of these activities separately, but before we do, here are some of the blessings that come because of these activities. Look at the list that follows.

A BLESSINGS LIST

Godly blessings include the 3 major Bible blessings that we have already studied - long life, wealth and honor. The Bible adds many other blessings to these 3. They are:

Health, Wisdom, Peace, Productivity, Children, Descendants, A good name, A godly spouse, Lands, Mercy, Favor, Miracles, Salvation, Light, Understanding, Leadership abilities, Supernatural Protection, Eternal inheritance, Supernatural anointing, Gifts of the Holy Spirit, Ownership of the earth, Fertility, Comfort, Strength, Fame, Glory, Righteousness, Answers to prayer, Patience, Joy, Angelic visits, The presence of the Lord, Abundant life, Godly fellowship, Maturity, Unity, and Freedom.

1. BLESSINGS IF YOU FEAR AND OBEY THE LORD

We have listed the 8 activities that produce the blessings list. Here is a brief summary on each of them. To start with, the fear of the Lord is the beginning of wisdom. Our need to fear the Lord is based on the premise that God is all powerful and wise, and we are frail and uninformed. As a result, we should be afraid to trust in our own wisdom. We must insist on getting our guidance from God. We call this the fear of the Lord. A blessing comes when we humble ourselves and position ourselves beneath the Lord, because God gives grace (all good things) to the humble. This is the fear of the Lord and the beginning of wisdom.

The world around us is full of dangers; peril can come from the wilds of nature to the handling of electrical circuits or nuclear waste. If an untrained person goes deep sea diving without adequate knowledge, they could die from pulmonary edema (bleeding in the lungs) or be eaten by a dangerous fish. Similarly, if an unskilled person climbs a telephone pole to tap some electricity from an overhead transformer, they would probably be electrocuted.

It would be very helpful to have a trained expert guide you on your dive or warn you of the dangers surrounding electrical transformers. It is not that you fear the instructor but it would be frightening to miss their advice. It always serves us well to have a wholesome fear or respect for the words of the expert. With the right kind of fear, the teacher's knowledge and power allow us to enjoy a deep sea dive or be saved from electrocution.

So it is with God: to fear Him means to fear what will happen if we miss His wisdom and power. As we humble ourselves under God's Holy Spirit, we come to the Expert of life for wisdom. Hearing and obeying the Holy Spirit protects us and leads us to godly blessings. The fear of the Lord is a solid foundation for all godly activity; it is the starting place for discovering real blessings.

On the contrary, to ignore God's Holy Spirit is suicidal. The ultimate failure in life is refusing to fear the Lord. That is when we ignore the wisdom of God and live according to our own understanding. Without the advice of the Expert, we can easily walk on a pathway that leads to hell.

2. BLESSINGS IF YOU SHUN EVIL AND EVIL PEOPLE

Secondly, godly blessings come if we turn away from evil and shun wicked people. This truth is repeated throughout the scriptures, but nowhere is it more clear than in the first Psalm. Here is a portion of Psalm 1 from the Amplified Version of the Bible.

"Blessed (Happy, fortunate, prosperous and enviable) is the man who walks and lives not in the counsel of the ungodly (following their advice, their plans and purposes), nor stands (submissive and inactive) in the path where sinners walk, nor sits down (to relax and rest) where the scornful (and the mockers) gather.

(Pslam 1:1)

Bad company corrupts good manners. It is one thing to reach out to evangelize or help the fallen, and quite another to receive their counsel or participate in the activities of their wicked behavior. Ungodly people are often very opinionated, but their counsel is a roadway that leads to failure and death, and their rebellious acts and attitudes lead to curses. Keeping one's self away from wicked influence will allow a person to embrace a godly influence, and that is positioning one's self for blessings.

Psalm 1 teaches us that we will be blessed if we do not walk, stand, or sit in the counsel of the ungodly. Having served the Lord as a minister of the gospel for most of my life, I have seen many people come to Christ in their youth, then fall away for a season. During their wayward years, an individual will seemingly reject every godly warning they are given; they cast the fear of the Lord to the wind. Often because of lustful pursuits, they abandon the ways of the Bible. While on this path, they do what is opposite to the teaching of Psalm 1; they listen to the counsel of the ungodly, walk in the path of sinful behavior and mock the people of God. This always results in rotten fruit and heavy losses. Walking in the counsel of the wicked leads to wrong choices, sinful activity, and if continued, it will lead to destruction.

After following the path of rebellion for 5 or 10 years, a terrible amount of damage can pile up. Many people spend the rest of their lives trying to recuperate from wrong choices they made while they were young. I think that most will repent later in life and still go to heaven when they die, but many forfeit their blessings here on earth.

God rewards righteous living. Taking a disciplined stand to shun evil behavior and wicked people will inadvertently produce great blessings in our lives.

3. BLESSINGS IF WE ENDURE HARDHSIP FOR RIGHTEOUSNESS' SAKE

We live in a fallen world, and many people endure hardship and traumas caused by others. When the people of God suffer injustice, God takes notice. He stores up blessings for those who will not compromise their walk of righteousness. Jesus taught about those who suffer injustice but walk uprightly in His famous sermon on the mount.

We read, *"Blessed are the poor in spirit ... Blessed are those who mourn ... Blessed are the meek ... Blessed are those who hunger and thirst for righteousness ... Blessed are the merciful ... Blessed are the pure in heart ... Blessed are the peacemakers ... Blessed are those who are persecuted because of righteousness ... Blessed are you when people insult you, persecute you and falsely say all kinds of evil against you because of me* [Jesus]. *Rejoice and be glad for great is your reward in heaven, for in the same way they persecuted the prophets who were before you"* (Mt. 5:3-12).

Every measure taken to endure hardship for Christ's sake is flagged with a promise of blessings. Each Beatitude begins not with a mention of a heroic action, but with the blessing. They all start with the words, "Blessed are [you]." God wants us to get the message that we will be rewarded if we endure hardship for righteous reasons.

As I read this Bible passage, I think of Mother Teresa; she fits the description. She was poor in spirit, meek, mournful, merciful, righteous, pure in heart, a peacemaker, and yet she stood firm against the unrelenting slander of wicked men and evildoers. Her amazing love and sacrifice is honored around the world and in heaven as well. I remember seeing her at a pro-life rally in the early 90's. She was tiny, old and very frail, but she influenced so many people. She was powerful. God used this Catholic nun to speak to the nations about the evils of abortion. Her love for life and for children was sacred; she defended the unborn with amazing tenacity. She was honored even more because of her unending work with the sick and dying people who lived on the streets of India.

From this humble servant came such extraordinary strength. I imagine that any military commander would love to have the conviction, the inner authority and the commanding presence that she possessed. The Catholic church is taking steps to honor her with, what they call, sainthood; she has found favor in the eyes of God and man.

Jesus tells us that blessings come if we take the high road that the martyrs travel on. We are promised blessings if we endure great hardship for righteousness' sake. Contrary to the dictates of common sense, Jesus even tells us to rejoice when we suffer misuse for doing the right thing. He says that martyrs will receive a golden crown, and the righteous who endure hardship will be showered with blessings. Every hurtful act perpetrated against a godly disciple is translated into a spiritual bar of gold on the other side of life.

Some would walk the high ground on good principle even if there were no blessings at the end of the day. God honors those people. Jesus taught His followers to lay up treasures in heaven because those are most valuable. Earthly treasures rot, get rusty and thieves break in and steal them, but eternal treasures are permanent.

4. BLESSINGS IF WE SHOW KINDNESS AND GENEROSITY TO THE POOR

In the book of James we read, *"Religion that God ... accepts as pure and faultless is this: to look after orphans and widows in their distress and to keep oneself from being polluted by the world"* (Js. 1:27).

In the Old Testament, Isaiah teaches us to help the poor. He says that this is God's chosen fast for us.

". . . to share your food with the hungry and to provide the poor wanderer with shelter – when you see the naked, to clothe him, and not to turn away from your own flesh and blood? Then your light will break forth like the dawn, and your healing will quickly appear; then your righteousness will go before you, and the glory of the Lord will be your rear guard. Then you will call, and the Lord will answer" (Isa. 58:7-9).

The Bible instructs us to share our resources with the poor. The Roman centurion mentioned in Acts 10 is a perfect picture of an individual whom God blessed because he feared the Lord and gave generously to the poor. Even though he was positioned under an ungodly government, his family's care for the poor brought them great spiritual blessings.

ZIMBABWE

I am reminded of one of the churches I visited in Zimbabwe, Africa. The people in the congregation were very poor. Some of them did not even have shoes and some wore clothes that were torn. Still these people were joyful. I am always amazed to find people who have so little, enjoying life so much. One thing in particular stood out with these people. Besides their regular offerings, the congregation brought food items for the poor. One brought an egg; another person brought a cob of corn, a banana or a small handful of rice wrapped in a used piece of plastic wrap. One person brought a skinny chicken with its legs and beak held-fast by elastic bands. A pile of food soon lay on the ground in front of the podium and remained there for the entire service. At the end of the meeting the host pastor said, "Let's gather up this food and find some person who is more needy than we are. We will give it to them."

I was impressed; I am sure that heaven was impressed as well and blessings will come to those who participated.

The Bible says, *"He who has pity on the poor lends to the Lord, And He will pay back what he has given"* (Pro. 19:17 - NKJV).

God gives a great return for those who lend to Him. He stands good on His word and pays back on behalf of the poor. He releases great blessings to those who show kindness to them. God has huge resources, and He gives huge dividends that are much greater than what was invested. The scripture says it is much better to give than it is to receive. The giver gets the joy of helping others plus they are reimbursed with blessings that are many times greater than their gift.

In Isaiah 58, God says that He gives direction, understanding, healing, protection and answers to prayer for those who give money to the poor. Isaiah adds an interesting feature to this teaching; he says that we should even be generous with our own family - our own flesh and blood. There is a blessing in taking care of our family. Sometimes helping our own flesh and blood can be the most difficult because we may have watched them in their rebellion; we have seen them make wrong choices. Perhaps, we warned them about the pitfalls of life. We told them how they could avoid those death traps, but they ignored our counsel and now come to us to bail them out.

Now they are lacking, and it could have been avoided. This is affecting the entire family, and it should not have happened. In this situation, it is easy to become hardhearted but God says that a blessing awaits those who give to the poor, especially when it is a family member. Whether it is a family member or a stranger, we are called to give, regardless of the wrong choices that may have caused their poverty.

5. BLESSINGS IF WE HELP LIBERATE THE OPPRESSED

God is the defender of innocent people who are oppressed. Tyranny, cruelty, injustice, an unfair balance and oppression of any kind is detestable to the Lord. Those who do these things bring curses and judgments on themselves and their families. Conversely, godly liberators will be blessed by God.

Isaiah wrote, *"Is not this the kind of fasting* [personal sacrifice] *I have chosen: to loose the chains of injustice and untie the cords of the yoke, to set the oppressed free and break every yoke?"* ... *"If you do away with the yoke of oppression, with the pointing finger and malicious talk, and if you spend yourselves in behalf of the hungry and satisfy the needs of the oppressed, then your light will rise in the darkness, and your night will become like the noonday. The Lord will guide you always; he will satisfy your needs in a sun-scorched land and will strengthen your frame. You will be like a well-watered garden, like a spring whose waters never fail. Your people will rebuild the ancient ruins and will raise up the age old foundations; you will be called Repairer of Broken Walls, Restorer of Streets with dwellings"* (Isa. 58:6, 9-12).

Those who free the oppressed will have many blessings afforded them by the Lord. They will have light in the darkness, guidance from the Lord, and a supernatural supply when others are in lack. They will be like a well of water and will have the honor of being used by God to restore families and communities back to strength.

WITH NO MALICIOUS TALK

An interesting teaching is added to this. The one who helps the oppressed must not point the finger with slander or gossip.

"If you do away with the yoke of oppression, with the pointing finger and malicious talk" (Isa. 58:9).

Malicious talk disqualifies the rewards of good works. In order for God to bless the hero, the liberator must also keep his tongue from speaking badly about others. Even when people have hurt us we must respond with forgiveness and blessings.

"Do not repay evil with evil or insult with insult, but with blessing, because to this you were called, so that you may inherit a blessing" (1 Pe. 3:9).

We do not render evil for evil but speak and give a blessing instead; then our good works will bring a good return. Those who fail this test cannot receive God's abundant blessings even though their lives are full of good works.

6. BLESSINGS IF WE MINISTER THE GOSPEL

"How beautiful on the mountains are the feet of those who bring good news, who proclaim peace, who bring good tidings, who proclaim salvation, who say to Zion, "Your God reigns!" (Isa. 52:7).

Paul quotes this scripture from Isaiah in his letter to the Romans and brings it into the New Covenant writings. He, like Isaiah, emphasizes the beauty and honor of those who preach the gospel of Jesus Christ (see Romans 10:14-15). Isaiah and Paul's message highlights the calling and service of the preacher; their feet are beautiful on the mountains.

These preachers are described as proclaiming salvation and bringing the good news of God's kingdom reign. It is not their mouths, however, that are said to be beautiful, but their feet. The most insignificant parts of the preacher, namely their feet, are beautiful to the Lord. God sees them positioned on the mountains, on the high ground of spiritual activity. The fact that these preachers are using their feet means they are busy; they are on the move and this is beautiful to the Lord. He honors them.

BLESS WORTHY MINISTERS

The Bible teaches that preachers are worthy of double financial blessings.

"The elders who direct the affairs of the church well are worthy of double honor, especially those whose work is preaching and teaching. For the scripture says, 'Do not muzzle the ox while it is treading out the grain', and 'the worker deserves his wages'" (1 Tim. 5:17-18).

This doctrine is not an isolated teaching; it is reemphasized in the Corinthian letter as well. *"Who serves as a soldier at his own expense? Who plants a vineyard and does not eat of its grapes? Who tends a flock and does not drink of the milk? Do I say this merely from a human point of view? Doesn't the Law say the same thing? For it is written in the Law of Moses: 'Do not muzzle an ox while it is treading out the grain.' Is it about oxen that God is concerned? Surely he says this for us, doesn't he? Yes, this was written for us, because when the plowman plows and the thresher threshes, they ought to do so in hope of sharing in the harvest. If we have sown spiritual seed among you, is it too much if we reap a material harvest from you? If others have this right of support from you, shouldn't we have it all the more? ... those who preach the gospel should receive their living from the gospel. ... I do all things for the sake of the gospel that I might share in its blessings"* (1 Cor. 9:7-12,14,23).

It is God's intention that His people participate in sowing blessings to His ministers, but the rewards that come to ministers are not just material ones.

Daniel says, *"Those who are wise will shine like the brightness of the heavens, and those who lead many to righteousness, like the stars forever and ever"* (Dan. 12:3).

Ministers who lead many to righteousness will shine like the stars forever; they will be honored and blessed throughout eternity. The Apostle Peter adds even more insight as he tells us that pastors and ministers can expect great blessings.

He says, *"Be shepherds of God's flock that is under your care, serving as overseerers - not because you must, but because you are willing ... And when the Chief Shepherd appears, you will receive the crown of glory that never fades away"* (1 Pe. 5:2,4).

A crown of glory is waiting for ministers of the gospel. Jesus also captured the truth of blessings for those who sacrificially serve as ministers as he taught his disciples.

He said, *"no one who has left home or brothers or sisters or mother or father or children or fields for me and the gospel will fail to receive a hundred times as much in this present age (homes, brothers, sisters, mothers, children and fields - and with them persecutions) and in the age to come, eternal life"* (Mk. 10:29-30).

Jesus promises an abundance of blessings for ministers of the gospel. Those blessings include houses, families, friends, and fields (financial blessings) in this life and eternal life and blessings in the here-after.

As a minister of the gospel, I declare that Jesus is faithful to His word. I have been a minister of the gospel for 40 years and my father and grandparents were ministers before me. When we minister and meet God's conditions, He always supplies the blessings promised in the list.

Personally speaking, God has promised me abundant blessings until the end of my life. I encourage you to stand in faith, as I do, and expect great blessings from the Lord as you serve Him, but let me put it in right perspective.

The other day, I was speaking to a pastor who was asking me to come and minister at his church. He said, "What do you charge for ministering? We cannot afford to pay you much when you preach for us, so will you still come?"

I replied, "It is my job to freely minister the gospel without any assurance of payment. It is your job to honor the man of God who ministers the gospel to you. In faith, may we both do our jobs well and if we do, then God will bless both the minister and those who receive the ministry."

7. BLESSINGS IF WE SUPPORT MINISTERS

It is no secret that wealthy women travelled with Jesus and His disciples. These servants of the Lord ministered to the ministers by supporting them financially.

We read, *"The Twelve were with him, and also some women who had been cured of evil spirits and diseases: Mary (called Magdalene) from whom seven demons had come out; Joanna the wife of Cuza, the manager of Herod's household; Susanna; and many others. These women were helping to support them out of their own means"* (Lk. 8:1-3).

As ministers of God, each of us has a different function. Some preach, others administrate and some support other ministers financially. Supporting ministry is just as important as praying for the sick or preaching. Every ministry endeavor requires a servant's heart and each receives blessings from the Lord. A partial list of ministries is recorded in Romans 12. Among them is the ministry of the giver.

We read, *"We have different gifts, according to the grace given us ... if it is contributing to the needs of others, let him give generously"* (Ro. 12:6, 8).

Like the many women who travelled with Jesus, some people are called to serve through financial giving. Among those in Christ's company was Joanna. Her husband was the manager of King Herod's house. She was, without a doubt, very wealthy. Although her husband was involved with an ungodly ruler, God allowed her to serve as a main financial supporter of Christ. Her giving probably involved great risk. The money was hers to give, but her husband's employer would likely have been very upset if he discovered that she was one of Jesus' supporters.

Cuza's wife, nevertheless, found her prophetic place; she had the ministry of supporting ministers. What an honor she had. We can be certain that God's blessings fell on her and her descendants. Scripture proves that Joanna was sacrificially committed to the cause of Christ; she was at the cross when Jesus died and was one of the women who went to visit the tomb of Christ on the first day of the week.

Giving to ministers has always been a doorway for blessings. A wealthy woman supported the prophet Elijah, and God blessed her with a child even though she was previously barren (see 2 Kings 4:8-17).

God also supported Elisha's predecessor, Elijah, in the same way.

God said to Elijah, *"Go at once to Zarephath ... I have commanded a widow in that place to supply you with food. ... [she said] "I don't have any bread – only a handful of flour in a jar and a little oil in a jug. ... a meal for myself and my son, that we may eat it – and die." Elijah said to her, "Don't be afraid. ... first make a small cake of bread for me and then make something for yourself and your son. For this is what the Lord, the God of Israel, says: 'The jar of flour will not be used up and the jug of oil will not run dry.' So there was food every day for Elijah and for the woman and her family. For the jar of flour was not used up and the jug of oil did not run dry, in keeping with the word of the Lord ... Some time later the son of the woman ... stopped breathing. ... Then he [Elijah] cried out to the Lord ... The Lord heard Elijah's cry, and the boy's life returned to him ... Then the woman said to Elijah, 'Now I know that you are a man of God and that the word of the Lord from your mouth is the truth'"* (1Kgs. 17:9,12-17,20-24).

Israel was experiencing a severe famine caused by drought, and the rains would not be coming for another 3 years. It seems strange that God commanded a poor destitute widow to support a minister during such a difficult season. It was, however, a doorway of blessing that God provided for her. She had only one final meal of bread left in her pantry and then she and her family would probably starve to death. She obeyed the Lord and gave what she had to the prophet, and God supernaturally supplied food for her family and for the prophet for the next 3 years. On top of that, at a later date, God raised her son to life after he had died. Powerful blessings came to a poor widow who gave generously to a minister of the Most High God.

It is very important to give to the ministry, but it is equally important to be directed by God in the giving. One should not give in response to guilt manipulation or coercion. Let a giver give generously and joyfully, but only as the Holy Spirit leads.

8. BLESSINGS FOR WORKING WITH DILIGENCE AND INTEGRITY

Wise business people in the secular world know that hard work and integrity will produce long-term profits. This may not sound very spiritual, but the Bible also teaches the principles of good work ethic and lets us know that God blesses those who adhere to them.

The Lord taught proper business behavior and hard work to the children of Israel. The Bible holds these standards high; they were taught by Moses and the prophets in the Old Testament and also by Jesus and the Apostles in the New Testament. We will highlight a few of these scriptures to help make the point.

DILIGENCE AND HARD WORK

While the entire Bible speaks of the benefits of diligence and hard work, the book of Proverbs gives us these principles in simple, brief statements.

We read, *"Lazy hands make a man poor, but diligent hands bring wealth"* (Pro. 10:4).

A diligent worker receives financial increase that leads to wealth.

Again we read, *"Diligent hands will rule, but laziness ends in slave labor"* (Pro. 12:24).

Hard work and diligence put an individual in the driver's seat instead of the back of the bus. Hard workers rule because they gain control of their situation. Their leadership comes because they are productive. They become owners of a business or are promoted within someone else's business because of hard work.

The opposite is also true: a person who is not diligent will face financial poverty, and if, by chance, their riches come through ill gotten gain, they will have poverty of soul. They will never be in control of their situation. They are slaves to trouble and anxiety because of their poverty. They always find themselves in a subservient situation where they must come and go at the command of others.

"Do you see a man skilled in his work? He will serve before kings" (Pro. 22:29).

A diligent person will develop great skills and become excellent in their field. This will open the doors to prosperity. A great example of a diligent worker is found in the description of the virtuous women. We read about her in Proverbs 31:10-31.

Here is a description of her diligence and hard work followed by a list of blessings that come to her as a result of her actions. This example is not about a specific individual but about any woman who will exercise diligence and hard work in a godly fashion. Notice her amazing diligence.

"She selects wool and flax and works with eager hands. She is like merchant ships, bringing her food from afar. She gets up while it is still dark; she provides food for her family and portions for her servant girls. She considers a field and buys it; out of her earnings she plants a vineyard. She sets about her work vigorously; her arms are strong for her tasks. She sees that her trading is profitable, and her lamp does not go out at night. In

her hands she holds the distaff and grasps the spindle with her fingers ... She makes coverings for her bed; she is clothed in fine linen and purple ... She makes linen garments and sells them, and supplies the merchants with sashes ... She watches over the affairs of her household and does not eat the bread of idleness"
(Pro. 31:12-19,22,24,27).

What a hard worker this woman is! The description of this woman's diligence and hard work seems to go on forever. My mother, my wife and my grown daughters fit this description, so I know first-hand that this description is attainable. Now here is a list of blessings that come to the virtuous woman as a reward for her diligence and hard work.

"Give her the reward she has earned, and let her works bring her praise at the city gate ... She is worth far more than rubies. Her husband has full confidence in her and lacks nothing of value ... She opens her arms to the poor and extends her hands to the needy ... she has no fear for her household; for all of them are clothed in scarlet ... Her husband is respected ... She is clothed with strength and dignity; she can laugh at the days to come. She speaks with wisdom ... Her children arise and call her blessed; her husband also and he praises her: 'Many women do noble things, but you surpass them all'" (Pro. 31:31,10-11,20-21,23,25-26,28-29).

To summarize, the hard working woman of God has earned many rewards; has become a valuable person; is reliable; has no financial lack; has resources to give to the poor; has no fears; receives much family respect; has strength and dignity; can laugh in the face of adversity; has gained wisdom, praise and recognition from her children; and is honored and praised by her husband.

Anyone who has all of these things will also have the spill-over blessings of peace, joy, faith, contentment, love and acceptance. The hard working, virtuous woman is greatly blessed by God.

INTEGRITY

The companion to hard work is integrity, and without it, everything else will eventually fail. In the world of money and industry, integrity means honest, righteous and fair dealings. Corrupt or crooked business dealings are like time bombs waiting to explode; they will always lead to destruction. Here are some scriptures that emphasize the importance of integrity:

"Do not steal. Do not lie. Do not deceive one another ... Do not hold back the wages of a hired man ... Do not do anything that endangers your neighbor's life ... Do not use dishonest standards when measuring length, weight or quantity. Use honest scales and honest weights" (Lev. 19:11,13,16,35-36).

The book of Deuteronomy encourages the same business ethics but also tells of God's blessings for those who follow them.

We read, *"You must have accurate and honest weights and measures, so that you may live long in the land the Lord your God is giving you"* (Dt. 25:15).

Proverbs says, *"The Lord abhors dishonest scales but accurate weights are his delight ... The integrity of the upright guides them ... When the righteous prosper, the city rejoices ... The wicked man earns deceptive wages, but he who sows righteousness reaps a sure reward."* (Pro. 11:1,3,10,18).

Integrity is rewarded by the Lord. He delights in honest gain and releases prosperity and joy to those who work hard and handle their business with righteous integrity.

SUMMARY

As we close this chapter, here is a summary of what will bring the blessings of the Lord into our lives. Some things, like the fear of the Lord, seem more spiritual while helping the poor and oppressed seem more compassionate and appropriate. Serving the cause of the gospel seems more religious, and good work ethic seems so practical and obvious. The Bible teaches that all of these things are important; they all bring God's powerful blessings. Use the whole recipe without missing any ingredient, and God's blessings will come to you and your family in great abundance.

Here then is a recipe for blessings:

1 lb. of - Fear the Lord.
2 lbs of - shunning evil.
1 cup of - enduring hardship for Christ's sake.
3 tablespoons of - giving generously to the poor
1 quart of – liberating the oppressed.
2 lbs of - ministering the gospel.
1 can of broth - to support ministers.
½ a gallon of – hard work with no compromise on integrity.

If a person does all of these things, godly blessings will most certainly follow them, and they will provide a gourmet meal for many generations to come.

Chapter Ten

BLESSING CHILDREN WITH YOUR HANDS

BLESSING YOUR CHILDREN

*H*ere are seven practical ways for parents to bless their children:

1. By speaking good words of encouragement and approbation over them.
2. By providing goods and services for them such as financial resources, training in the useful skills of life and a godly education.
3. By helping them find the right doors for advanced education, business, ministry and social opportunities that will lead them toward their godly best.
4. By laying your hands on them with faith-filled prayers to impart God's grace into their lives.
5. By being a godly example for them to follow, for they will be formed more by your actions than your words.
6. By providing a stable home, a spiritual and healthy environment that is conducive to godly growth and maturity.
7. By clearing away the negative things from your past (things such as Generational Curses) that can be passed on to your children so they will inherit a good name and a clean template and be able to better fulfill their destiny in God.

These blessings that come from parents are in most cases, self evident. The one that I feel needs to be further addressed is number 4. "To bless your children: By laying your hands on them with faith-filled prayers to impart God's grace into their lives."

THE LAYING ON OF HANDS

The importance of the laying on of hands is noted in the book of Hebrews where it is listed as one of the six foundational doctrines of the church.

We read, *"Therefore let us leave the elementary teachings about Christ and go on to maturity, not laying again the foundation of repentance from acts that lead to death, and of faith in God, instruction about baptisms, the laying on of hands, the resurrection of the dead, and eternal judgment"* (Heb. 6:1-3).

The book of Hebrews lists 6 foundational teachings about Christ. The first 3 involve our coming into relationship with Him. They are repentance, faith and water baptism. The last 2 involve what happens after we die; they are the resurrection and eternal judgment. The doctrine in the middle involves God moving through human agents; it is called the laying on of hands.

The doctrine of the laying on of hands tells us that between our coming to Christ and the time of our death, God wants to use us for the release of His blessings. A powerful release of God's anointing will flow through human hands.

WHEN HANDS AND FAITH CONNECT

God can do anything without the use of human agents, but He has chosen to involve people as ambassadors and representatives. The saints have been assigned to distribute His blessings through their hands. This requires faith, obedience and timing, but once those elements are in place, a minister's hands become holy conductors; they function as if they are the hands of God.

When a person is given authority they may release blessings upon those who are under their government, care or ministry. There is a heaven-sent expectation that power and blessings will be passed on through hands that are directed by hearts of faith.

We read in the Bible that through the laying on of human hands, God anointed priests; commissioned preachers and ministers; ordained kings; healed the sick; cast out demons; imparted peace; and released parental blessings to the next generation. Blessings flowed continually through the hands of powerful people as they prayed over those in need.

PARENTS WHO BLESS CHILDREN

God will not ignore a child's free will, but He has put laws of authority in place that cannot be denied. He will bless children and grandchildren, when godly parents pronounce blessings over them by the laying on of hands. Even with rebellious children, God will release a level of holy pressure and persistence that is almost irresistible if parents will continue to bless and not curse them. The prayers and blessings of parents that are transmitted through the laying on of hands will widen the door for God's effective power to reach even the most difficult children.

DREAMS INSPIRE PRAYER

I am convinced that no person receives God's blessings unless some other person prays for them. Even when we do not know a person, God can lead us to pray for them. I think of the time I saw a young lady's face in one of my dreams.

She had an olive skin tone with a small mole on her right cheek. Her hair was long and jet black. She was about 21 years old, and I thought, in my dream, that she was of Spanish descent. Her face was presented to me in a picture frame. I did not discover her name nor any part of her story, but her face stayed before me for what seemed about half a minute, and that was the whole dream.

When I woke, I prayed for the young lady's salvation and for the blessings of God to come upon her. The picture of her face was indelibly printed on my mind and I prayed for this nameless person many times over the next year. For the next couple of years I kept my eyes open in case I might meet this lady and discover her story, but I did not meet her. I think I will meet her in heaven, and she will thank me for coming into agreement with God for her salvation. For me, it was a joy to partner with God on her behalf.

PARENTS ARE COMISSIONED

Combined with the power of target prayer, a parent has been commissioned to lay their hands on their children to release God's blessings. This should be done on a regular basis and also on special occasions. It should be done at times of transition throughout a child's life. It should also be done spontaneously as the Holy Spirit prompts a parent.

Parents should lay their hands on the head of their child and say something like, "My son, (or my daughter,) today I release God's blessings upon your life. May you receive angelic protection, favor with those around you, success with whatever you put your hand to, and the anointing of the Holy Spirit to teach and train you. I speak open doors for God's favor to be in your life. I speak these words over you in faith in the mighty name of Jesus."

POWER IN A GRANDPARENT'S HANDS

If curses can be passed down from great, great grandparents, (see Exodus 20:4-5) we can be sure that blessings can be transmitted through grandparents, as well. Some parents are young and may not recognize the power of God in their hands or in their prayers, but most godly grandparents know. They have learned to lay their hands on their grandchildren and release God's blessings. Most grandchildren will let grandparents bless them, for godly grandparents often have a gentle way about them that is endearing for a child of any age.

FATHERS WHO BLESS

This hands-on-anointing is especially powerful when it is released through a father or one standing before God, in the place of a father. Do you remember the Bible story of Isaac and Jacob? Isaac had twin sons, Esau and Jacob. Isaac was old and blind, and the time came to release the blessings of the family inheritance to his sons. Esau had been born just moments before Jacob and as such, he was the first born and was entitled to the greatest blessing; it was his birthright.

Rebekah, their mother, wanted Jacob to have the first blessing because Jacob was godly and Esau was rebellious. She convinced Jacob to pretend that he was Esau; so Jacob went into his father's tent acting as though he was Esau, and he received the primary birthright blessing.

"Jacob said to his father, "I am Esau your firstborn.... give me your blessing."

"He [Isaac] *blessed him and said, ... 'May God give you of heaven's dew and of earth's richness – an abundance of grain and new wine. May nations serve you and people bow down to you. Be lord over your brothers, and may the sons of your mother bow down to you. May those who curse you be cursed*

and those who bless you be blessed'" (Gen. 27:19,27-29).

Later Esau, who was out hunting, came to receive his father's blessings. Notice the power of the blessings that the father had already given to Jacob; they could not be reversed.

"After Isaac finished blessing him and Jacob had scarcely left his father's presence, his brother Esau came in from hunting ... Isaac trembled violently and said, 'Who was it, then, that hunted game and brought it to me? I ate it just before you came and I blessed him- and indeed he will be blessed! ... Your brother came deceitfully and took your blessings'" (Gen. 27:30,33,35).

Regardless of the unscrupulous manner with which Rebekah and Jacob deceived Isaac, the point I wish to make is regarding the power of a father's blessing. When a godly father lays his hands on his child and blesses them, that child is blessed by God.

PLEASE UNDERSTAND

Parents and grandparents, please understand that you are ministers of heaven on behalf of your children. Just like the prophets and ministers of the Bible who laid their hands on the heads of men and women to bless, heal, ordain kings or anoint priests; lay your hands on the heads of your sons and daughters and release them into God's purpose and blessings. Be led by the Holy Spirit, for the things you speak will activate eternal dynamics over the lives of your children.

Chapter Eleven

BLESSINGS FROM KINGS
AND RULERS

NATIONS RECEIVE BLESSINGS AND CURSES

God has established the nations. Scripture says, *"From one man he made every nation of men, that they should inhabit the earth; and he determined the times set for them and the exact places where they should live. God did this so that men would seek him . . . and find him"* (Acts 17:26-27).

God gave the nations their boundaries and their appointed time so that the people of those nations might seek him. It is God's desire that the people of every country would find Him and be blessed. Most nations, however, like many families, have inherited a massive mixture of blessings and curses from previous generations.

A detailed list of national sins that produced on-going curses can be found in Psalm 106.

"When our fathers were in Egypt, they gave no thought to your miracles ... they rebelled by the ... Red Sea ... they gave in to their craving; in the wasteland ... At Horeb they made a calf and worshipped an idol ... They forgot the God who saved them ...
So he said he would destroy them – had not Moses ... stood in the breach before him to keep his wrath from destroying them. Then they despised the pleasant land; they did not believe his

promise. They grumbled in their tents and did not obey the Lord. ... They yoked themselves to the Baal of Peor and ate sacrifices of- fered to lifeless gods; they provoked the Lord to anger by their wick- ed deeds ... By the waters of Meribah they angered the Lord ... for they rebelled against the Spirit of God ... They did not destroy the peoples as the Lord commanded them, but they mingled with the na- tions and adopted their customs. They worshipped their idols, which became a snare to them. They sacrificed their sons and daughters to demons. They shed innocent blood, the blood of their sons and daughters whom they sacrificed to the idols of Canaan, and the land was desecrated by their blood. They defiled themselves by what they did; by their deeds they prostituted themselves. Therefore the Lord was angry ... with his inheritance. He handed them over to the na- tions, and their foes ruled over them" (Ps. 106 - selected verses).

The entire nation of Israel was judged repeatedly because of their repeated sins. I have purposely recorded this long list of horrifying sins to show the reader that God is amazingly merciful. Even after this devastating list of sins, the nation still had hope. We find that Moses and Phinehas, (who we previously mentioned) were godly he- roes who intervened, stopped the sin and halted a plague that had killed 24,000 people (see Psalm 106:10,11 and Numbers 25:1-13). They stopped the complete annihilation of Israel. As a result, Phine- has was blessed with righteousness for endless generations. Nations whose leaders or populous participate in godly service or wicked sin receive national blessings or curses and those blessings or curses are generational. The laws of sowing and reaping that apply to nations are still in effect today just as much as they were in ancient times.

THE STANDARD OF LIVING

The standard of living in every nation is a direct result of the bless- ings or curses they have earned. The nations are set on scales that tip toward greatness or disaster with blessings on one side and curs- es on the other. The balance of blessings and curses come from the historical behavior of a nation's leaders and its population. One criminal in a nation will not bring destruction upon the entire country, but a wicked leader, a wicked government or if a great number of a nation's citizenship act wickedly, then the scales will tip toward judgment and destruction. The tipping of the scales can lead to extreme judgments and even complete annihilation.

On the other hand, the scales can tip in the opposite direction as a nation or its leaders extend extraordinary kindness to those in need. That is how a nation can be honored as the greatest nation on earth.

Sodom and Gomorrah suffered annihilation because of their horrific sins. The men of Sodom had opportunity to repent when the angels resisted them, but they continued to press towards Lot's house in their pursuit of wickedness (Genesis 19).

Wicked nations are still capable of receiving God's blessings. The people of Nineveh may have been just as wicked as the people of Sodom but they repented when they heard the preaching of Jonah the prophet (Jonah 3). Because they repented, God lifted the judgment of annihilation off of them and that generation was spared.

In the New Testament, Jesus cursed the cities of Capernaum, Bethsaida and Korazin because they had seen most of His miracles, and yet they did not repent of their wickedness. Seventy percent of all of Christ's miracles happened around the Sea of Galilee, in the vicinity of these 3 cities. That is why God expected more from them. God's mercy has always been extended to displace judgment, but many nations reject God's mercy; they fail to repent.

God's heart for the nations is heard in the words that He spoke to His chosen people. He said, *"if my people, who are called by my name, will humble themselves and pray and seek my face and turn from their wicked ways, then I will hear from heaven and will forgive their sin and will heal their land"* (2 Chr. 7:14).

Blessings are not extended to nations because of their faith in Jesus alone, nor are they cursed because they lack a faith in Christ. Although faith in God will lead to blessings, nations are judged by their leaders' and the majority of their citizen's behavior. Curses or blessings fall upon nations because of how they treat their citizens and how they treat the peoples of other nations.

GOD WILL BLESS THE NATIONS

1. God will bless the nations who pursue justice and mercy.
2. He will bless the nations who rescue the oppressed or extend compassion to the poor.
3. He will bless the nations who send out ministers of the gospel.
4. He will bless the nations that promote biblical standards of righteousness.
5. He will bless the nations who have learned to bless Israel.

God will curse those nations that shed innocent blood, oppress their citizens, encourage corruption, promote violence, worship demons or revel in wickedness and sexual perversion. A curse brings punishment and it will result in natural disasters, financial depression, poverty, and civil unrest.

NATURAL DISASTERS

Natural disasters are not always judgments from God, but many are. The earthquake that swallowed Korah (Numbers 16:31-35), the flaming meteor shower that struck Sodom (Genesis 19:23), the drought in King Ahab's time (1 Kings 17:1, 18:1) and even Noah's global flood (Genesis 7:11-24) were natural disasters, and each of these examples were judgments (curses) from God.

The book of Revelation warns us of the great tribulation. It will bring a series of natural disasters almost as severe as Noah's flood. They will come as judgments from God because of mankind's evil ways. The great tribulation is the result of global curses that have piled up. The cup of poison in the nations of the world are almost full, and the judgments of God are about to fall. Even during the great tribulation, however, God's mercy will abound.

Many disasters are a necessary part of nature. Some natural disasters must come to keep our climate and environment refreshed and balanced. A volcano, for example, will release carbon emissions that will shield the earth from the suns burning rays. A forest fire will clear the land for new growth and this will help sustain wildlife. A forest fire is the only way that some pinecones, for example, will open up and release their seeds. Even hurricanes and water tornadoes are needed to stir up the depths of the sea. These violent acts churn the silt from the ocean floor, and this fills the oceans with much needed nourishment. This, in turn, feeds plankton and the increased number of plankton, provides food for larger creatures. What, to the untrained eye, looks like muddy water, will sustain life in the sea. I once went scuba diving a couple of days after a hurricane had flared up hundreds of miles away from our location. We had no hurricane winds where we were but we still had to call off our dive. The waters, that were usually clear, were filled with so much silt that our visibility extended no more than two feet in front of us. Although we did not see evidence of this hurricane on the land or in the air around us, its power moved through the waters and churned them up hundreds of miles away from its source. Even great floods serve to redistribute huge amounts of soil that replenish the valleys for better agricultural returns.

While not all natural disasters are judgments from God, it appears that many are. When great numbers of people are killed because of a natural disaster, I am convinced that a 2 sided edge of God's sword is at work. One side of the sword will judge a nation because of wickedness that has been encouraged or permitted. The other side of God's sword may be a surprise to some. On occasion, God removes His people from the evil of the earth in order to keep them from torturous pain and to bring them into His eternal blessings.

The Bible says, *"The righteous perish, and no one ponders it in his heart; devout men are taken away, and no one understands that the righteous are taken away to be spared from evil. Those who walk uprightly enter into peace; they find rest as they lie in death"* (Isa. 57:1-2).

And again we read, *"Precious in the sight of the Lord is the death of his saints"* (Ps. 116:15).

Recently, in the USA, we experienced a natural disaster which I believe was a judgment from God. A dreadful hurricane named Katrina struck the Gulf Coast. New Orleans took the brunt of the hurricane's wrath. This city was the center for voodoo witchcraft; it had the highest crime rate in the country and the city celebrated sexual perversion in such a flagrant manner that it compared with the worst in the country. Curses follow such wickedness, and in this case, many died during this natural disaster. No doubt, many godly people were taken away by the catastrophe as well. Only God can sort out the details of such a situation, but we look back and see both the kindness and the severity of God.

BLESSED IS THE NATION

"Blessed are the people whose God is the Lord" (Ps.144:15).

The nations that rightly boast of great prosperity, strength, peace and equity for their people are the nations that have behaved in such a manner as to evoke God's blessings. Some have shared these blessings for a season but misused their privilege, entertained wickedness on a large scale, and eventually fell into ruin. It would require a volume of books to uncover the history of blessings and curses on the nations. Whatever a nation sows, however, it will surely reap.

Scripture says, *"Righteousness exalts a nation, but sin is a disgrace* [reproach] *to any people"* (Pro. 14:34).

THE UNITED STATES

I believe the United States is the greatest nation on the earth (besides Israel). This honor has been given to her by God because of the godly behavior of some of her leaders and many of her people. Regardless of many global criticisms, people from around the world want to live in the USA.

In the United States, many recognize the delicate scales that tip on one side toward blessings and on the other side toward curses and judgments. The United States, in my opinion, is perhaps the most misunderstood nation in the world, largely due to the propaganda of a biased media that paints the US in a bad light. It is not that the USA is without error, but the amazing amount of good is often down-played or ignored, and biblical godliness is mocked by sinners who want to justify a godless lifestyle.

God continues to bless the United States because many of her leaders and many of her citizens endeavor to follow godly principles for justice and mercy. Here are the 5 emphases (as previously listed) that release God's blessings upon the USA.

1. **The generous giving of financial aid to poor people around the world**
   The financial aid and generous giving to the poor that comes from the government and the peoples of the USA far exceeds that of any other nation. God takes notice of this (Acts 10:1-4).

2. Her consistent support of Israel

Whoever blesses Israel (God's chosen people), God will bless (Genesis 12:3, 27:29).

3. The USA has come to the aid of many peoples and nations who have been oppressed

They are the only nation in history who have consistently defeated oppressive regimes and not taken possession of the land they conquered. They have given conquered lands back to the indigenous peoples who live there and provided aid to help those nations rebuild their infrastructures.

4. Many in the USA, including presidents, have confessed a living faith in Jesus Christ

This is a nation of faith. Her churches are filled with godly, faith-filled, praying, disciples of Christ. They are as salt and light in the nation and in the world. God blesses the nation because of them.

5. Many Americans have stepped forward to be ministers of the gospel

Some may not perform this task well, but God loves ministers of the gospel and blesses the land that supports them.

God has blessed the United States because of these godly acts of righteousness and heroism. A spiritual battle continually rocks the United States over issues such as the family, human rights, the protection of life, sexual decency, care for foreigners, economic equity and extending aid and military help for downtrodden people around the world.

Political elections in the USA bring these issues to the forefront. I have no doubt that one issue in recent elections is far more important to God than any other issue. All other issues pale compared to the issue of abortion. I believe this to be the main issue that voters should look at to determine who they should vote for as President.

I do not understand a Christian who would vote for any person who is not completely prolife.

Abortion is popular in the nations of the Western world, but it still remains a huge battle front in the United States. Our failure, however, to stop government sanctioned killings of unborn children in this land is an abomination to God. This terrible act is present and popular in the United States, and it will bring curses and judgments from God on any nation, including the United States of America.

Already, the USA suffers unnecessary judgments because of abortion, the public encouragement of the Gay agenda, and the celebration of witchcraft and sexual perversions. The USA must keep the scales tipped in favor of blessings if she is to continue to be the greatest nation on the earth.

NATIONAL EXAMPLES OF CURSES

The rise of Communism and Nazism seemed to start with great success, but they quickly suffered their demise. Both regimes were brutal; they massacred God's chosen people, the Jews, and oppressed anyone who differed from their ideologies. Both Germany and Russia were guilty of the shedding of innocent blood; they murdered multitudes of people. Their own people have suffered greatly because of the sins of these regimes. They were judged by God, dishonored among the nations, and the generation who participated in the crimes of Nazism and Communism were cursed. Many of those curses have been passed on to their descendants today. Even today, many are in need of healing, deliverance and the breaking off of generational curses because of those evil years. God continues to reach out His hand of mercy to those who desire His grace. Multitudes have received healing and freedom from those judgments and are leading their families in the ways of the Lord.

RULERS HAVE FAR REACHING AUTHORITY

I encourage every person who reads this book to prayerfully consider their own nation and insist on supporting righteous leadership. The power that national leaders hold is far greater than their ability to manage an economy, promote good standards for education or secure their borders against enemies. Their most important work is to lead their nation in godliness and righteousness. It is most important that their actions please Almighty God. If they do, God will bless them and the nation that is under their oversight.

It is likely that whatever decisions are made in the halls of government today will eventually produce blessings or curses over a nation. The ramifications of these decisions will fall upon the generations that follow. Our children will reap the spiritual results of the decisions that governing leaders are making today.

You may not see yourself as a political person. Perhaps you think that the political world does not affect you and your family. Nothing could be further from the truth. Rulers have far reaching authority; they can open spiritual doors of blessings over your community. They can also release a whirlwind of judgment if they promote wickedness.

It is the mandate of God's people to pray, participate in, and promote the good news of the gospel. The preaching of the gospel is the power of God unto salvation, and salvation at the grassroots level is the only true and lasting hope for any nation. God has made the nations and given them their allotted time and boundaries so that the people of those nations might seek and find Him. He has also placed His church and you as an individual in the nations for such a time as this.

"I urge, then, first of all, that requests, prayers, intercession and

thanksgiving be made for everyone - for kings and all those in authority, that we may live peaceful and quiet lives in all godliness and holiness. This is good, and pleases God our Savior, who wants all men to be saved and to come to a knowledge of the truth"

(1 Tim. 2:1-4).

PART TWO

CURSES CAN BE BROKEN

Chapter Twelve

CURSES ARE REAL

A WITCHDOCTOR'S CURSE

I met James Santhosham in Madras, India. He is a fine pastor of a local church, but as a boy he had been cursed by a witch doctor. He told me his story....

James came from a remote, forest village in the back-woods of India. It was a poor community that was mostly cut-off from the outside world. A Hindu priest, or "swami," resided over the village. The swami moved among the people like a professional witchdoctor. He wielded great influence and authority because all of the villagers were dedicated Hindus and he was their spiritual leader.

When James was born, the swami said, "The stars are not lining up for this boy, therefore, he is cursed. He will bring trouble to all who associate with him. The entire village will suffer because of him."

Word got out and town gossip spread these evil words, keeping them alive. As James grew up he was rejected by the people of his village. Only his immediate family would pay attention to him.

James became the town pariah; when crops failed or disease took the life of a villager, James, inevitably, was to blame. Children outside of his family were forbidden to play with him, and adults in the village would scowl at him whenever they happened upon him. His entire family was shunned because neighbors would say, "The family must be evil to have brought such a wicked child into the world."

Over the years, James became a catch basin of rejection and depression. He learned to hate the other villagers and finally he hated himself. A bitter root grew within him because of unforgiveness and hopelessness. Soon evil spirits taunted and tormented him. They accused him of being wicked even when he did no wrong. He was a total failure in life. The pain of rejection brought such despair that James could not bear it, and he decided to kill himself.

James ran away from home, and on three occasions, he tried to take his life. Once he tried to hang himself from the branch of a large tree, but the branch broke. On two occasions, he waded out into the Bay of Bengal, hoping that the ocean would swallow him up and he would drown. Both times, the pounding surf threw him back to the shore. He was unsuccessful even at killing himself, and eventually, he lost his nerve.

After his failed suicide attempts, James resolved that his fate was to live in horror and unrelenting torment. He believed that it was his destiny to live a life of suffering, and he accepted his fate. Soon he became one of the millions of destitute people who live on the streets of Madras. He ate garbage, became a professional beggar and stole whatever he could to survive. Filth and darkness swallowed him, and ill health battered and broke him. Any dignity afforded to humanity had long departed, and James fell into depravity. It was there that hope beyond hope suddenly came and rescued him.

CURSES CAN BE BROKEN

"Youth With A Mission" (YWAM) workers are among the most effective evangelists in the world. When the Lord led them to James, it seemed that he was more dead than alive, but they possessed a healing secret. The workers had the power of God's Holy Spirit living in them, and they knew how to minister compassion and love. They brought a message of salvation, forgiveness of sins, and heaven's healing power to James Santhosham.

At first, James went along with their foreign teachings because of the food and shelter they offered, but soon James realized that a wonderful change had come over him since the YWAM workers had prayed for him. Like some kind of magic, he experienced peace and joy for the first time in his life. Everything began to change for James. They introduced him to Jesus Christ, and he received forgiveness of sins. He learned to forgive the people who had tormented him, and curses were broken off of his life. Healing came to James' body and soul. He renounced his evil past, embraced the Living God and became a born-again Christian.

James joined the YWAM team in Madras and was nursed back to health. Every day his life became better than it was the day before. Past judgments were broken off and he was delivered from tormenting demons and evil spirits. The love of Jesus broke through and the light of God changed him completely. Purity came to his heart, freedom came to his mind, and a lovely smile came to his face. James had an amazing conversion.

James became a student in training at the YWAM Discipleship Training School. He was taken on as a new recruit and soon was on the streets sharing the love of God with others. In his own rite, James became a minister of the gospel.

PREPARATIONS FOR POWER

A year or so passed since James found faith in Christ. He had experienced God's love, and this led him to think about his family and the people of his village. Even though he had suffered because of them, he had a new love in his heart and wanted to help them. James decided to go back to his village and preach salvation. He wanted his people to know the amazing love that God had given him. The Holy Spirit began leading James back to the source of his pain. He had mixed feelings; he thought about their hatred for him and what they might do, but James pressed through his fears. Finally, he gathered courage and made the long journey back to his village.

Upon his arrival, the villagers not only rejected him, but beat him severely. A mob came upon him and roughed him up so badly that he almost died. They dragged his limp, unconscious body out of the village and threw him on a brush pile at the side of the road. He was like the wounded man who fell among thieves in the story of the Good Samaritan - he was half dead (Luke 10:25).

James, however, did not die; he revived and slowly made the long, arduous journey back to the YWAM base. There, he was nursed to health a second time. James was discouraged and confused; disappointment overcame him. Even though he did not understand, God had not forsaken him. James knew how much God had done for him, but he could not figure out what had gone wrong. He thought that God's power would have protected him, and the message of God's love would have been irresistible. Nothing happened as he had hoped, but James continued to pray for his people.

God heard James' prayer and did not forget his village; He had a plan. Six months after his first attempt, James gathered enough courage and returned to his people for a second visit. The day he arrived, his younger brother died, and as one would expect, everyone blamed James. Normally, they would have attacked him, but they held off in reverence for his dead brother. The family was in grieving and preparing for the funeral pyre. Although hatred was boiling in their hearts, they decided to release their anger on James at a later date.

James went to his family home. There, in a tiny room with a mud floor and a thatch roof, lay a cold, dead body on a roughhewn wooden table. His brother had been his only friend in the village and now he was gone. James looked upon his ashen face and saw the dreadful burn marks on his legs and feet where town officials had burnt them with fire to be certain he was dead.

James did not know what to do, but God was with him. He closed the door and got down on his knees beside his brother's body. James faced an impossible situation. He cried out to God in prayer. With loud crying and tears, he called for heaven's mercy. Many layers of wicked curses were covering his family and his village; but God desires to break curses. The prophet Ezekiel proclaimed the word of the Lord.

He said, *"I* [God] *looked for a man among them who would build up the wall and stand before me in the gap on behalf of the land so I would not have to destroy it* (Ez. 22:30).

Israel, at the time when Ezekiel wrote these words, was overcome with curses because of the terrible sins that were rampant in the nation. God was using Ezekiel to call his people to be curse - breaking intercessors. Dark judgments can be removed. God is looking for people who will come into agreement with him so that deadly curses might be lifted.

While James was praying, he was building a wall and standing in the gap before the Lord. He did not understand all that was happening in the spirit world, but he kept praying. God had him in what seemed to be a timeless prayer capsule, and James gained super-natural energy to continue his vigil of intercession.

AN OPEN HEAVEN

No one opened the door or interfered with the man in mourning, and the prayers of James Santhosham did not stop. After 24 hours the spiritual atmosphere lightened, the darkness lifted and the power of God fell upon the village. Suddenly, his dead brother coughed and came back to life. He sat up and James embraced him and gave him some water. James was extremely weak, but he managed to cradle his brother in his arms and carry him outside.

The villagers could not believe what they were seeing. God Almighty poured out his mercy upon the village, and the people saw a demonstration of His mighty power. The heavens opened; the eyes of the villagers opened, their hearts opened, and now they were made ready to open their ears and listen to what James had to say. He preached the good news of Christ. The Holy Spirit moved upon them with wisdom and revelation, and that day, at least it seemed to James, the entire village was converted to Christ. Even the swami repented of his sins and acknowledged Jesus Christ as Lord. Holy Spirit revival came to the village of James Santhosham.

After telling me his story, James said, "Would you like to shake the hand of one who has been raised from the dead? My brother is sitting right there."

I looked to the other side of the room. There was his brother. He was now a pastor and a minister of the gospel just like James. I for sure wanted to meet him, and I did.

INCANTATIONS

In many nations, curses come because of the incantations of witch-doctors. Witchdoctors are the professional spiritual leaders of many pagan religions. Depending on their culture and religion, they have different names, different techniques and different powers. The results of their work, however, is the same. Like the swami in the Santhosham story, they knowingly or unknowingly, work with Satan to perpetuate curses. Many are deceived to think they are doing good, but all of their activities lead to sickness, ruin and death.

If people know how to walk with God they need not fear any witchdoctor. Their curses are not effective when a saint remains under the protective shield of godly faith. The shield is available for those who embrace the work of the cross and the provisions of God.

Scripture says, *"Like a fluttering sparrow or a darting swallow, an undeserved curse does not come to rest"* (Pro. 26:2).

A witchdoctor's curse will not affect a saint in right standing with God. A curse cannot settle on people without a legitimate reason. If, however, anyone aligns themselves with those who practice witchcraft, they are in trouble. If, like James Santhosham, they or their families are under the authority of a witchdoctor, then the words of a dark priest will have power over them.

James broke away from a canopy of curses through the saving grace of Jesus Christ. He discovered that he had authority with God, and he returned to the source of those curses with the life giving power of the gospel. Christians equipped with the love of God and the gifts of the Holy Spirit are far more powerful than any curses or demons.

Jesus said, *"The   theif* [Satan] *comes only to steal and kill and destroy; I have come that they may have life, and have it to the full"* (Jn. 10:10).

Jesus has come to change the spiritual environment of people's lives. He comes to take us from the kingdom of darkness and to bring us into the kingdom of light. He sends forth those who have become disciples as ambassadors. They are assigned to bring liberty and light to a dark, demonized world.

COMMON CURSES

This book will help equip God's people for supernatural works of service. We will investigate many kinds of curses, and discover that many curses do not come from witchdoctors. They are often judgments that come because of the terrible sins that we or our ancestors have committed. Here is a list of possible sources of a curse:

1. Professional witches or witchdoctors
2. Parents, teachers or spiritual leaders who have authority
3. Ourselves, due to our own sins or judgmental words
4. From generations past because of our ancestor's sins
5. From God, because He judges vile abominations

My goal in writing this section of the book is twofold: first, I wish to expose the pitfalls that bring curses upon people; secondly, I will show what Christ has done for us so that we and our families may be set free from curses. Without the power of God's Holy Spirit and faith in the Lord Jesus Christ, it is impossible to be freed from the judgment and penalties of curses. With Christ, however, every prisoner can be set free and every curse can be removed. All of the instructions we need can be found in the Bible. All of the wisdom we need can be found by hearing the voice of God's Holy Spirit. All of the power we need will come in the name of Jesus. Let the journey begin.

Chapter Thirteen

CURSES FROM GOD

A FOUNDATION FOR RUIN

Curses are more than fairy tales, folklore and the stuff of legends; they are a very real demise in every society. They are a present cause of ruin, the greatest hindrance to personal peace and prosperity. They may affect a person while they are still in their mother's womb, giving them a poor start in life. Curses will stick to most people like a spiritual genetic code; they will be ever-present until they die. Those curses, in most cases, are usually passed on to the next generation.

Curses bring poverty, debilitating addictions, unrelenting sicknesses and relational strife. Some people have more curses than others, but curses are common in every country and culture. Most people are born into families that are fighting their way through heavy thickets of dark curses. Whole generations are caught in a web of formidable judgments, and many individuals will add a few more curses to the malaise before they die.

A SWORN JUDGMENT

Curses may come from God. These curses are called sworn judgments. Notice these verses from Deuteronomy: *"If you do not obey*

...[the] decrees I am giving you today, all these curses will come upon you and overtake you ... The Lord will send on you curses, confusion and rebuke in everything you put your hand to"

(Dt. 28:15-20)

People receive curses from God because of certain kinds of sin against the Lord and humanity. Witchcraft, occult practices, sexual perversions, killing the innocent or injuring the handicapped are a few of the sins that will bring serious judgments to people. To the surprise of many, it is God who sends these curses. He brings judgment when heinous crimes are committed because He is the Judge of heaven; He is the defender of the weak and the protector of the innocent. He watches over the widow and the orphan.

Scripture says, *" 'Vengeance is Mine, I will repay,' says the Lord"* (Ro. 12:19).

ABORTION

When I was a young pastor I prayed for a young, single Christian woman who was told by her doctor that she had a medical problem and could never have children. God healed her, and later, she committed fornication and became pregnant. Then the woman had an abortion.

Sometimes Christians fall into sin, and God will forgive them. The shedding of innocent blood, however, brings a curse; God is the avenger of an unborn child. What would happen if this girl repeated this sin, and over time, she had many abortions? No doubt, a powerful generational curse would come upon her. She can still be forgiven, for the Bible teaches that all sin is forgiveable except blaspheming the Holy Spirit (see Mark 3:28,29).

Even when forgiveness is granted, however, a curse may remain. When a person repents of their sins, they are given a ticket into heaven, but that does not mean that all of their problems in this life are now behind them. Many Christians struggle under great difficulties. A curse will linger until a person meets God's conditions, and it is broken off by the power of the Holy Spirit. God swears to judge the wicked, and that judgment is called a curse. All who have had an abortion or participated in procuring one will be under a curse until that curse is effectively broken. These people may still go to heaven, yet they will suffer all kinds of trouble in this life because of the sworn judgment that hangs over them.

CURSES ON ISRAEL

Curses came upon Israel many times because of their sins. Thousands of years ago, Daniel prayed this prayer:

"All Israel has transgressed your law and turned away, refusing to obey you. 'Therefore, the curses and sworn judgments written in the Law of Moses, the servant of God, have been poured out on us, because we have sinned against you. You have fulfilled the words spoken against us and against our rulers by bringing upon us great disaster'"
(Dan. 9:10-12).

Curses and sworn judgments fell on Israel. Notice the pattern:

1. Israel committed curse deserving sins.
2. Words or curses were spoken against them.
3. God released those curses and judgments against Israel.
4. God punished Israel.
5. God found and raised up Daniel, the intercessor.
6. Daniel began to pray that the curses would be lifted.

Daniel, the prophet, was an intercessor (prayer warrior) and a hero of the faith. He was a curse-breaker, a deliverer and a champion for his nation. These verses from Daniel help us learn about curses. They are part of Daniel's petition for national amnesty. The interssesor is pleading with God for sworn judgments to be lifted off the people. That is what intercessors do.

ADAM'S CURSE

Generational curses came upon humanity when sins were committed by the first family. All people on the planet are under a curse because of Adam and Eve's sin in the Garden of Eden. A sworn judgment and a generational curse came on the human race because Adam consorted with Satan, took his counsel and committed treason against the Almighty.

That is witchcraft; it is an abomination to the Lord. Witchcraft always brings a curse. All who turn to the occult bring sworn judgments on themselves. They are cursed, and those curses are always passed on to their children. The Lord cursed all women because of Eve's sin and all people because of Adam's sin.

To Eve he said, *"I will greatly increase your pains in childbearing; with pain you will give birth to children. Your desire will be for your husband, and he will rule over you"* (Gen. 3:16).

"To Adam he said, ... "Cursed is the ground because of you; through painful toil you will eat of it all the days of your life. It will produce thorns and thistles for you, and you will eat the plants of the field. By the sweat of your brow you will eat your food until you return to the ground since from it you were taken; for dust you are and to dust you will return ... So the Lord God banished him from the Garden of Eden to work the ground from which he had been taken" (Gen. 3:17 -19,23).

The curse that fell on the human race was a judgment from God. It has been passed down from generation to generation, and some aspects of that Adamic curse will be in effect until the end of the millennial rule of Christ.

During the thousand year reign of Christ on the earth, we are told, *"... he who dies at a hundred will be thought a mere youth; he who fails to reach a hundred will be considered accursed"* (Isa 65:20).

Although some people will be immortal, others will die during and at the end of the millennium reign of Christ. That tells us that the Adamic curse is still in effect for some people. Notice that full freedom from the Adamic curse is not announced until the last chapter of the Bible, after the new millennium is over.

As eternity begins, we read, *"No longer will there be any curse"* (Rev. 22:3).

If the Adamic curse was totally removed when we become born again Christians, we would not become old and die. Some, in error, have preached that if a person has enough faith, they can stay the hand of death over their lives right now. All who have preached this message have eventually died, and usually, they have left a congregation of disillusioned saints behind them. I have met some of them. The doctrine of never dying applies only to those who are alive and remain until the second coming of Christ. The rest of God's people will die and experience the resurrection.

Yes, Adam's curse was legally removed at the cross, but the full outworking of it is still in progress. The book of Revelation must unfold before the full benefits of the cross will come. For details on this theme, I suggest that you read my book *Unexpected Fire – A Powerful New Study of the Book of Revelation.*

Unlike the Adamic curse, most judgments do not endure for such a long period of time, but all curses have the power to interfere with 3 or 4 generations of people within a family or community. They must be broken.

JUDGMENTS HERE ON EARTH

Judgments in this life are very different from those declared on Judgment Day, in eternity. Every person will be judged by God or Jesus at the end of their lives. In eternity, everyone stands alone either before Christ or before Almighty God. At that time, it will not matter what their parents or the rest of their family may have done; they will be judged individually and personally on their own merits. On that day, those in Christ will find that His death paid for their sins and wiped away all eternal judgments against them.

Judgments in heaven are one thing, but judgments on earth are quite different. Some judgments will come upon people while they are still alive. Here on earth, judgment is usually a package deal. Curses fall on nations, communities and families. They affect all who are within those demographics. For example, if a nation is cursed because of the abortions committed in it, then natural disasters sent from God may hit all who live there, even those who committed no abortions. Understand that entire families who are descendants of serial killers will find poverty, disease and premature death looming over them for many generations. The only solution for those families is to break free from those curses.

CURSES CAUSED BY OTHERS

Daniel is an example of a person who suffered because of other people's sins. He was a good man, yet he came under a national curse.

Scripture says of him, *"They [his attackers] could find no corruption in him* [Daniel]*, because he was trustworthy and neither corrupt nor negligent. Finally these men said, "We will never find any basis for charges against this man"* (Dan. 6:4-5).

Daniel was above reproach; he had committed no sin worthy of a curse, yet he suffered pain and trouble with the rest of Israel because judgment in this life is a package deal. He was guilty by association. Many have suffered and died because of curses even though they were not the ones to blame for the sins of their ancestors or their community. That is the power of a curse; it paints with a broad brush. Generational curses must be broken so that families may be set free from these punishments. Once free, they will be able to receive all of God's blessings that have been assigned to them.

GOD WILL NOT IGNORE WICKEDNESS

Wickedness is a gross crime committed by one human being against another or against The Almighty. The Lord cannot allow some things to go unpunished.

He says, *"A man reaps what he sows"* (Gal. 6:7).

When wicked people sin, they may think that they are getting away with horrendous evil and that no one has seen their actions, but God sees and releases generational curses on them.

In this fallen world, people are not always protected from evil men or women, but this life is only a blip on the computer screen of eternity. God allows sin to continue in this world; even gross violations against humanity are not automatically stopped. The Bible teaches that God will rescue many from suffering only when they enter into eternity. In the ages to come, multitudes will be healed and blessed; they will become joint-heirs with Christ. He will wipe away all tears from their eyes, and there will be no more pain.

It is difficult for some to understand, but scripture says, *"Some faced jeers and flogging, while still others were chained and put in prison. They were stoned; they were sawed in two; they were put to death by the sword. They went about in sheepskins . . . destitute, persecuted and mistreated - the world was not worthy of them"* (Heb. 11:36-38).

These verses give examples of the work of wicked people. For some reason, God did not stop the evil. Those wicked people who perpetrated the pain, however, received curses on their lives and families. The children of these people may be innocent, but they will suffer punishment because of their ancestor's sins. That is a generational curse, and unless it is broken off of them, they will be hindered in their progress and suffer much affliction in this life. Many people who go to heaven will be among those who have lived under a curse. Those judgments, however, will not continue beyond this life, for Christ *" ... will wipe every tear from their eyes. There will be no more ... crying"* (Rev 21:4).

The judgment of generational curses is summed up and spoken of in plain terms in the book of Numbers.

We read, *"The Lord is slow to anger, abounding in love and forgiving sin and rebellion. Yet he does not leave the guilty unpunished; he punishes the children for the sin of the fathers to the third and fourth generation"* (Num. 14:18).

A similar word is recorded in Exodus 34.

We read: *"The Lord, the Lord, the compassionate and gracious God, slow to anger, abounding in love and faithfulness, maintaining love to thousands, and forgiving wickedness, rebellion and sin. Yet he does not leave the guilty unpunished; he punishes the children and their children for the sin of the fathers to the third and fourth generation"* (Ex. 34:6-7).

BREAK THE CURSES NOW

Why should we wait until we get to heaven when we can break the generational curses now? Many have demonic interference in their lives because of a generational curse. Others have sickness, poverty or

addictions that they cannot be free of because they have curses.
They love the Lord, but they are not free.

While serving as a pastor for more than thirty-five years, my wife
and I ministered to thousands of people who thought that they would
never be free from certain pressures, traumas and addictions. We
have seen so many people set free from enormous problems, but only
after curses were broken off of their lives.   Thousands have experienced great change because of this ministry.

GOD IS MERCIFUL

Even though judgments must come, it is God's desire that His
mercy triumph over judgment. Jesus paid for all human sin and all
curses on the cross, but it is up to us to apprehend all that Christ afforded us. No person, this side of heaven, has fully received all that
was provided for in the cross. There is still more that we can take
hold of in this life. One of the benefits of the cross is the removal of
curses, but this is not as simple as some might think. We will discover the work of the cross for the removal of curses in the next
few chapters.

Chapter Fourteen

CURSES AND THE CROSS

THE POWER OF THE CROSS

Some two thousand years ago, Jesus died to pay for the sins of the world. Since the creation of man, no act for humanity has been more loving or more powerful. God made humankind in his own image. He made man for fellowship and partnership with himself. It was no surprise to God, however, when people lost their way and were separated from him. He knew what would happen. Humans would sin and mar the great opportunity they were given. That is why, even before the foundations of the world, God determined that Jesus would die for the human race. He reconciled humankind back to Himself.

The instrument of redemption was a Roman cross. Both Italians and Jews were fulfilling the edicts of the Almighty when they participated in crucifying Christ. They were not the real Christ killers, as many throughout history have stated. It was God who designed the death of his Son. Nothing in all of time or space has ever been more costly or more valuable than this sacrifice.

From the moment of Christ's death, payment was laid on the table, and man's sin was covered in full. That is why no sin, sickness, act of wickedness or curse can keep a human soul beyond the reach of God's grace. The act of the cross was so powerful that it completely covered every weakness known to humanity, even curses.

Two exceptions for forgiveness can put a person in hell. Only these remain as lasting deterrents to a man or a woman's salvation. One is the blasphemy of the Holy Spirit, and the other is a person's stubborn will and persistence in resisting God. Both of these, in my opinion, are difficult to accomplish, especially when someone is praying for you.

1. Blaspheming the Holy Spirit is a complete rejection and scandalizing of God from a person who has been a mature minister of Christ. That person must have understood deep spiritual teachings and experienced the supernatural power of miracles.

2. The other great impediment to salvation is an individual's persistent rebellion against God. The Almighty will not violate the free will that He has given humankind. If someone really works at it, they can miss heaven and forfeit their God given destiny. God will continuously reach out to them in His great mercy, but they can consistently and persistently refuse Him all of their days and, consequently, end up in Hell.

HELL IS FOR EVIL PEOPLE

Hell is not for those who missed a step, fell occasionally or, because of ignorance, did not know how to find God. Hell is for those who categorically and persistently rebel against God. It is for evil people. Multitudes will mess up their lives in this world, but will be redeemed and rescued in the end because of the authority of the cross. Do not underestimate the power of the cross.

We cannot understand every blessing that has been extended to us because of the cross and we do not see every effort that God extends to a lost soul to beckon them to salvation. No man or woman can enter heaven except through Jesus Christ, but the Holy Spirit works in ways beyond the eyes of earth to bring people to Christ. We will all be surprised to see who has made it into God's kingdom when Judgment Day arrives. We will be even more surprised when we hear the stories of how those people got there. The thousands of stories of salvation that I have heard continue to amaze me. God, the maker of every man, will find a way through Christ for most people to enter heaven. Such is the power of the cross.

IN HONOR OF GRANDPA DEREK

As I approach a more detailed study of the significance of the cross, I would like to, once again, give honor to my grandfather Derek Prince who now stands in the presence of the Lord. I know of no Bible teacher who has communicated the divine exchange of the cross better than he. I love the Bible teachings he brought on so many Bible themes. I have a special place of gratitude in my heart because of what I have received through him. On a more personal note, I am grateful and blessed to be named after Derek Prince. His first name is really Peter. I am honored to be his name sake. In many ways, I stand on his shoulders and carry much of his message and ministry. I am thankful for his commissioning in my life and for such a godly heritage.

Derek Prince taught the divine exchange. He said, and I paraphrase from many of his sermons, "On the cross, Jesus took everything about us that was bad, and in exchange, he gave us everything about Himself that was good."

Here is the essence of what he taught concerning the power of the cross. I have added some details to the list. This list is not exhaustive, but it helps us understand the power of the cross.

On the cross, Jesus took:
1. Our sin and gave us His righteousness
2. Our rejection and gave us His acceptance
3. Our ignorance and gave us His wisdom
4. Our sickness and gave us His health
5. Our shame and gave us His glory
6. Our weakness and gave us His power
7. Our poverty and gave us His wealth
8. Our failures and gave us His success
9. Our curses and gave us His blessings
10. Our death and gave us His resurrection life

TAKING HOLD OF THE DETAILS

No one on earth has taken hold of every benefit that was afforded them on the cross. Some people may think that they took hold of everything in the cross the moment they were saved. The truth is, however, that some things will not be fully claimed until we are in heaven. Nevertheless, even on this side of heaven, we can possess more than what we have received so far.

The Bible says, *"for God does not give the Spirit by measure* (Jn. 3:34 - NKJV).

God does not give His Holy Spirit by measure, but we receive it in measure. God does not limit what you can have, but all of us fail to take everything we can. If we, by faith, will receive more, then we will have more. God will not stop the flow of blessings at His end if we meet the necessary requirements at our end.

GRACE IS AN OPPORTUNITY

Mercy and grace are two great gifts that God continually pours upon the human race. Although they may look similar, mercy and grace are very different.

Mercy is God's undeserved kindness. He will have mercy on whomever he will have mercy. A person does not need to do anything to receive God's mercy. The Lord chooses to extend His mercy to whomever He wills.

Grace is also God's underserved kindness, but unlike mercy, we must do something to receive it. Grace is always an opportunity. The cross, for example, is an instrument of God's grace. Jesus died for every person on the planet when He hung on the cross, but only those who call upon Him will be saved. Even though the benefits of the cross are for everyone, people have to do something to receive those rewards. Salvation and all other blessings afforded man on the cross are opportunities.

To use an example, no one needs to suffer from rejection, for Christ took our rejection and gave us acceptance on the cross. Many Christians, however, suffer from rejection. Freedom from rejection is an opportunity, but many believers have failed to take hold of it. That is how it is with every detail of the cross. Each detail is a provision of grace, an opportunity to embrace. It cannot be earned, but it must be embraced. Every aspect of the cross must be specifically claimed. That is our personal journey of sanctification. Even though we may be saved from the consequences of our sins so that one day we will go to heaven, there are many other details of the cross that we should take hold of. One of those details is the removal of curses.

The Bible says, *"Christ redeemed us from the curse . . . by becoming a curse for us, for it is written: 'Cursed is everyone who is hung on a tree.' He redeemed us in order that the blessing given to Abraham might come to* [us] *through Christ Jesus*   (Gal 3:13-14).

Even if you have been a Christian for years, you may still need to have curses broken off of your life. Regarding the work of the cross, there is a difference between what is yours legally and what is yours experientially. Legally, everything that Christ accomplished on the cross belongs to you, but experientially, you may not be enjoying the good of it.

I do not participate in lotteries, but many people do. If someone wins the lottery, they are the legal winners and perhaps millions of dollars now belong to them. If, however, they do not claim their prize, the money that is rightfully theirs remains out of reach, and it is of no use to them. They, in fact, may live in poverty. To claim their winnings, they cannot just announce their winnings in their bedroom. They must go to the right place and follow the procedure to obtain their prize.

Christians have legal ownership of the cross and all of its benefits, but unless they take hold of their blessings, they may still live in poverty. The removal of curses has been paid for on the cross, but we still have to claim our prize. When we go to claim what belongs to us, we may find a legal battle before us. There may be some work to do on our part.

Scripture says, *"work out your salvation with fear and trembling, for it is God who works in you to will and to act according to His good purpose"* (Php. 2:12-13).

If a generational curse hangs over our lives, it is there because of a legal spiritual judgment. Breaking legal judgments will involve an act of claiming our legal rights in Christ. This battle for sanctification may involve acts of repentance, renunciation of things like witchcraft, forgiveness of others who have hurt us, and a verbal declaration to cut those curses from us. Later in our study, we will deal with the steps we should take for the removal of stubborn curses.

Chapter Fifteen

CURSES, DEMONS AND ANGELS

ANGELS ARE COMING

*E*veryone has angels attending them unless the angels have been driven off. People are made in the image of God, and at birth, an angel is assigned to care for each of them. All children have a guardian angel.

The Bible says, *"Take heed that you do not despise one of these little ones, for I say to you that in heaven their angels always see the face of My Father who is in heaven"* (Mt. 18:10 - NKJV).

Notice that all children are automatically children of God. They are connected with the Father in heaven. Each baby has an angel. There are billions of people on the planet, and that tells me there are billions of angels as well. God is no respecter of persons; He is not racist, nor is He biased in his love for people. God loves people, and all are made in His image. One of the assignments of angels is to serve those who will inherit salvation. Once a person becomes a Christian, even more angels will attend them. It is the place of angels to protect people, to help provide for their needs and to help them fulfill their destiny in God.

PROVISION ANGELS

A year ago, I had an amazing spiritual encounter. It began at 3 o'clock in the morning. Suddenly, in a dream, an angel shouted, "Look!" It was so loud that I bolted out of bed and my body was shaking because of the power of the angel's voice. Like those who shout "Come," in the book of Revelation, this angel had a voice like thunder. I walked around the house asking God what He wanted me to see, but I discovered nothing. I went back to sleep and had an amazing dream.

In the second dream, God showed me some of the angels that have been assigned to serve me. I was sitting at a table with some friends. I knew that I was about to receive a meal, but it seemed a long time coming from the kitchen. Suddenly, an angel began walking toward me. He was a tall man dressed in a three piece suit. I knew that he was in charge of serving the meal. Without looking at me directly, he came and stood at one side to oversee the operations. We waited, what seemed for a long time, and then another angel came. This time the angel looked like a woman, tall, and thin, with short hair. She was average looking but, like the first angel, she walked toward me with her head held high and an air of dignity surrounded her. In her hands were two trays, each with a pedestal. On top of the trays were two fabulous supreme pizzas. They were the best looking pizzas I had ever seen. The angel stopped in front of me and placed the pizzas on a separate serving table. She proceeded to lift one of the pizzas and place it in front of me. Suddenly, she tripped and the pizza flew through the air. The tray shot out of her hand and landed strategically on the floor so that the pizza landed on it safely. Although it was a bit disheveled, the pizza did not touch the floor. I looked at the angel in charge as if to say, "What is going on here?"

He leaned forward and graciously placed a huge glass bowl full of orange ice cream in front of me. It had sections of tangerines lying on top of the ice cream. I said, half jokingly, "I see we are having dessert first."

The angel just returned to his position. He said nothing, nor did he smile or look at me directly. Immediately, the other angel placed the pizza in front of me, and I woke up.

Then the Lord said to me, "These are some of your provision angels. It is their place to look after you, to see that your needs are met, and that you are protected. They will help you fulfill your destiny."

For the longest time, I sat in awe before the Lord. I was so thankful for the revelation. Then I asked the Lord, "Why was the angel so clumsy as to trip and drop the pizzas, and why was the meal so long in coming from the kitchen? I have always thought that the angels were more professional than that.

Instantly, I felt the Holy Spirit speaking to me. He said, "The angels are neither clumsy nor slow, but you did not see the demons tripping the angel when she proceeded to serve you. Nor were the angels slow in preparing the meal in the kitchen, but they were resisted by demons. Whenever your provisions are slow in coming, or they come in an unusual manner, it is because your angels have experienced resistance from demons. If you pray and stand in faith, the angels will continue to solve problems, rearrange circumstances and make sure that your blessings get through."

ANGELS ARE WAITING

Angels, like God's people, are in partnership with Him. They are constantly being sent to earth to help us. When we pray in faith and our prayers are in line with God's will, we attract angels. Our prayers and our godly behavior allow clear paths for their involvement in our lives. In effect, we roll out a red carpet and welcome their partnership when we pray. All of our activities are meant to be complimented by angels. The angels of God set up camp around those who fear the Lord (Psalm 34:7). For Christians who want to fulfill their calling and destiny, angels are not a luxury, they are a necessity.

Angels are waiting to come and help us. When we sin, speak evil of others or refuse to walk in faith, the angels hesitate and even retreat. We can drive them away from us by participating in darkness. Even our own guardian angel will eventually depart if we persistently walk in defiance toward Almighty God. Even in those cases, all is not lost for the faithful prayers of other people will allow a sustained presence of angels to protect and help us. It will be limited, though, and the spiritual warfare surrounding those people will be intense.

DEMONS WAIT AS WELL

Like angels, demons are also real. They are servants of Satan, and they do what he does. The Bible tells us what he does.

It says, *"The theif* [Satan] *comes only to steal and kill and destroy; I* [Jesus] *have come that they may have life and have it to the full"* (Jn. 10:10).

Demons cannot live inside of people just because they want to, nor can they destroy us easily. They must find a legal pathway into our lives. When angels depart from us because of our sin, the way is made clear for demons to come. Demons love it when we sin. It is like honey for a fly; they are waiting for an opportunity to connect with us. Our willful acts of sin give permission for evil spirits to entice us. Then they find a way to trouble us. Their goal is to steal, destroy, and ultimately rob us of our lives through sickness or trauma.

Even when we have not committed a curse-causing sin, our ancestor's sins may have opened the doors for demons to get involved in our lives.

As godly lives and effective prayers roll out the red carpet to welcome the presence of angels, so curses lay out the welcome mat for demons. Because a curse is a legal judgment that often comes as a punishment from God, the demons have legal permission to cause trouble. Curses are one of the main reasons why evil spirits persist in their attacks against some Christians. They claim legal rights to trouble and torment people because of generational curses. When legal curses are broken, demons lose their footing and are greatly weakened in their battle against believers.

SPIRITUALITY IS PROGRESSIVE

Both blessings and curses tend to accumulate. In other words, the more we live in godly obedience, the more blessed our generations will be; the more we participate in wickedness, the more generational curses will fall upon us and our children. Blessings welcome angels; curses open the door for demons.

Some people live in constant pain. Due to their own sins and the number of curses over them, some people are swallowed up in demonic torment and trouble. Conversely, those who walk with God and live under the amazing blessings of a godly heritage experience an abundance of righteousness, peace and joy. Every step they take in life is filled with God's grace.

Both blessings and curses can become more intense as time passes. Godly people who become more godly will experience more and more blessings, while the ungodly experience the growing accumulation of evil.

People can live in a measure of heaven or hell here on earth. The adage, "hell on earth," is very real for those who experience it.

Concerning the righteous, however, the Bible says, *"The path of the righteous is like the first gleam of dawn, shining ever brither till the full light of day"* (Pro. 4:18).

DEMONIC ATTACKS

For the sake of clarity, it must be noted that a godly life is not free from demonic attack. In this life we will have tribulation. We live in a fallen world, and Satan looks for every opportunity he can find to hinder the work of God and the blessings of the saints. There are definite seasons of struggle that everyone must face in life. This is especially true if someone is an effective minister of the gospel. The devil hates the work of God; he hates being pushed back by the saints and will do all he can to retaliate.

That is exactly what happened to Jesus. At the very moment that His earthly ministry was about to emerge, Satan met him in the wilderness and tempted him for 40 days. A spiritual battle followed, but in time, it came to an end.

The scripture reads, *"And the devil left him* [Jesus] *for a season and the angels came and ministered to him"* (Mt. 4:11).

It is expected that Christians will be hassled by men and demons because of their faith. These attacks, however, should be seasonal, not constant. The life of a believer should be filled with peace, joy, goodness, and outstanding blessings. It is not normal for a saint in right standing with God to live in constant strife or trouble. Overwhelming trouble is often a sign of generational curses that have left an open door for demonic attack.

The gifts of the Holy Spirit have been given to us to ward off the devil's cronies. The keys of the kingdom (Holy Spirit authority) must be used to bind the works of Satan. While ministering in the power of the Spirit, it is necessary for Christians to break the ancestral curses off of their lives. When they do this, they slam shut a door of demonic interference.

Chapter Sixteen

NEW TESTAMENT CURSES

CURSES ARE STILL IN EFFECT

Many believers have not been taught about curses, and still others believe that they were in effect in bygone times but do not exist today. Perhaps others think that if they do exist, they are only in countries where paganism and witchcraft are commonplace. They portray the attitude that certainly curses are not functional in the lives of normal people in the developed nations of the West. No doubt, many believers think that Christians who are living under the New Covenant cannot be affected by curses from generations past.

Nothing could be further from the truth. Curses are affecting most Christians today, and people need to have those curses broken off of them and their families.

CURSES ARE IN THE NEW TESTAMENT

Let us study the scriptures to see if curses can affect Christians today. We have already discovered that curses and blessings are woven into the fabric of the Ten Commandments. Even though we know that the Ten Commandments are still godly principles for every culture in our world today, some might think that their position in the Old Testament scriptures disqualifies them from being part of the New Covenant. Of course, this is not true, but let us look further.

Let us look to the New Testament to help bring the subject of curses forward in our thinking.

JESUS TAUGHT ABOUT CURSES

Jesus spoke about curses. In the Gospels we discover that He pronounced curses over people, cities, nations and even trees. For example, He pronounced judgments over Korazin, Bethsaida and Capernaum.

Jesus said, *"Woe to you, Korazin! Woe to you, Bethsaida! If the miracles that were performed in you had been performed in Tyre and Sidon, they would have repented long ago in sackcloth and ashes. But I tell you, it will be more bearable for Tyre and Sidon on the day of judgment than for you"* (Mt. 11:21-22).

Concerning Capernaum, Jesus said, *"And you, Capernaum ... you will go down to the depths ... it will be more bearable for Sodom on the day of judgment than for you"* (Mt. 11:23-24).

Jesus also cursed or placed a judgment on the city of Jerusalem.

He said, *"O Jerusalem, Jerusalem, you who kill the prophets and stone those who sent to you, how often I have longed to gather your children together, as a hen gathers her chicks under her wings, but you were not willing. Look, your house is left to you desolate. For I tell you, you will not see me again until you say, 'Blessed is he who comes in the name of the Lord'"* (Mt. 23:37-39).

Korazin, Bethsaida and Capernaum were cursed because they had seen so many miracles, yet they were full of unbelief. Jerusalem was cursed because they had killed the prophets and rejected Jesus, the Giver of life. Even though the curse on Jerusalem will not remain, it will be in effect until the Jewish people open their heart. to Jesus. That is when they will experience their revival.

On another occasion, Jesus cursed the Jewish people.

He said. *"the kingdom of God will be taken away from you and given to a people who will produce its fruit"* (Mt. 21:43).

The Jewish people were cursed. For a season, the kingdom of God was taken from them and given to another people who would be fruitful (the Gentile Church). This happened because the builders, (The Jewish Leaders) rejected the chief cornerstone, Jesus. One day, the curse will be lifted, and God will restore Israel.

Jesus also cursed a fig tree for not bearing fruit. Once again, He was showing his disciples that the Jewish people (represented by the fig tree) were cursed because they were given so much, yet because of their sin, they were not bearing fruit.

We read, *"as they went along, they saw the fig tree withered from the roots. Peter remembered and said to Jesus, 'Rabbi, look! The fig tree you cursed has withered!'"* (Mk. 11:20-21).

Both Jesus and Paul taught us not to pronounce curses. They told us to bless and not to curse (see Matthew 5:44, Luke 6:28 and Romans 12:14). Abused, violated and mistreated people can curse their offenders if they have legal grounds to do so. We are specifically taught, however, to bless those who curse us. Our own personal repentance, walking in righteousness, extending forgiveness, and blessing others is an antidote that shields us from the curses that others would pronounce on us.

THE DISCIPLES KNEW ABOUT CURSES

The early disciples believed in curses. They understood the teachings of the Old Testament and what it said about curses. Like all good Jews, they were students of the scriptures and knew its instructions.

When a Jewish man, who had been blind from birth, came before Jesus, they asked the Lord if the man's blindness was the result of a generational curse.

"As he went along, he saw a man blind from birth. His disciples asked him, 'Rabbi, who sinned, this man or his parents, that he was born blind?'" (Jn. 9:1-2).

A person who was disadvantaged from birth was thought to have a curse because of their parent's sin. The disciples of Jesus, along with the entire population on the planet, at that time, knew that generational curses were real.

THE APOSTLES KNEW ABOUT CURSES

Although scripture recommends that wounded people should not retaliate by pronouncing curses, the apostles cursed people who practiced witchcraft, especially when those people were interfering with the gospel.

Peter and John went down to Samaria, and during that time, they cursed Simeon the sorcerer. He was a wizard who wanted to use the power of the Holy Spirit for selfish gain.

They said to him, *"May your money perish with you, because you thought you could buy the gift of God with money"* (Acts 8:20).

They cursed Simeon's pocket book.

Paul also cursed a Jewish sorcerer, a false prophet named Bar-Jesus who opposed the gospel and tried to turn serious seekers away from the Lord.

Paul said to Bar-Jesus, *"'You are a child of the devil and an enemy of everything that is right! You are full of all kinds of deceit and trickery ... Now the hand of the Lord is against you. You are going to be blind, and for a time you will be unable to see the light of the sun.' Immediately, mist and darkness came over him, and he groped about, seeking someone to lead him by the hand"* (Acts 13:10-11).

When Paul cursed the sorcerer he became blind.

Peter cursed Sapphira because she conspired with her husband to deceive the entire Christian community and test the Holy Spirit during a season of revival.

Peter said, *"'The feet of those who buried your husband are at the door, and they will carry you out also.' At that moment she fell down at his feet and died"* (Acts 5:9-10).

As Peter pronounced the curse, Sapphira fell to the ground and died.

The Apostle John speaks of the active strength and power of curses.

He says, *"If anyone sees his brother commit a sin that does not lead to death, he should pray and God will give him life. I refer to those whose sin does not lead to death. There is a sin that leads to death. I am not saying that he should pray about that. All wrongdoing is sin, and there is sin that does not lead to death"*
(1 Jn. 5:16-17).

Although many evangelical Christians seem to be unaware of these verses, the Bible teaches that there are two kinds of sins: one that leads to death and one that does not lead to death. I believe the sin that leads to death is a curse-causing type of sin. The effects of those sins, while a person is still here on earth, cannot be removed by a simple prayer. John said, *"I do not say that he should pray for that"* (1 Jn. 5:16).

A simple prayer will not remove curses. The removal of curses requires: humility, obedience, repentance, forgiveness, and Holy Spirit authority because the requirements of a legal judgment must be overturned and broken. The work of the cross must be applied to one's life to break curses.

CURSES IN THE FUTURE

At the end of the age, the great tribulation will come to earth. During the tribulation, powerful prophets will curse communities and individuals who persist in vile rebellion against God.

We read, *"If anyone tries to harm them* [the prophets]*, fire comes from their mouths and devours their enemies. This is how anyone who wants to harm them* [the prophets of God] *must die. ... they* [the prophets] *have power to turn the waters into blood and to strike the earth with every kind of plague as often as they want"* (Rev. 11:5-6).

These anointed prophets will curse communities with plagues and even curse wicked individuals, and those people will die.

During the new millennium, after the return of the Lord, some people will live to be a thousand years old. If during that time, a person dies having reached only one hundred years of age, it will be because they were cursed.

"he who dies at a hundred will be thought a mere youth; he who fails to reach a hundred will be considered accursed" (Isa. 65:20)

At the very end of the millennium, after Satan is released from the abyss and finally thrown into the lake of fire, all curses will be completely destroyed. At that time, even the Adamic curse will be removed.

Regarding eternity, the Bible says, *"No longer will there be any curse"* (Rev. 22:3).

CURSES ARE REMOVED THROUGH THE CROSS

We have seen several scriptures where the men of God cursed wicked people. The Bible teaches that curses are very real and are still in effect today. The Bible also teaches that Jesus became a curse for us so that we might receive the blessings promised to Abraham (See Galatians 3:13,14).

CONCLUSIONS ABOUT CURSES

Before looking through the scriptures to discover what kind of sins cause curses, it was necessary to show the reader that curses are real, and that they are spoken of at great length even in the New Testament. In fact, curses are mentioned, activated or taught about from one end of the Bible to the other. They are included in the scriptures from Genesis to Revelation. Our study shows that curses are very real; they must not be ignored because they are far reaching, and they are very powerful.

It is the privilege of every believer to minister the grace and power of God. Holy Spirit empowered saints can partner with God to open prison doors and break generational curses. They can release the power of the cross and set captives free. They can lead families to their God-given blessings. That is their inheritance.

Chapter Seventeen

WHEN GENERATIONAL CURSES CEASE

SOUR GRAPES

*T*here was a famous saying in Israel: *"The fathers have eaten sour grapes, and the children's teeth are set on edge"* (Jer. 31:29).

This proverb means that when the fathers commit terrible sins (eat sour grapes), the consequences of their sins are passed on to their children as a curse (the children's teeth are set on edge).

Generational curses have been in effect since the days of Adam. Many, however, believe that generational curses ceased with the New Testament. This is often supported by, what I believe to be, a misuse of scriptures found in Jeremiah and Ezekiel. They say that some-time in the future, generational curses will not exist. Further study of these scriptures show that, indeed generational curses will cease, but that day does not come until the millennium reign of Christ. This chapter in my book explains that generational curses are still in ef-fect today, and that the scriptures in Jeremiah and Ezekiel refer to the new millennium, which takes place after the second coming of Christ.

JEREMIAH AND EZEKIEL

Read all of Jeremiah 31 and Ezekiel 18 and you will find God's promise that generational curses will cease at some designated time in the future.

We read, *"In those days people will no longer say, 'The fathers have eaten sour grapes, and the children's teeth are set on edge.' Instead, everyone will die for his own sin; whoever eats sour grapes – his own teeth will be set on edge"* (Jer. 31:29-30).

Ezekiel says, *"As surely as I live, declares the sovereign Lord, you will no longer quote this proverb in Israel. For every living soul belongs to me, the father as well as the son ... he has done all these detestable things, he will surely be put to death and his blood will be on his own head. But suppose this son has a son who sees all the sins his father commits, and though he sees them, he does not do such things: He does not eat at the mountain shrines or look to the idols of the house of Israel. He does not defile his neighbor's wife. He does not oppress anyone or require a pledge for a loan. He does not commit robbery but gives his food to the hungry and provides clothing for the naked. He withholds his hand from sin and takes no usury for excessive interest. He keeps my laws and follows my decrees. He will not die for his father's sin; he will surely live. But his father will die for his own sin"* (Eze. 18:3-4,13-18).

These scriptures do not suggest the removal of personal curses, for what a man sows he will surely reap, but they speak of the removal of generational curses. At some time in the future, the judgments for such sins will no longer be passed on to the children. It is clear that both scripture passages in Jeremiah and Ezekiel refer to a future date. The NIV Study Bible footnotes (copyright 1995, page 1169) tell us that the people of Jeremiah's day had misinterpreted Exodus 20:5 and Numbers 14:18, believing there was no such thing as generational curses.

But the truth is that generational curses were still as much in effect in Jeremiah's day as they are today. The context of this promise to remove generational curses points to the new millennium. I have listed below many verses from this chapter to show that this was not referring to Jeremiah's day, nor was it referring to the first coming of Christ. These verses speak of Israel's revival and her end-time blessings. These blessings did not come to Israel during the time when Christ walked the streets of Jerusalem, or when He died on the cross, as some suggest. After ministering to them, Jesus did not leave these blessings with the Jewish people. In fact, at that time, He cursed them, telling them that their house would become desolate (Mt. 23:37-38, Jn. 12:12-13) and the kingdom of God would be removed from them - for a season (Mt. 21:43). The blessings for Israel that are mentioned in Jeremiah coincide with the removal of generational curses, and these blessings begin just before and during the great millennium (see my study book on Revelation called *Unexpected Fire*).

Some might suggest that these blessings were really promised for the Gentile Church and not for the people of Jacob. That erroneous teaching is called "Replacement Theology" and fails to discern that Israel will come to her Messiah and receive all of her promised blessings at the end of the age. There are verses that tell of these end-time promises and connect them with the removal of generational curses.

Any true historian will testify that these promises for Israel have not yet been fulfilled. Israel's history, so far, has been quite the opposite of what is recorded here. It has been full of sorrow and pain. Only since 1948 have these promises even begun to be fulfilled. These blessings will not come in full measure until after the second coming of Christ.

In the same chapter that promises that generational curses will cease, we discover blessings that will not be fulfilled until the millennium.

Here are the millennium blessings: *"I will come to give rest to Israel, ... I will build you up again, ... Again you will plant vineyards on the hills of Samaria, ...There will be a day when watchmen cry out on the hills of Ephraim, 'Come, let us go up to Zion, to the Lord our God' ... See, I will bring them from the land of the north and gather them from the ends of the earth ... Hear the word of the Lord, O nations; proclaim it in distant coastlands: He who scattered Israel will gather them and will watch over his flock like a shepherd. For the Lord will ransom Jacob and redeem them from the hand of those stronger than they. They will come and shout for joy on the heights of Zion; they will rejoice in the bounty of the Lord ... They will be like a well-watered garden, and they will sorrow no more ... I will give them comfort and joy instead of sorrow ... 'So there is hope for your future', declares the Lord ... 'The days are coming', declares the Lord. ... 'Just as I watched over them to uproot and tear down, and to overthrow, destroy and bring disaster, so I will watch over them to build and to plant,' declares the Lord. In those days people will no longer say, 'The fathers have eaten sour grapes, and the children's teeth are set on edge.' Instead everyone will die for his own sin"* (Jer. 31:2,4,5,6,8,10,11,12,13,17,27,28,29,30).

THE NEW MILLENNIUM

So, at the end of these verses, we discover that generational curses will be removed, but not until the millennium reign of Christ when the other promises in the same chapter are fulfilled. To suggest that these verses prove that generational curses have been removed now is to take verses out of their biblical context.

All of the global traumas mentioned in the book of Revelation are a product of generational curses that come due at the end of the age. At the end of that tribulation period, Christ will return and set up His earthly kingdom, and the new millennium will begin.

During the millennium, both mortals and immortals will live side-by-side on the earth. We know this is true because the millennium begins with the resurrection of the dead. Those in Christ will receive glorified bodies and become immortal, but they are not the only people who will be present on earth during the millennium.

Do you remember the story Jesus told of the guests at His wedding feast? Some did not wear the right wedding clothes and were removed and sent to hell (Mt.22:11).

After the thousand years are over, Satan is released for a season to tempt the nations. He gathers a multitude for war and they march on Jerusalem. Before the battle begins, fire falls from heaven, and God Almighty kills them all (see Revelation 20:9-10). That means that some people in the millennium are not immortal because they are able to die (for a more detailed study on this subject, see my book *Unexpected Fire*).

During the millennium, generational curses do not exist, as we learned from the prophecies of Jeremiah and Ezekiel. Personal curses, however, will still be in effect for individuals and for nations. Mortals can die during the new millennium, and that is the product of a curse. Death will not come because of any generational curse but only because of a personal curse. Let me remind you of the following verse:

Speaking of the new millennium, we read: *"Never again will there be in it an infant who lives but a few days, or an old man who does not live out his years; he who dies at a hundred will be thought a mere youth; he who fails to reach a hundred will be considered accursed"* (Isa.65:20).

The Lord tells us that He is prepared to curse nations during the new millennium by releasing a drought over their land.

We read. *"Then the survivors from all the nations that attacked Jerusalem will go up year after year to worship the King, the Lord Almighty, and to celebrate the Feast of Tabernacles. If any of the peoples of the earth do not go up to Jerusalem to worship the King, the Lord Almighty, they will have no rain. ... This will be ... the punishment of all the nations that do not go up to celebrate the Feast of Tabernacles"* (Zec. 14:16-19).

IN CONCLUSION

In conclusion, only at the beginning of the new millennium are all generational curses removed. During that time, personal, self-induced curses will still be in effect. In the days of the new millennium, however, there will be no generational curses and the following verses will be fulfilled:

"In those days people will no longer say, 'The fathers have eaten sour grapes, and the children's teeth are set on edge.' Instead, everyone will die for his own sin; whoever eats sour grapes – his own teeth will be set on edge" (Jer.31:29-30).

Finally, at the end of the new millennium, after the thousand years are over, even self-induced curses will be removed. I remind you of this verse from the last chapter of the Bible:

"No longer will there be any curse. ... They will see His [God Almighty's] *face, ... And they will reign for ever and ever"* (Rev. 22:3,4,5).

At the end of the new millennium, when every vestige of every curse is finally removed, we will be able to see God Almighty, face to face. We will live and rule with Him forever.

Chapter Eighteen

SIGNS OF A CURSE

AN OVERVIEW OF LIFE

*E*very person on the planet experiences trauma, but I am thankful for the countless blessings that my family and I have enjoyed. I love the Lord; I love the Father, Son and Holy Spirit. I love my Father's world which is bursting with creative life. I love my family for their special place in my life. I love people, for each human being is a treasure from heaven; each one is made in the image of God. I love serving God in the ministry; it is thrilling to see people healed and set on course with their predesigned destinies. I love life, for it is a journey of outstanding discovery and amazing blessings. My family and I have never been financially wealthy, but we have always had what we needed and, most of the time, our lives have been great. Loving and enjoying life like this is normal because God, the Giver of all gifts, loves to give good gifts to His children.

My family and I, however, have also had times of loss and pain. We have had our share of suffering and struggles, and that is normal too.

Scripture says, *"He causes his sun to rise on the evil and the good, and sends rain on the righteous and the unrighteous"* (Mt. 5:45).

Some of our struggles have been attacks brought on by demons because they are set on stealing, killing and destroying all who are made in the image of God.

The Bible says, *"In this world you will have trouble"* (Jn. 16:33).

Not all trouble comes from demons; some are self-inflicted because of wrong choices and mistakes. I am thankful that once we learn to walk in the ways of the Lord, our mistakes are for learning and not punishment.

Some struggles come because we exist in a fallen world. We live in a world that is under curses and judgments. As we consider the fall of Adam, we see that all troubles and struggles on the earth are part of some curse. In eternity, there will be no more tears or crying because even the Adamic curse will be totally removed (Rev. 22:3).

During this present age, we accept light afflictions as a normal part of life. It is the struggles that are not normal that are the focus of this book. We ask the questions: "Are there generational curses in our lives or over our families? Are there devastating troubles that go beyond the norm? Do we suffer from debilitating traumas that seem particular to us?" If so, we want them removed.

GENERATIONAL SIGNS

It is not normal to have unrelenting troubles or suffering. If we see repetitive patterns of excessive trauma repeated over and over again, we are likely experiencing the effects of a generational curse. This is especially true if the problem does not make sense, if there seems to be no rhyme or reason for such a high level of trouble. We are not looking for a one-off problem but a trauma or battle that is constantly before us; one that keeps showing up generation after generation.

Here are 12 serious questions you should ask yourself:

1. Do you have continuous poverty in your family regardless of the jobs you have or how hard you work? Does it seem that you can never get ahead financially even though you work hard and the money that your family makes should be enough?

2. Are there so many divorces in your family that a couple who has not been divorced seems to be the exception?

3. Are there patterns of debilitating or lethal diseases that continue with each generation? Even if the doctors say it is genetic, it may still be a sign of a generational curse.

4. Are there perverted sexual strongholds that imprison and control the lives of grandparents, parents and children in your family? These signs are often accompanied by evil activities and abuse.

5. Is there a pattern of infertility, debilitating reproductive problems, cancers involving the reproductive system, hysterectomies, inability to carry children to full term or other reproductive problems that show up generationally?

6. Do accidents resulting in physical harm or death occur so often that it appears that your family is accident prone?

7. Are there repeated instances of mental illness throughout your generations?

8. Are there repeated incidents of demonic haunting, spirit sight-

ings or supernatural traumas in your homes that are witnessed by different members of the family?

9. Do several family members live most of their lives in a state of panic, fear, worry, pessimism and anxiety?

10. In your linage and family, are there premature, untimely or uncommon deaths that occur far too often?

11. Is there a history of addictive behavior that every generation in your family fights? It may involve alcohol, drugs, sexual perversions, gambling, eating, spending, stealing, fighting or other addictions.

12. Is there a pattern of alienation and separation with other people so that your family cannot keep jobs, enjoy school or community events, stay long-term with a church, get along with friends or neighbors or keep from fighting with other members in the family?

If you answered yes to one or more of these questions, it is likely that your family is under the influence of a generational curse. I am reminded of the proverbial comic strip character with a rain cloud positioned over his head. It may be sunny all around, but wherever they go the rain cloud follows. Some individuals and families live under a spiritual rain cloud because of curses. No matter what they do, they cannot get free from disproportionate troubles.

FIRST GENERATION CHRISTIANS

Throughout my life as a minister, I have been especially impressed with first generation Christians. These folk had parents who were not practicing believers, so they were not raised with a supportive Christian family.

Usually a huge amount of negative baggage was passed down to them from previous generations. They have battles to fight that people raised in godly homes do not have to face. It is common place for them to battle addictions, demonic strongholds and disproportionate baggage. Since becoming believers, they have taken a stand to change the family pattern. They have drawn a line in the sand and said, "As for me and my house, we will serve the Lord."

Demon spirits who have lived with a family for generations are given notice once people become Christians. The demons must leave, but they put up such a fierce fight for as long as they can. That means that these new Christians find themselves facing unnatural hardships within the family and with life in general. They must learn to be overcomers. For these people especially, it is important to break off generational curses.

If you are a first generation Christian, the first thing I want to do is commend you: well done! I have the highest regard for you. Hold fast and press into God; He will prove Himself faithful to you and bring you and your family onto the road of ever-increasing blessings.

Understand, however, that you will pay a price in order to receive all of God's blessings. You will face an even greater battle as you take your stand to bless the next generation. If you continue to walk with God, your children and grandchildren will not have to fight the intense battles that you are fighting. Strongholds will be broken, and you will pass on many new freedoms. Your descendants will know greater blessings than you did because the kindness of the Lord is accumulative. Both blessings and curses can increase with each generation, and you are now a doorway for God's blessings for your family.

A PASTOR'S PLEASURE

Joy and I have been pastors for more than 40 years. We have seen so many young people come to Christ, and many of them came from families where strife and chaos were common. Often, new believers are coming from dysfunctional families. It has been our joy to see people healed, become stable and receive unexpected blessings from God. Soon, other members within their families come to Christ. We have witnessed magnificent generational transitions come to entire families. In each case, there were serious bumps along the road; the wonderful spiritual shift is not without trauma.

In the early years, as a family comes to Christ, it may seem like they are on a rollercoaster ride. They usually experience joyful advances and some very real setbacks as well. Change is met with resistance, for it is not easy to shift from lifelong habits of addiction and abuse. Some members of the family prove to be stronger than others, and they are set in place to hold the others up. They will pray, counsel and encourage each other, and if they are not too demanding or legalistic, the weaker members will be held on course as lots of sacrificial patience and love is extended. When one falls, the others help them get back on their feet. In time, the entire family is better, and some will excel as champions of Christ.

Individually, they enter the process of sanctification, and this may include: curse breaking, deliverance, dedications, habit changing, and life altering revelations from the Holy Spirit. As they move forward, they mature in Christ. This can happen very quickly or come over a long period of time, but the blessings of God will eventually overtake them. Then they become a lighthouse of hope for many other families.

There are always things to work through as we press toward the blessings of God. At different times and seasons, the Holy Spirit will reveal areas where our sanctification needs improvement. At those times, He will bring to our attention things such as generational curses. The signs of curses will become evident as people receive a revelation of a family's negative patterns or baggage. It is not time to blame our ancestors, but it is time to break strongholds that have left an open door for demons to conspire against us. We should not reject all that has come to us from our ancestors, but we should renounce and reject the areas that have brought curses. They must be removed.

LOOK FOR THE SIGNS

I do not recommend that anyone go on a witch hunt, looking for dark secrets in the family closet, but ask the Lord to reveal any spiritual forces that are interfering with your family. As the Holy Spirit leads you, look for the signs of a curse. I encourage you to look over the list of 12 symptoms of curses that I described earlier in this chapter. If the Lord uncovers areas of darkness, then deal with those curses.

Line up with God and do what is necessary to move forward in faith. Later in our study, we will walk you though the steps that lead to freedom. You may need a minister of the gospel who has authority and understanding to help you on your journey. That is why God gave apostles, prophets, teachers, evangelists and pastors to the church. He does not expect us to get everything we need without the help of other ministers.

You are responsible for your life. Do not continue in unnecessary struggles. As you deal with your personal situation, come into unity with family members and walk through the process of sanctification for your generation. God will show up and change will come.

This is the pleasure of pastors, ministers and saints. Jesus came to set the captives free, and He commissions His workers to do the same. In the next chapter, we will look through the scriptures to discover which sins bring curses on families. This will help us discover the roots of some of our family problems. Pray and let the Holy Spirit teach you. He is faithful to accomplish every good work in your life.

Chapter Nineteen

CURSES ARE A CHOICE

CURSES ARE STILL IN EFFECT

Many believers dismiss the Old Testament teachings as invalid truths for this generation. They may be guilty of selective reading, accepting the things they like and rejecting what they don't like from the scriptures. The Old Testament is the word of God, and the teachings of Christianity are a continuation of God's word. Some Old Testament truths have received a spiritual upgrade, and those changes are described in the apostolic writings (the New Testament). We should not reject or adjust any Old Testament teaching unless the New Testament instructs us to. We still embrace the Ten Commandments, for example, even though they are found in Exodus 20. We accept the stories and lessons of the patriarchs as foundational to our faith, and we love the miracles, the Proverbs, the Psalms, and the prophecies of the Old Testament. All of that is part of the word of God.

Blessings and curses are also mentioned in great detail in the Old Testament. We must not ignore the reality of curses just because we read of them in the Old Testament. The remedy for curses can only be found in Christ and the authority of His cross, but how curses come and the power they possess is taught in the Old Testament.

OPPORTUNITY TO CHOOSE

Deuteronomy chapters 27 to 30 give us amazing understanding of the doctrine of curses. God spoke to the Jewish people.

He said, *"This day I call heaven and earth as witnesses against you that I have set before you life and death, blessings and curses. Now choose life, so that you and your children may live"* (Dt. 30:19).

Alongside of Israel, the opportunity to embrace blessings is given to all people. The laws of sowing and reaping along with judgments and blessings are available to people of every nation. In every case, the ramifications are generational; it is for you and your children.

Scripture says, *"so you and your children may live"* (Dt. 30:19).

Deuteronomy chapter 28, verses 1 to 68 are completely devoted to the explanation of curses and blessings. The first 14 verses highlight the blessings of God, and the remaining 54 describe the effects of curses. The blessings of God include the blessings of promotion in the city and in the country, the grace to have children and the gift of economic prosperity, good and plenteous food sources and all of one's paths and journeys being blessed. The person who is blessed by God is protected from enemies, and everything they are called to put their hand to will prosper. The blessed person receives honor and abundance under an open heaven as they walk in obedience before the Lord.

To sum it up, the scripture says, *"The Lord will make you the head, not the tail, ... you will always be on top, never at the bottom"* (Dt. 28:13).

Many who refuse to believe in curses feel free to quote these verses that speak of success in the first part of the chapter. It is easy to agree that blessings are available to all who will walk with God. The rest of the chapter, however, describes trouble and curses and how judgments come to people who walk in wickedness.

This scripture section starts with the words, *"However, if you do not obey the Lord your God and do not carefully follow all of his commands and decrees I am giving you today, all these curses will come upon you and overtake you"* (Dt. 28:15).

The following 53 verses give a most devastating description of failure, chaos and destruction that come to individuals and families who fall under the judgments of curses. The description of curses is far more detailed than that of blessings. It is wrong to accept the teaching of the first 15 verses and reject the rest of the chapter. Scripture teaches us that judgments follow vile behavior.

It says, *"The Lord will send on you curses, confusion and rebuke in everything you put your hand to, until you are destroyed and come to sudden ruin because of the evil you have done in forsaking him"* (Dt. 28:20).

A LIST OF CURSES

The devastating curses that are listed in Deuteronomy 58 include: plague, disease, wasting disease, fever, inflammation, scorching heat, drought, blight, mildew, a bronze sky and an iron earth, rain turning to dust and powder, defeat before enemies, horror, bodies becoming carrion, boils of Egypt, tumors, festering soars, the incurable itch, blindness, no success, oppression, being robbed with no rescue, your spouse being stolen, an unlivable house, unreapable harvests, unusable herds, unkeepable children, unstoppable family calamity, madness, incurable boils, forcible thefts, cruelty, scorn, ridicule, locust, worms, fallen harvests, captive children, hunger and thirst, nakedness and dire poverty, serving your enemies, an iron yoke on your neck, destruction, siege, attacks, cannibalism, no compassion for family members, hatred within families, lingering illness, dread, every kind of sickness, reduction of offspring, no geographical stability, being scattered from one end of the earth to the other, anxiety, despair, no confidence, terror, selling oneself into slavery, rejection, overpopulation, the superiority of aliens in the land, and borrowing but not lending.

To sum it up the scripture says that the alien among you will, *"be the head, but you will be the tail. All these curses ... will be a sign and a wonder to you and your descendants forever because you did not serve the Lord your God joyfully and gladly in the time of your prosperity"* (Dt. 28:44,45,46).

If these traumas are piling up around you and your family, then most certainly, your family has the signs of generational curses. If these horrors are present in your family, however, there is hope. The Lord tells us that we may choose life and blessings and be rid of these calamities. How much more is His deliverance available to us through the blessings of the New Covenant than it was under the Old Covenant? What will you and your family choose?

A TIME INTERVAL

Most of us are wired for immediacy. When we do something good, we want to see quick rewards for our actions. Speed and convenience are at the top of the wish list in modern society. We want fast meals, fast working diet plans, quick studies, easy money, sudden materialism, instant recognition, undeserved health, spontaneous wisdom and immediate spiritual growth.

Even Jesus had to grow in favor with God and with man. Time and even some hardships are a necessary prerequisite for maturity and strength. While God is the Giver of all good gifts, He does not take short cuts as He develops quality in His people. The journey is as important as the gift at the end, and many gifts from God will only come as we walk along the path.

Scripture says it like this, *"The path of the righteous is like the first gleam of dawn, shining ever brighter till the full light of day"* (Pro. 4:18).

The lion's share of God's blessings are not instantaneous but accumulative and progressive. They start with a gleam and end in amazing brilliance. Notice the New Testament teaching on this theme of waiting for the blessings to come.

It says, *"through faith and patience inherit what has been promised"* (Heb. 6:12).

It takes faith and patience to inherit God's blessings; they are not immediate. Patience is a fruit or trait of the Holy Spirit. Those who walk with God choose blessings; in time, they receive the benefits of patience and faith. Those who endure receive the rewards; they discover the blessings that emerge, line upon line, over their lives and families.

DETOXIFICATION

The blossoming of blessings is intensely beautiful, but the systematic unfolding of trauma that comes from curses is intensely painful. Both are choices that we make; eventually our choices bring far reaching results. Our choices may start as small decisions, but continuing on our chosen paths may lead us to opposite extremes. Two people from the same family may start the race at the same place but end up with opposite finish lines. An individual's choices will make all the difference in the end.

It is much easier to make right choices in the beginning than it is to undo the effects of wrong choices from the past. Still, recovery and attaining God's blessings are available to all. We call this process sanctification. It begins with a decisive and determined choice to turn around. The process of sanctification is like an addict breaking free from addictions by going through a detoxification program. The process may be similar to extreme dieting. It may be like a person who is 200 pounds overweight who finds the discipline, the diet and the exercise program to loose excess weight and keep it off. Many people are able to do this because they make the right choices and act in strict compliance with those choices.

The detoxification process to be free from curses starts with a choice. It cannot, however, be accomplished by discipline alone; it requires a miracle from God. If we fail to choose God, we will never be free of curses. As we continue to choose Him, He continues to release an anointing for change.

The choice that makes the difference will involve dedication, submission, forgiveness, receiving the powerful ministry of curse breaking, deliverance and healing. We must turn from our wicked ways and walk with the Lord. In the place of wrong choices, we learn to do that which is godly and good and that brings blessings. There are many levels and steps, and we must continue to make right choices. This is the journey of the just, and each stage of it will bring new results.

Stopping a run-away train or turning an ocean liner that is cruising at full bore, takes time. The results of right choices will also take time. Some blessings will appear immediately, but others come along the way. In time, the blessings will come. They will percolate through the limestone pores of life and fill the empty spaces with goodness. Through patience and intimacy with the Lord the dry places will become saturated with pools of delight. Where darkness once reigned, the Holy Spirit will bring refreshment. Little by little, all things will become new and improved and life will get much better. Soon, some of the pools of living water will become wells and fountains for others who need help. The one who was previously cursed becomes blessed and then they become a channel of life for others. The wounded and dysfunctional can become a bright light. They can become a fountain of life for others. The choice is yours; the Lord has laid the choice before you. This day you may choose blessings or curses. Choose blessings so that you and your children may live.

Chapter Twenty

WHAT SINS CAUSE CURSES?

A LIST OF SINS

As we continue to study Deuteronomy chapters 27 to 31, we discover an eye-opening list of sins that cause curses. It is not an exhaustive list, for there are other sins not mentioned here that bring curses. This list is, nevertheless, far reaching; it will give us a detailed picture of what God will judge. From this list we will discuss 10 different sins that result in curses. There are two other curse-causing sins mentioned in the Bible that we will also look at.

The list includes: 1. witchcraft, 2. rebellion toward parents, 3. crooked business behavior, 4. abusing the handicapped, 5. withholding justice from immigrants, 6. abusing widows and orphans, 7. sexual perversions such as bestiality, 8. sexual perversions such as incest and child abuse, 9. murder, 10. assassinations, 11. not paying one's tithes and offerings and, 12. anti-Semitism. In this chapter we we will focus on the sin of witchcraft.

WITCHCRAFT

The curse-causing list of Deuteronomy 27 begins with witchcraft.

We read, *"Cursed is the man who carves an image or casts an idol – a thing detestable to the Lord"* (Dt. 27:15).

The image or idol mentioned here is a statue or picture of a deity. It is a false God that has been created for the purpose of worship. Exodus says, *"You shall have no other gods before me"* (Ex. 20:3).

This is the first of the Ten Commandments. When people make an idol and worship it, they will, inevitably, be worshipping a demon. Behind every idol is a demon. When we look to any spiritual source other than the God of the Bible for counsel, help, or as a focus to give homage, we are practicing witchcraft. In essence, we have created an image and put it in the place of Almighty God. There are thousands of different faces, programs and presentations that offer spiritual help or enlightenment. They include all non-Christian or non-Jewish religions, all New Age spiritualisms, all idols and all fortune-telling mediums.

Demons are supernatural creatures who live in rebellion and defiance against the Lord Jesus and God Almighty. They may present themselves as angels of light and act as counterfeits of God. Every time a person reaches out for any spiritual or supernatural benefit in any direction apart from Jesus, God the Father or the Holy Spirit, they are interacting with demons. It may be done in ignorance or in vile rebellion against God, but the results will be the same; demons will run to the opportunity. The evil spirits will come with lies, false teachings, superficial help, momentary pleasures and great deception.

DEREK AND LYDIA MINISTER

I am reminded of the story that my grandfather, Derek Prince, told me. He said that a mother once brought her child to Lydia and him for prayer. The child was about 10 years old but had faced a debilitating disease since infancy. She had received some healing at a church, but it did not last, so she went to a fortune teller. Then the sickness left, but it returned years later, and the mother knew they needed help.

After inquiring, Derek and Lydia discovered that the fortuneteller had given the child a locket that was not to be removed from her neck nor was it to be opened. Grandma Lydia opened the locket and in it was a piece of paper. It was a document from the fortuneteller and it read, "I will keep this child's body well until her soul is found in hell."

They destroyed the locket and ministered curse-breaking and deliverance over the mother and the child. The child was healed. The well-meaning mother had not understood the ramifications of her actions; by going to the fortuneteller, she committed an act of witchcraft, and that brought a curse on her and her daughter. Praise God for the ministry of Lydia and Derek Prince and the power of God to break curses.

People may think they are finding what they are looking for when they seek help from a spiritualist; but in the end, they will open the doors for destruction. Demons may be hidden or disguised at first; they may even come in a cloak of kindness. Their ultimate goal, however, is to manipulate, misuse an individual, and then destroy them.

All who journey down this path practice the sin of witchcraft – a thing detestable to the Lord. Witchcraft is the main reason why God's judgment falls on people. It will always result in generational curses. The pain and trauma that follow will be deep-seeded, difficult to remove and extremely troublesome.

WITCHCRAFT IN AMERICA

One Sunday morning, 35 years ago, we were enjoying a wonderful time of worship at our church, when suddenly a woman cried out. She erupted with a blood-curdling scream that rose high above the sound of praise. Over and over again she yelled, "They're drinking her blood, they're drinking her blood!"

Nothing like this had happened in our meetings before, but we knew without a doubt that we were experiencing a demonic manifestation. Quickly, I made my way to where the woman was and began to speak forcefully to the demons that were in her. She was in a trance and no matter what I did, the demons paid no attention.

After several unsuccessful attempts, her husband and a few of the ushers led her to a back room so as not to disturb the service any further. The worship, now mixed with fervent prayer, continued as we confronted demons in the back room. They continued to pay no attention to us as they wailed their eerie announcement, "They're drinking her blood!" The 25 year old woman starred off into space with lifeless eyes and a flush color in her face. Suddenly she stopped screaming. She then slumped over and fell into a deep sleep.

Her husband told us that this had happened about once a month since they were married. She would sit up in bed and scream these words for 20 minutes. Each time, she would be in this trance-like state. He would be unable to wake her, and in the morning, she would remember none of it. We prayed over her and sent them home with the promise that we would visit them the following evening.

The next day, we fasted and prayed and went to the couple's home in the evening. The lady was pleasant, sitting on a chair and in her right mind. We asked as many searching questions as we could, but neither the wife nor the husband had any explanation for the bizarre events that had taken place. Both were from Christian homes, and she was the daughter of a Pentecostal pastor. Both of them had become Christians during their childhood, and to our knowledge, they had not lived wicked or rebellious lives.

Again, we prayed earnestly over the woman and rebuked the demons forcefully in Jesus name. We had her repent, forgive and renounce, and for more than half an hour, we prayed fervently, but neither the lady nor any demon spirit gave any supernatural response. Then the Lord spoke to me, and I said, "Let us stop what we are doing and ask God to give us the missing key."

We got down on our knees and began to seek the Lord. Suddenly, I found myself asking God to bring to the lady's remembrance the secret thing that she had forgotten. In just a moment of time, the woman began sobbing as if a dam had opened up inside of her. She was so emotional and so distraught that she could not speak clearly for more than 10 minutes. She just sobbed and sobbed, over and over again. Finally, she gained her composure and told us that she remembered something that had been removed from her memory until now.

When she was 12 years old, she went on vacation with her girlfriend's family and they took her to a witches coven. Hundreds of people gathered somewhere in a forest outside of Chicago. She told us that she witnessed a human sacrifice; a pregnant woman was killed on an altar. They proceeded to remove the unborn child from her womb and then drink the baby's blood.

She said that, at the time, she was put under some kind of spell, and after it was finished, she was brought before a satanic priest. He prayed over her, saying that she would not be able to remember any of the events she had seen that night.

We led the lady through a time of repentance and renunciation. Then we prayed and cast the demons of witchcraft and murder out of her. She fell to the ground and the demons left her immediately.

The occult is very much alive and functional here in America. Most expressions of witchcraft in the USA are not as dramatic as the witchcraft story that I have just told you, but all forms of witchcraft are diabolical. They are just as dangerous and just as problematic as what happened to this young girl.

WITCHCRAFT IN THE NATIONS

Deuteronomy gives a partial list of the different expressions of witchcraft.

It says, *"Let no one be found among you who sacrifices his son or daughter in the fire, who practices divination or sorcery, interprets omen, engages in witchcraft, or casts spells, or who is a medium or spiritist or who consults the dead. Anyone who does these things is detestable to the Lord"* (Dt. 18:10-12).

Servants of Satan are very active in every nation. Some practice ritualistic sacrifices, and others practice the casting of devilish curses. They aim at destroying every good and godly virtue in society. Many people dominate and manipulate others through the practice of witchcraft and sorcery.

Most people will not engage in such blatant evil, but will still get involved in areas of the occult that seem more innocent. The occult may be divided into three parts.

1. Divination is seeking spiritual information from any source other than God. This includes such things as fortune telling, horoscopes, transcendental meditation, and séances.

2. Sorcery is the use of physical objects to bring curses or to provide spiritual power and false blessing. These include such things as charms, crystals, voodoo dolls, animal entrails, and symbols such as pentagrams and broken crosses.

3. Witchcraft in its truest sense is the power branch of the occult. It includes human sacrifice, death threats, incantations, curses, ritualistic abuse and control of people's lives through spiritual manipulation, abuse, seduction or oppression.

Many people stay far away from sorcery or witchcraft, but they still practice divination. Others, who would not knowingly indulge in the darker expressions of the occult, still participate by enjoying various forms of demonic entertainment. These include satanic videos or board games that can open spiritual doors that lead to witchcraft. They include the role-playing of dungeons and dragons and Ouija boards. Under the guise of entertainment, many people feast on demonic movies. New demonic movies seem to come before the public more frequently than changes in the weather. People can also become hooked on witchcraft by involving themselves in secret societies such as Free Masonry, the Klu Klux Klan and various Mormon cults. At first, some of these societies may seem righteous and even helpful, but many secret societies lead to satanic activities of witchcraft. They are an abomination to the Lord.

INCREASE OF THE OCCULT

As the Revelation apocalypse approaches, Satan knows that his time is short. He is doing everything within his power to draw souls into his occult web. His demons blind the eyes of those who do not want to see the light of the Gospel. Demonic forces sugar coat occult activities by making them pleasurable and entertaining. They may even present their schemes as acts of righteousness by connecting them with good works, or they may wrap them in sensuality and seduce the world through sexual pleasures. They buy the souls of humanity with materialism and financial gain so people will compromise and throw godly behavior to the wind. Man's lust is the very thing that Satan uses to drag him into the sin of witchcraft. People may enjoy the momentary pleasures connected with the occult, and they may tell themselves that it is their privilege, their choice and their right to do what they want. That is rebellion, and rebellion is like the sin of witchcraft. Persistent rebellion always leads a person down the road toward the occult.

Depart from, renounce, and remain far away from all forms of witchcraft. Guard your heart against the subtleties of rebellion. This is no game. It is time to stand firm on the Rock, Christ Jesus. All other ground is sinking sand.

Chapter Twenty-one

MORE SINS
THAT CAUSE CURSES

A HEAVY WARNING

As we continue to study Deuteronomy chapters 27 to 31, we discover more of the sins that bring curses. Every person is a sinner until God forgives them through the power of the cross, but not every sin produces a curse. Some activities however, are so heinous to God that they do cause judgments and curses. These judgments result in pain and suffering. In the previous chapter, we isolated 12 such sins and we have already discussed the first one on the list, the sin of witchcraft. Let us look at the others.

DISHONORING PARENTS

The scripture says, *"Cursed is the man who dishonors his father or his mother"* (Dt. 27:16).

During the time of Israel's history, when these words were written, it was a serious crime to rebel against one's parents. A young person who persisted in rebelling and dishonoring his parents would bring a curse upon themselves. In fact, the town's people would kill them.

"If a man has a stubborn and rebellious son who does not obey his father and mother and will not listen to them when they discipline him, his father and mother shall take hold of him and bring him to the elders at the gate of his town. They shall say to the elders, "This son of ours is stubborn and rebellious. He will not obey us. He is a profligate and a drunkard." Then all the men of his town shall stone him to death. ... All of Israel will hear of it and be afraid" (Dt. 21:18-20,21).

I am sure that this was not a common occurrence because young people would be afraid to disobey. Instead of a mother saying, "Wait until your father gets home," she might say, "Change your behavior, or we will take you to the elders at the gate."

If a youth violently attacked one of their parents they would be stoned to death immediately (see Exodus 21:15).

Honoring parents, on the other hand, brought great blessings (see Exodus 20:12 and Deuteronomy 5:16). Scripture says that honoring parents is the first commandment that God promises to bless. He says we will live long on the earth if we honor our mother and father.

It would be a horrible thing to ask the town to stone your child. I can understand why young people behaved themselves back then. Today, such harsh measures are forbidden by law, but I have seen parents so hurt and so angry with their rebellious children that they came to the end of their patience and wanted to disown them.

Many movies, TV programs, music videos, websites and media presentations encourage young people to rebel against their parents. As a pastor, I have estimated that more than half of all church members coming for counsel and advice are looking for help for their troubled families, and many of those cases involve rebellious children. Rebllion is an epidemic in our society.

Think for a moment of the vast number of rebellious young people in America, and realize the strongholds of curses on the nation that have come for this reason alone - not to mention the many other curse-causing sins that have filled our land.

Many people who are past their youth have come to Christ, and now have children of their own. They remember the season of their own rebellion and regret the way they treated their parents when they were young. Some have curses on their lives and will reap sorrow with their own children because of what they did.

If this is your story, then go back to your parents and repent of your sin and rebellion against them, even if it happened long ago. If your parents hurt you, forgive them. Then break off those curses in the name of Jesus. Furthermore, do all you can to honor and bless your parents from this day forward. Honoring parents does not mean agreeing with everything they do, but loving them and showing kindness to them. If they are messed up parents, then pray for them, love them and let God change them; changing your parents is not your responsibility. If you partner with God, through prayer and good works, miracles will come.

CROOKED BUSINESS BRINGS CURSES

The list of curse-causing sins from Deuteronomy 27 continues. The third one in the list involves crooked business.

Scripture says it like this: *"Cursed is the man who moves his neighbor's boundary stone"* (Dt. 27:17).

In ancient times, a property line was marked by a boundary stone. It represented the covenant or business agreement between neighbors. If a person moved the stone to gain more land, without the neighbor's consent, he was breaking a business agreement; he was stealing.

Today, we mark properties with registered surveys and metal rods that go deep in the ground. It is not so easy to move a neighbor's boundary stone, but there are many kinds of boundary stones. Any business agreement, contract or covenant is a boundary stone. If we move it, we can cheat someone in business and fail to keep our part of the agreement. God judges crooked business behavior.

Many church goers have a disconnect that separates church-life from business, but God makes no such distinction. When you sign a business agreement, shake hands on a financial matter or give your word, you are held accountable by God. Financial agreements, investments, loans or work that you promise to do, should not be altered or changed without the consent of the other person in the business agreement. Many brothers and sisters in church families are guilty of such defaults. If you fail to fulfill your part of the business agreement and the other person suffers loss because of it, that is stealing and a curse will follow.

We could talk about breaking treaties with Native American peoples, business scams in society or delinquent and fraudulent companies. Entire nations have been cursed because of broken treaties or criminal behavior in high places. Crooked government activities that are allowed to flourish will bring curses on government workers. Corruption in institutions or companies will result in curses coming on the owners, the CEOs and even the employees of those companies. Entire nations suffer poverty, lack and shame because of crooked business. Some countries do not function without illegal bribes and unjust measures. Books could be written to describe the corruption of people in every nation on the planet. Some nations are worse than others, and they incur more curses. Usually the level of curses is directly related to the lack of Judeo-Christian ethics and standards within the nation.

Let us, however, focus on our personal and family behavior, for that is where we have direct responsibility. The pastor's study is a place of enlightenment; over the years, many have come into my office to tell of a church member who is defrauding them. They have borrowed money or agreed to do work for them. The individual was given a loan or a payment, but the due date has passed, and the party has failed to pay back the loan or keep their part of the agreement. Often, the promised work was not completed, and the owing party will not answer their phones. They may have stopped coming to church. The person who was cheated does not want to take a fellow church member before the law, so they come to the pastor for help.

I am convinced that thousands of Christians have borrowed money from other Christians for an investment, business start-up or because they were in dire straits. They promised to pay back their friends in 3, 6 or 12 months. Two years later, the borrower's situation has not improved and they are avoiding them. Without going to the lender to work the problem out responsibly, the faulty Christian has stolen from their friend and curses will come. This is so common that every church that I visit around the country seems to have a problem like this. The consequences are far reaching; individuals, families and whole churches come under a cloud of debilitating judgment because people have moved their neighbor's boundary stone.

I use the church scenario as an example, but all business with Christians or non-churched people must be handled with honesty and integrity. God expects us to fulfill all business agreements and contracts and will hold us accountable if we fail to do so. Good business behavior is a serious matter with God; it involves a covenant and it must not be broken. Always fulfill your business agreements on time and give more than what is required. Use just scales, give excellent work and pay back your debts on time and with a bonus thank-you gift, especially if the loan comes from an individual person rather than an institution. If you do these things God will bless you.

HANDICAP ABUSE

Concerning handicap abuse, I am not referring to parking in a handicap spot without good reason; but even something as small as that, I personally cannot do. Taking advantage of the disadvantaged is terrible and it will bring a curse from God.

The Bible says, *"Cursed is the man who leads the blind astray on the road"* (Dt. 27: 18).

People who are mentally, physically or socially handicapped are often preyed upon by crooked business people. They target the aged, the weak-minded and those who are desperate. Scam artists are cursed people. They are not only taking advantage of whoever they can, but they are soliciting the help of other workers who are looking to make a fast dollar. In effect, these people are leading the blind astray on the road.

All people must be treated with dignity and respect, regardless of their disposition in life. The Bible teaches that those who are less comely should, in fact, receive more honor.

Corinthians says, *"those parts of the body that seem to be weaker are indispensible, and the parts that we think are less honorable we treat with special honor ... But God has ... given greater honor to the parts that lacked it"* (1 Cor. 12:22-23,24).

Mentally handicapped, physically handicapped, the aged, children, street people, and any others who are disadvantaged for one reason or another should be given more dignity, honor and care. Woe to the person who takes advantage of any one of them. God is the defender of all of these people and will bring severe judgments to those who abuse them.

Abusing the handicapped or disadvantaged can include aborting a handicapped child, and sexually, mentally or physically abusing children, the aged, the mentally or physically handicapped, street people, the poor, or those who are disadvantage because of their addictions. Abuse includes stealing property, goods or finances from them. It also includes pushing them to the back of the line concerning jobs, opportunities, privileges or blessings.

As with other curse-causing sins, handicap abuse is prevalent in our society. It is the responsibility of every good person to guard against these abuses and to bring justice to those who hurt the underprivileged. We should go out of our way to extend help and care to those who are weaker or more needy than ourselves.

IMMIGRANT ABUSE

Before leaving this chapter, let us look at the subject of immigration. God includes this theme in His list of curse-causing sins. God loves people no matter where they are from, what they look like or what their background is. He hates racism and will judge a racist person. Today, we in America are facing the matter of illegal immigration. All people should ask the Lord and then judge their own hearts to determine if they have God's perspective on foreigners who come to the nation.

The Bible says, *"Cursed is the man who withholds justice from the alien"* (Dt. 27:19).

God gives every nation their boundaries and their appointed time (Act 17:26). This is important because God does not want a one world government until righteousness rules in the new millennium. He gives nations a manageable opportunity to release blessings over their ethnic peoples. Some nations have perpetuated ungodly behavior and have brought great judgments upon themselves; others have had godly leaders who brought blessings. It is not right that a nation open their doors for curses. Israel was warned by God that they should love the people of other nations but not succumb to their wicked ways or embrace their ungodly behavior. A nation must guard itself against evil.

That is why a nation should have borders and be able to control who comes into the land and, to an extent, what those people bring with them. A nation must secure her borders to protect her people and guard her environment.

A nation, however, must welcome all strangers and foreigners into the land, provided they will respect her foundations and keep her laws. A country's policies should not be racist, but screening criminals and trouble-makers is essential.

Once people enter a nation, they must be treated with respect, dignity and justice. Whatever inalienable rights belong to citizens also belong to strangers. These are non-negotiable rights given by God to every person. It is our place to love all immigrants.

Criminals who are immigrants must be justly tried and be given opportunity for reform, if they are legally living within the boundaries of a nation. They should be treated appropriately under the guidelines of a godly justice system. A society should do their best to help them get on their feet, and they should guard against injustice. Immigrants often need help, and a godly nation should extend help to them and their children in any way possible. God loves people, and the nations are called to represent Him.

If a criminal, however, is in a country illegally, it is not inappropriate to deport them back to the country they came from. The civil government of a nation is mandated by God to protect its citizens.

Chapter Twenty-two

CURSE-CAUSING SINS CONTINUE

GOD IS SERIOUS

We are studying the list of curse-causing sins from Deuteronomy chapter 27. We have looked at witchcraft, rebellion toward parents, corrupt business practices, handicap abuse and the ill treatment of immigrants. We will continue with the list, starting with the sin of mistreating widows and orphans. This is a very serious matter with God, for He is the defender of those who cannot defend themselves.

MISTREATING WIDOWS AND ORPHANS

The Lord God Almighty watches over widows and orphans.

He says *"Cursed is the man who withholds justice from ... the fatherless or the widow"* (Dt. 27:19).

Every child, no matter their ethnicity or cultural background, is made in God's image. He loves children. They are His inheritance, and from the moment of conception, He is their defender and has given every child their own guardian angel (see Matthew 18:10).

Jesus warned against hurting a child. He said it would be better for a person if a thousand-pound mill stone were tied around his neck and he was thrown into the sea, than for that person to hurt a child (see Matthew 18:6, Mark 9:42 and Luke 17:1).

Pure religion, as defined in the Bible, is helping widows and orphans and keeping yourself from spiritual pollution (see James 1:27). The scriptures call us to care for widows and orphans from start to finish. The oldest book in the Bible is Job, and in it we discover that Job opened the first home-based orphanage to care for the fatherless (see Job 29:12,13,16,17, 31:16-22).

The Mosaic Law laid out God's instructions for the people of Israel. He mandated care and protection for widows as well as for orphans (see Exodus 22:22 and Deuteronomy 24:19,27:19).

The books of Psalms and Proverbs, the teaching of the prophets, the ministry of Jesus and the apostolic teachings all emphasized caring for widows and orphans. I will share some of the verses in the Bible that speak of God's heart to care for widows and orphans. By looking at these sample verses we discover that God gives great attention to the matter. For further study, see Psalms 10:17-18, 68:5, 82:3, Proverbs 23:10,11, 19:17, Ezekiel 22:7,29,30, Isaiah 1:16,17,23, 58:6,7,12, Daniel 4:27, Jeremiah 7:6, 22:3, Hosea 14:3, Malachi 3:5, Amos 6:3-7, Luke 4:14,18, Acts 6:1-3 and James 1:27.

For the purposes of this book, we cannot record all of these verses, but here are several sample verses that emphasis the fact that God defends the fatherless and seriously warns all who would misuse them.

"A father to the fatherless, a defender of widows, is God in his holy dwelling" (Ps.68:5).

"Defend the cause of the weak and fatherless; maintain the rights of the poor and oppressed. Rescue the weak and needy; deliver them from the hand of the wicked" (Ps. 82:3-4).

"Do not ... encroach on the fields of the fatherless, for their Defender is strong; he will take up their case against you" (Pro. 23:10-11).

Carefully read the excellent words of Job. *"If I have denied the desires of the poor or let the eyes of the widow grow weary, if I have kept my bread to myself, not sharing it with the fatherless – but from my youth I reared him as would a father, and from my birth I guided the widow – if I have seen anyone perishing for lack of clothing, or a needy man without a garment, and his heart did not bless me for warming him with the fleece from my sheep, if I have raised my hand against the fatherless, knowing that I had influence in court, then let my arm fall from the shoulder, let it be broken off at the joint. For I dreaded destruction from God, and for fear of his splendor I could not do such things"* (Job 31:16-23).

Proverbs and Job emphasize the fear of God and declare that He is the Defender of widows and orphans. Proverbs warns us not to mistreat them, for God, their defender, is strong. Job said that he was fearful and dreaded the thought of what might happen to him if he overlooked the orphan or the widow. He says that if he did, His arm should be broken off, for God, in all His splendor, will avenge the fatherless and the widow.

Job lived before the Jewish law was written, yet he understood the laws of blessings and curses. He knew that God's judgments would fall on those who mistreat widows and orphans. Any society that does not care for their widows and orphans will bring curses on their nation.

SEXUAL PERVERSIONS

In our study of Deuteronomy 27, we come to the sins of sexual perversions. While each of the other sins in the list are spoken of in their own single verse, sexual perversions cover 4 verses. The two areas of sexual perversion in this list that are singled out as most detestable to the Lord are incest and bestiality.

Regarding incest, the Scriptures say, *"Cursed is the man who sleeps with his father's wife ... Cursed is the man who sleeps with his sister ... Cursed is the man who sleeps with his mother-in-law"*
(Dt. 27:20,22,23).

Sexuality is designed by God to be covenantal; it is only permitted when marriage vows are made. The act of sex between husband and wife is an expression of deepest intimacy. All other sexual encounters are inappropriate and some are diabolical perversions. Incest, the sex act with a family member other than a marriage partner, is called inbreeding. This sexual perversion is one that God will judge. It involves covenant breaking, betrayal, and evil conspiracies under one's own roof. It involves a level of deception and darkness that is demon-inspired. Those who cross the line to commit incest, rebel against their own conscience and rebel against God.

BESTIALITY

Bestiality, the act of having sex with an animal, is likewise a dark perversion. The sex act is precious and holy, designed by God as the expression of covenant and love between a married couple.

The Bible says, *"Cursed is the man who has sexual relations with any animal"* (Dt. 27:21).

It is difficult to think of such a dark perversion, but it happens, and the fact that it is in the ancient writings of the Bible tells us that it has happened for thousands of years. This act is inspired by demons and is closely connected with witchcraft. It is one method demons use to degrade and destroy humans. Disease and demon possession will follow this act. A person who lowers themselves to such sin will become evil-minded; they will become demented. Demon spirits cannot simply enter a human being at will. That is because all humans have a God-given protection against such creatures. When a person commits a perverse or vile sin, rebels against God or participates in some form of witchcraft, they open a legal door, and in effect, welcome demons to come and dwell inside of them. Even drug and alcohol abuse will remove God-given protections within one's mind and make a person susceptible to demonic indwelling.

An animal can be demon possessed. We discover this from the story in the Bible that tells of Jesus casting 6000 demons out of a man. The demons went into 2000 pigs. The pigs became so tormented that they committed suicide by running down a steep cliff and drowning themselves in the lake (see Luke 8:26-37).

Animals are weak creatures and are no match for demon spirits, but demons do not prefer to live inside of animals; they prefer people. If, however, a person chooses to have sex with an animal, be sure that demon spirits will enter the animal to transfer into a human host through the act of perverted intercourse. Whenever two have sex, they become one in body and spirit. This also means that a spirit within one individual or creature can migrate to the other during the sex act (see 1 Corinthians 6:16-17). Bestiality is a legal door of entrance for demons to travel into a person; it is a filthy abomination to the Lord.

THE SIN OF MURDER

There is a difference between murder and killing someone in the act of self defense. Killing someone in the defense of one's nation, in a time of war is also not murder. Murder is the shedding of innocent blood or killing someone when you have no right from God to do so. An individual must not kill as an act of aggression or retaliation. Civil governments have been empowered by God to take a life in the purposes of justice. Soldiers, the police and magistrates have been empowered to take a life in order to protect the people who are under their care.

The Bible says, *"Cursed is the man who kills his neighbor"* (Dt. 27:24).

God alone is the Giver of life, and only He and those He authorizes may take a life. Those who commit murder will bring a curse on themselves. Murder includes having an abortion, killing an innocent person, killing someone during a robbery or a violent act of racism, killing someone because of domestic revenge, euthanasia, infanticide, genocide or ritualistic sacrifice.

A person having an abortion or a doctor procuring one is committing a crime against God and humanity. Curses will follow those who participate in the taking of any innocent life and there are none so innocent as unborn children. All who have participated in an abortion need to repent of this terrible sin. They need forgiveness from God, the creator of life. They need curses and judgments broken off of them so that they and their children will be free from the consequences of a curse.

I have singled out the act of abortion because it is so common in almost every country on the earth today. Whole nations are cursed because their leaders have put laws in place to allow legal abortions. When God looks down on our political election, the issue of abortion stands above all others. It is the one issue that should sway a Christian's vote. All other civil matters are less important than the protection of human life, and the more innocent that life is, the more

God will defend it.

Murder of any type will bring a curse. Genocide or infanticide where large numbers of a population are murdered by a dictator or a political party will invoke the wrath of God. Today curses hang over many nations because of this horrible crime. The book of Revelation is God's ultimate response to this and other curse-causing sins. How many years of God's mercy and grace do we have before global judgment falls? Even now, curses are unfolding over individuals, families, communities, and nations.

HIRED ASSASSINS

A hired assassin will bring a curse upon his family.

The Bible says, *"Cursed is the man who accepts a bribe to kill an innocent person"* (Dt. 27:25).

I am not saying that a person who acts on behalf of a godly government to kill a wicked terrorist is cursed. It is the assassin who kills outside of God's directives and laws who will be cursed. He is one who kills for a bribe. This is the way of gangs, thugs, conspirators, crooked business people, cover-ups from corrupt governments, mafia type syndicates who exercise criminal activity, and of course, it is the way of terrorists. All who participate as hired hit men under these directives bring curses on themselves and on their descendants for generations.

ANTI-SEMITISM

Besides the curse-causing list of Deuteronomy 27, I am mentioning 2 other notable sins because the Bible speaks of them in clear terms. One is the sin of Anti-Semitism; that is the hatred and persecution of the Jewish people.

God said to Abraham, *"I will bless those who bless you, and whoever curses you I will curse"* (Gen. 12:3).

When Isaac blessed Jacob (Israel), he gave a similar word.

He said, *"May those who curse you be cursed and those who bless you be blessed"* (Gen. 27:29).

A man named Balaam was hired to curse the Israelites, but God stopped him.

We read: *"But God said to Balaam, 'Do not go with them. You must not put a curse on those people, because they are blessed'"*
(Num. 22:12).

God hates racism. He made all people and made all nations so that people from every nation might seek and find Him. He adds to His love for all nations a special grace for the Jewish people. I do not think it is because they deserve it; they do not behave as extra special people. God, however, made a covenant with their father Abraham and promised a special blessing for his descendants through his son Isaac. So a spiritual law has been put in place: whoever blesses the Jews will be blessed, and whoever curses them will be cursed.

This angers the devil and he does whatever he can to incite individuals and nations against the Jews. For centuries and millenniums, nations have hated and cursed the Jews. The Israelites have been persecuted like no other ethnic group in history. Many Jews have made many serious blunders, including rejecting the Messiah, the Lord Jesus, but God will keep His word concerning them.

He says, *"As far as the gospel is concerned, they are enemies on your account; but as far as election is concerned, they are loved on account of the patriarchs, for God's gifts and his call are irrevocable"* (Rom. 11:28).

Greeks, Romans, Catholics, Protestants, Reformers, Crusaders, Russians, Europeans, Nazis and Muslims, to name only some of the guilty parties, have each taken turns in cursing themselves with the sin of anti-Semitism. As they persecuted and killed Jews, they sowed into their own destruction. Judgments and curses have falen on individuals, families and nations because of how they treated the Jews.

Concerning this, God has made a promise to the Jews: at the end of the age, He will judge the nations for how they have treated them.

He says, *"I will gather all nations and bring them down to the Valley of Jehoshaphat. There I will enter into judgment against them concerning my inheritance, my people Israel, for they scattered my people among the nations and divided up my land. They cast lots for my people and traded boys for prostitutes; they sold girls for wine"* (Joel 3:2-3).

I am not alone in believing that America is so blessed because she has, for the most part, blessed Israel. The nations who come against Israel, especially from this time forward, will injure themselves and bring curses on their people. Israel is God's inheritance and His choice. All who fight against them will have to fight against God.

TITHES AND OFFERINGS

The subject of tithes and offerings is mentioned extensively in the Bible, and it warrants a book of its own. In summary, the Bible teaches that believers who do not pay tithes and offerings are robbing God. They bring a curse of poverty on their families.

Scripture says: *"Will a man rob God? Yet you rob me. "But you ask, 'How do we rob you?' In tithes and offerings. <u>You are under a curse</u> – the whole nation of you – because you are robbing me. Bring the whole tithe into the storehouse, that there may be food in my house.*

Test me in this," says the Lord Almighty, "and see if I will not throw open the floodgates of heaven and pour out so much blessing that you will not have room enough for it" (Mal. 3:8-10 - emphasis mine)

These verses on tithes are not isolated from the other curse-causing sins. A couple of verses earlier in the same chapter of Malachi, a list of curse-causing sins is given. Let us read verse 5 and discover the lead-in to the subject of curses caused by not paying tithes.

" 'So I will come near to you for judgment. I will be quick to testify against sorcerers, adulterers and perjurers, against those who defraud laborers of their wages, who oppress the widows and the fatherless, and deprive aliens of justice, but do not fear me, 'say the Lord Almighty" (Mal. 3:5).

This chapter lists witchcraft, adultery, perjurers, oppressors of employees, abusers of widows and orphans, oppressors of immigrants and those who do not pay tithes and offerings as sins that bring curses.

Believers are not exempt from the curse of not paying tithes anymore than they are exempt from other curse-causing sins such as witchcraft or oppressing widows and orphans. In fact, judgment will apply to believers more specifically, for how can a heathen who does not even believe in God, be expected to give tithes and offerings to Him?

MORE CLEARLY

Let me present the situation to you more clearly. It is as if God is saying that everything on the earth is His, and you work for Him. At the end of the day, you may receive your wages for the work you do. He says that you may keep 90% of the business profits. A minimum of 10% (a tithe) must go back to the owner of the business (God). If you keep all of the work profits, God says that you are robbing Him of His share and a curse will follow. That 10% of your income is not yours but God's, and He will hold you accountable for it. You must pay the tithe so there will be food in His house.

Tithing is a matter of faith. Those who refuse to tithe tell God they do not trust Him with their well-being. They are afraid that they will not have enough for themselves if they give 10% of their earnings to the Lord's work. The Lord asks us to test Him and see that He will come through. He will open the windows of heaven and bless those who give, but those who refuse will be cursed.

This is not a teaching for the Old Covenant alone; it transcends history. Before the giving of the Old Testament Law, tithing was practiced. It is also confirmed in the New Testament through Christ's teaching and in the book of Hebrew. Some argue that we should be giving much more to the Lord than just 10%. I agree, but God insists on this minimum, and those who refuse will curse themselves and their families.

Offerings, on top of the tithes, are required by the Lord as well. The amount of the offerings are not specified but mentioned in general in the verse from Malachi that we quoted. Offerings are free-will gifts that we give to those in need as the Holy Spirit directs us. Blessings will follow those who give generous offerings when they give with a cheerful heart of faith.

REMOVING THE CURSES

The last three chapters that you have read in this book have focused on the sins that cause generational curses in people's lives. The list of curse-causing sins has included:

1. Witchcraft
2. Rebellion toward parents

3. Corrupt business behavior
4. Abusing the handicapped
5. Withholding justice from immigrants
6. Abusing widows and orphans
7. Sexual perversions such as bestiality
8. Sexual perversions such as incest and child abuse
9. Murder
10. Assassinations
11. Anti-Semitism
12. Not paying one's tithes and offerings

All of these sins bring curses, but they were paid for by Christ's death on the cross. Sanctification is God's opportunity for freedom. Let us do whatever is necessary to change our ways, repent of our sins, break the generational curses, and come into the flow of God's blessings. Let the light of God shine. It is time to receive ministry. It is time for change!

PART THREE

HOW TO MINISTER
EFFECTIVELY

Chapter Twenty-three

AN INTERCESSOR'S POWER

ISRAEL'S SINS PILE UP

*T*he sins of Jerusalem, during the days of Ezekiel the prophet, were detestable to the Lord. Ezekiel was called to prophesy over the city to give her fair warning and opportunity to escape the pending curses and punishments.

In Deuteronomy 27, we discovered a list of sins that bring curses and these same sins were evident in Jerusalem in Ezekiel's day. They include: witchcraft (idol worship), dishonor towards parents, crooked business dealings, handicap abuse, immigrant abuse, widow and orphan abuse, the sexual perversion of incest, the sexual perversion of bestiality, the shedding of innocent blood, murder, and assassinations of innocent people.

Ezekiel chapter 22 tells us that Jerusalem was guilty of all of these sins. Here are some tell-tale verses:

"O city that brings on herself doom by shedding blood in her

*midst and defiles herself by making idols, you have become guilty
... In you they have treated father and mother with contempt; in
you they have oppressed the alien and mistreated the fatherless and
the widow. ... and they commit lewd acts. In you are those who dishonor their fathers' bed; ... another shamefully defiles his daughter-
in-law, and another violates his sister, ... In you men accept bribes
to shed blood; ... Her officials within her are like wolves tearing
their prey; ... to make unjust gain. ... The people of the land practice extortion and commit robbery"* (Eze. 22:3-4,7,9,10,11,12,27,29).

In addition to the list of curse-causing sins mentioned in Deuteronomy 27, Ezekiel 22 mentions 12 more sins that Jerusalem was guilty
of. They include: despising God's holy things, eating at the mountain
shrines, priests teaching that there is no difference between the unclean
and the clean, priests doing violence to God's Law, desecrating and
not keeping the Sabbath, causing God to be profaned, slander, violat-
ing women during their period, committing a detestable offense with a
neighbor's wife, charging excessive [financial] interest to make unjust
gains from neighbors, oppressing the poor and forgetting the Lord.

Ezekiel describes the curses and judgments that will follow Jerusalem's sins. They include; their days coming to a close, being
made an object of scorn among the nations and a laughingstock to
other countries, mockery, turmoil, being scattered among the nations, lack of rain, destruction, and experiencing God's wrath.

MERCY OVER JUDGMENT

Israel was guilty of many curse-causing sins, and history tells us
that the judgments attached to those sins came upon her. This
is a sad story, especially when we know that God prefers mercy
over judgment. At the end of the chapter, God, speaking through
Ezekiel, makes a profound statement.

The Lord says, *"I looked for a man among them who would build up the wall and stand before me in the gap on behalf of the land so I would not have to destroy it, but I found none"* (Eze. 22:30).

God is the defender and the avenger of the weak and innocent. Justice demands that God fight for them. He cannot turn his back on the fatherless, the widow, the poor, the stranger, and the righteous.

The matter of man's abuse looms large, and so many are caught in the web of curse-causing sins. What does God require to satisfy judgment and extend mercy to those who deserve to be punished? He has the power and the right to lift the punishments off of sinners and stay the hand of destruction, but certain conditions must be met.

THE POWER OF THE INTERCESSOR

When people sin, God chooses intercessors to help Him. An intercessor is one who prays for others so that the Lord will extend mercy. The role of the intercessor, however, is more than prayer; intercessors are God's friends and are given the power of partnership with Him. When intercessors pray, God releases mercy.

We will discuss the amazing power of Christ's cross which saves us from sin. It is the reason for forgiveness and salvation under the New Covenant, but the intercessor's role was functioning long before the New Covenant was established. Abraham, Moses, Daniel, and every spiritual hero in the Old Testament was an intercessor. Look at what the Lord did because of Moses.

The Israelites had sinned, *"So he* [God] *said he would destroy them - had not Moses, his chosen one, stood in the breach before him to keep his wrath from destroying them"* (Ps. 106:23).

The task of the intercessor is to stand in the breach. It is to do whatever is necessary to break curses and judgments over people so they may receive God's blessings. God is looking for the person who will build up the wall and stand in the gap – that person is an intercessor. The following list helps us see the things that an intercessor might do to accomplish the two goals of wall building and gap standing. Here are the curse-breaking tasks of the intercessor and a person in the Bible who accomplished the task.

An intercessor will:

1. **Negotiate** with God through bargaining prayer, in order to remove the punishment of a curse (Abraham - Gen. 18:20-33, Moses - Ex. 32,33).

2. **Identify** with those being judged in order to receive their punishment if needs be (Daniel - Dan. 9:4-19).

3. **Preach** repentance to the sinners in question, to affect godly sorrow and behavioral change (Jonah - Jnh. 3:1-10).

4. **Rescue** those in distress by removing their oppressors or by delivering them from abuse, sickness or poverty (Job – Job 29, 31).

5. **Restore** the lifestyle of the afflicted by helping them stand on their own two feet, so they may repossess the years that the locust and caterpillar have eaten (Elisha - 2 Kgs. 4).

6. **Cry out** to God for His mercy because He is longsuffering, compassionate and full of kindness (Elijah - 1 Kgs. 17:20-21,18:36-41).

7. **Break** personal and generational curses by releasing God's authority through the spoken word (Jesus - Lk. 4:18-19).

THE CROSS AND THE INTERCESSOR

Since Jesus died on the cross, the way has opened for every person to come into God's throne room for help in time of need. An intercessor has more authority under the New Covenant than they did under the Old Covenant because the punishment for man's sin has now fallen on the crucified Christ. The punishment that fell on Jesus deflects the judgment that sinners deserve, and this comes into effect as those people meet God's requirements of repentance, godliness and faith.

The intercessor may identify with and pray on behalf of a fallen or victimized person for a season, although a sinner must ultimately choose life for themselves. The more an intercessor functions in their ministry, the more God will respond. God will send angels to assist; He will protect the defenseless, open doors of opportunity, hold back demonic aggression, and orchestrate the situation around the life of a sinner to open their eyes, soften their hearts and lead them to righteousness. The passionate intercessor who hits the target will do exactly what God is looking for. He is looking for a man (or a lady) who will build up the wall and stand in the gap before Him on behalf of the land (multitudes, families and individuals) so that He will not have to destroy it (them).

A SUMMARY

In conclusion, Israel, and more specifically, Jerusalem, is our example. Her people were committing a vast amount of curse-causing sins and God warned them of the judgments that would follow if change did not come. The Lord announced that He was looking for an intercessor to build up the wall and stand in the gap so that He would not have to judge Israel. It is not His desire to judge, but He will if He has no other recourse. An intercessor could have turned the tide and worked with God to remove the curses off of Israel, but no intercessor could be found in Ezekiel's day. God was bound by justice;

He had to pour out His wrath on the Jewish people (Eze. 22:31).

We thank God that many people are eternally saved even though their lives on earth may be ruined because of curses. We also thank God for His promise of restoration for the Jewish people at the end of the age.

We have studied curses, seen the desire of God's heart and the power of the intercessor. The scriptures reveal these dynamics as they applied to Israel, but they apply to people of every nation. Sin has brought curses on nations and families, and God looks for intercessors who have understanding and power to break those curses and lead multitudes into His purpose. God is a rescuer, a redeemer, a restorer, and a creator of righteousness in people. Intercessors work with Him to make it all happen. I encourage you to walk close to the Lord, become God's friend, and you will be called to the amazing power of the intercessor. God is looking for partners; He is looking for you.

Chapter Twenty-four

POWER TO OPEN THE HEAVENS

CLOSED DOORS

*T*here are none so sad and none more pitiful than those who have closed hearts and closed hands, who live behind closed doors, in spiritual prisons, under a closed heaven. They are people who have become captives because of a curse. They are always in pain, always in failure, always in lack and they have no relief or hope in sight. That is a description of dark depression, and unless things change it will lead to ultimate destruction.

THE MINISTER'S KEYS

The Bible shows us that ministers of Christ are empowered to open things that are closed. Notice some of the things that must be opened.

1. **Open Faces** (hearts and hands) - 2 Cor. 3:18-20, 4:1-2 - *"where the Spirit of the Lord is, there is freedom. And we, who with **unveiled** [open] **faces** all reflect the Lord's glory, are being transformed*

into his likeness." As we seek the Lord, pray and worship, a devotional key is given to us. This allows the nature of Christ to be reflected in us and through us. This tenderness will open the hearts and hands of others.

2. **Open Eyes** - Acts 26:17-18, 2 Cor. 4:4 - The Lord said to Paul, *"I will rescue you from your own people and from the Gentiles. I am sending you to them to **open their eyes** and to turn them from darkness to light, and from the power of Satan to God."* Paul and all ministers have been given the gospel key to open the eyes of those who are spiritually blind.

3. **Open Doors** - Col. 4:3 - *"And pray for us, too, that God may **open a door** for our message, so that we may proclaim the mystery of Christ."* Many doors can be opened and new ground can be taken with the apostolic key.

4. **Open Prisons** - 2 Cor. 10:3-5, Lk.4:18 – *"On the contrary, they have divine power to demolish prisons." "...proclaim freedom for the prisoners."* Ministers are called to **open prisons**. We will discuss the intercessor's key later in this chapter.

5. **Open Heaven** - Jn. 1:51 – Jesus said to Nathanael, *"you shall see heaven open, and the angels of God ascending and descending on the Son of Man."* The disciples would see an **open heaven**. That means that angels are bringing messages, protection, miracles, provisions, and blessings from heaven. Using the angelic key is the sign of God's blessings and favor.

Jesus commissions all of His ministers to open hearts, hands, eyes, doors, prisons and the heavens. He gave us His authority for this very reason.

He said to His disciples, *"I will give you the keys of the kingdom of heaven; whatever you bind on earth will be bound in heaven, and whatever you loose on earth will be loosed in heaven"* (Mt. 16:19).

The Lord sends fire with His angels and keys with His disciples. These keys open things that have been shut tight by sin, curses and demons. The keys represent authority. With the keys we can open the doors to let God's blessings in and lock the doors to keep the devil out.

Among the many keys that Christ gives, I can identify at least 5. Five is the biblical number for God's grace. Imagine that you have a key ring with 5 keys dangling from it. Each key has a name engraved on it.

The **Devotional Key** is for opening hearts and hands.

The **Gospel Key** is for opening eyes.

The **Apostolic Key** is for opening doors.

The **Intercessor's Key** is for opening prisons and breaking curses.

The **Angelic Key** is for opening the heavens.

Ministers of the gospel are ministers of good news; they come to change the atmosphere and to open that which has been closed. Jesus is the best example of a minister. Here is a description of what Christ did; it is a job description for all ministers who follow Him.

Jesus said: *"The Spirit of the Lord is on me, because he has anointed me to preach good news to the poor. He has sent me to proclaim freedom for the prisoners and recovery of sight for the blind, to release the oppressed, to proclaim the year of the Lord's favor"* (Lk. 4:18-19).

Jesus is anointed, He preaches, brings good news, sets prisoners free, opens blind eyes, rescues the oppressed, and releases God's favor. He is our example. We are called to do what He did.

Notice the 5 keys of the kingdom that He mentions in His job description:

The Devotional Key to open hearts (The Spirit of the Lord is on me.)

The Gospel Key to open eyes (To preach good news to the poor)

The Apostolic Key to open doors (To proclaim freedom for prisoners, recovery of sight for the blind)

The Intercessor's Key to open prison (To release the oppressed)

The Angelic Key to open the heavens (To proclaim the year of God's favor)

Whether Jesus preached to one or two or to the multitudes, He brought good news. He inspired hope and faith by opening the eyes of those who lacked vision. He gave new beginnings to people like the woman taken in adultery, to forsaken lepers and despised Samaritans. He opened prison doors, broke curses and set demoniacs free. He cast out demons and healed the sick. Jesus opened the heavens over people's lives as He called them into the ministry and blessed them with the ministry gifts of His Holy Spirit.

ALL CAN MINISTER

Jesus said, *"And these signs will accompany those who believe: In my name they will drive out demons; they will speak in new tongues; they will pick up snakes with their hands; and when they drink deadly poison, it will not hurt them at all; they will place their hands on sick people, and they will get well"* (Mk. 16:17-18).

Miracles and wonders follow when a believer uses the keys of authority that they have received from Christ. These keys are for all believers who will walk the road of the disciple. Many people live in spiritual prisons, and many are tormented or oppressed by demon spirits. At least one third of Jesus' ministry was breaking curses and setting people free from spiritual prisons. If these signs follow believers, then the ministry of deliverance and curse breaking should certainly be exercised by all who follow Him as ministers of the gospel.

DEMOLISHING PRISONS

Counseling has its place; financial aid or good advice is won-derful, but often we need a miracle to change someone's situation. That is why God has commissioned His people to break curses, set prisoners free from demonic oppression and to heal the sick.

Scripture says: *"For though we live in the world, we do not wage war as the world does. The weapons we fight with are not the weapons of the world. On the contrary, they have divine power to demolish strongholds"* (2 Cor. 10:3-4).

Let us understand the following words. A strong box is a safe, and a stronghold is a prison. There are many kinds of spiritual pris-ons. A prison is a place where one is held against their will. This scripture describes the stronghold of wrong thinking. That is a mindset contrary to the ways and knowledge of God; it leads a person into spiritual darkness.

Wrong thinking, however, is not the only prison. Other prisons include poverty, debt, addictions, loneliness, violence, depres-sion, sickness, fear, and demonic control. Jesus has given us the keys of the kingdom of heaven that enable us to open these prison doors. The verses of scripture that we have just quoted, however, take us to another level. Jesus came to do more than open prison doors and set the captives free; He came to demolish the prisons.

We have been given divine power to demolish strongholds

that have been built as a result of curse-causing sins. Believers are called to be demolition workers; they are to open prison doors, lead the captives to freedom, then destroy the prison. The Bible says that we have divine power to make this happen. Divine power is God power; it is not of this world. In other words, we can bring the good news, heal the sick, drive off demons and then destroy all the curses that brought the trouble and trauma. The curses must be broken and demolished.

MINIMUM, MEDIUM AND MAXIMUM PRISONS

Because of curses, some people are in minimum security prisons. They live in bondage, although it is often a secret prison. Their behavior seems normal to all who meet them but they are not free. They function quite well, and they are allowed to come out of their spiritual prison on weekends to go to church, but they are still not free.

When more curses pile up, people find themselves in medium security prisons. They are living with heavy addictions and are always failing, falling, and struggling. Everyone who is close to them knows that they are living in a nightmare of chaos and pain. They are fighting with demonic spirits. They may even attend church meetings on occasion, but usually, they are so imprisoned that they cannot even meet with God's people or live a righteous life.

Some people are under so many curses that they are in maximum security prisons. They are totally demonized and controlled by evil. They have no peace but live in constant torment. Many of these people are in institutions, but in countries like India, you may see them lying naked in the street covered with dirt and manure, completely devoid of a sound mind.

The more curses a person has, the stronger are the prisons they live in. That means that more power and anointing are needed to set them free and demolish their prisons.

THE PRISON WARDEN

Jesus taught, *"But if I drive out demons by the finger of God, then the kingdom of God has come to you. When a strong man, fully armed, guards his own house, his possessions are safe. But when someone stronger attacks and overpowers him, he takes away the armor in which the man trusted and divides up the spoils ... When an evil spirit comes out of a man, it goes through arid places seeking rest and does not find it. Then it says, 'I will return to the house I left"* (Lk 11:20-22.24).

If a strong box is a safe, and a stronghold is a prison, then the demonic strong man is the prison warden. He is the demon that rules over the prison guards (the other demons who live in a person). A curse becomes a prison and the demons guard or hold a person in it. People cannot escape because the curses and sworn judgments have real authority over them.

Ministers of Christ cast demons out of people and set them free from prisons. At that point, a prison should be demolished so that the demons have no legal right to return. This happens when the minister breaks the curse and removes the legal judgment that hangs over the freed prisoner.

The freed prisoner must cooperate with the minister as well. He must not go back into the prison. He must allow his thoughts and actions to come under the obedience of Christ (see 2 Corinthians 10:3-4). He must become a disciple whose life is led by the Holy Spirit.

When a captive who has been set free walks with the Lord then angels, church members and the Holy Spirit come to ward off returning demons and help protect the freed prisoner. If the prison of curses has been demolished, he is on the right road to enjoy a life of blessings.

THE GLORY OF HIS SAINTS

It is the glory of all believers to be ministers of the gospel. Nothing is more exciting or more meaningful than seeing lives change through the power of the Holy Spirit.

Permit me to get a little personal. You have been called to make a real difference in this world, and you can do that by helping people. If you live by the power of the risen Lord, then you can make this declaration for yourself. I encourage you, right now, to stand to your feet and proclaim the following paragraph out loud. Do it with all of the faith that God gives you. Make the following confession and prayer as an anointed minister of the gospel:

"The Spirit of the Lord is on me,

Because he has anointed me to preach good news to the poor.

He has sent me to proclaim freedom for the prisoners

And recovery of sight for the blind,

To release the oppressed,

And to proclaim the year of the Lord's favor."

"I will, by God's grace, fulfill this assignment, for I am a believer, a child of God, a disciple of Christ, and a minister of the good news. I have been saved and sent by God for this purpose. Oh Lord, I dedicate my life to you for the work of the ministry. Let your powerful anointing rest on me. Teach me to be an able minister of the gospel. Teach me to break curses, to cast out demons, to demolish prisons, to heal the sick and to set people on the pathway of blessings. I pray this prayer in faith for the glory of God in my life. In Jesus' name, Amen!"

Chapter Twenty-five

EQUIPPING FOR POWERFUL MINISTRY

A MATURE INSTRUMENT

Ministering to people is never complete with one prayer or experience. There are many stages in the process of healing and the development of spiritual maturity. Commitment, deliverance, freedom, healing, stability, the fellowship of the Holy Spirit, serving, purpose and destiny, are all important parts of our growth. This is called the process of sanctification. It literally means, "to be made holy." It involves being called from darkness to light and being progressively changed into the image of Christ. Finally, it involves being set apart for purpose and ministry. Everyone who receives ministry should one day become a minister.

Christian ministry is progressive. If we make an initial commitment to Christ and receive no other ministry, we may be like an instrument that is only playing one note, even though it was designed to play many notes on a vast musical scale. People are fearfully and wonderfully made in God's image, but everyone needs more of Christ in order to reach their potential. Ministers may fail to help people find spiritual health and purpose because they only minister a fraction of what is possible or intended.

All ministers need more teaching and much more preparation. As we press into God, we will be continually stretched and equipped to serve God's people better. Effective ministry is why God raised up ministers in the first place. It is why He gives them wisdom, powerful preaching, anointed prayers, ability to instruct and equip, gifts of the Holy Spirit, far reaching vision and amazing supernatural authority. All of this has been given to help people.

The work is not finished when ministers extend kindness or give a fine teaching. Ministry involves bringing people into positive change. Healing and deliverance may be required. Even then, the minister's role may not be complete; they are not only assigned to get the darkness out but also to put the light in. People need restoration, value, dignity, an array of ministry gifts and a picture of their destiny. All ministers have been called to equip God's people so that they may come to maturity and do works of service (see Ephesians 4:11-13).

One step toward healing and maturity will lead to the next step, for the path of a believer gets brighter and brighter until they reach the full brightness at noon day. Many changes in a disciple's life will come directly from the Holy Spirit, but some will require the personal assistance of ministers. This is especially true if a person has many curses, if they are new believers or if they are transitioning to a new level of ministry or purpose.

Every human personality is more beautiful and more extensive than we can understand, and even with the power of the Holy Spirit, no person can minister everything by themselves. That is why God has designed His church to be a team of workers. Together the members of Christ's church serve as many great channels for God's grace to flow through. Each member has a different expression of the Holy Spirit, and each is called to be a worker. When the whole body of Christ does the whole will of God, there will be no lack. Every instrument can be developed to play wonderful masterpieces for the glory of God.

THE 10 GUIDELINES OF MINISTRY

For many years, my wife Joy and I have travelled extensively, ministering in hundreds of churches and praying for multitudes of people. We have seen thousands of people healed and set free from demonic oppression. As we have ministered, God has taught us about the different levels of ministry and how we can help people on their journey no matter what they are in need of. In the next several chapters, we will focus on ministering to people, including the breaking off of generational curses. To start with, we will give an overview of the 10 guidelines for ministry that we have discovered. After outlining the list, we will look at each of the guidelines in more detail. Notice that the first 4 guidelines involve God's grace functioning in the personal life of the minister.

1. Live as a branch connected to and abiding in the vine.

2. Minister with the anointing of the Lion and the Lamb.

3. Conform to the shining character of Christ.

4. Depend on the supernatural gifts of the Holy Spirit.

5. Break generational curses.

6. Cast out demons.

7. Heal the broken hearted.

8. Heal physical bodies.

9. Restore value and dignity.

10. Release God's purpose and destiny.

ABIDING IN THE VINE

Before leaving this chapter we will get started with our ministry list. Here is the first of 10 guidelines that all of us should embrace. The Bible calls it "Abiding in the Vine".

The Lord said, *"I am the vine; you are the branches. If a man remains in me and I in him, he will bear much fruit; apart from me you can do nothing"* (Jn. 15:5).

Abiding in the vine is fellowship with the Holy Spirit. He lives inside of us, teaching us and leading us on a moment by moment basis. We abide in Him as we focus on Him, communicate with Him, listen to His voice, and walk in obedience to the directives that He gives us. If we fail to do our part, we will not be led by Him or receive His power. If, however, we do our part, He guarantees to do His part.

Jesus (or the Spirit of Jesus – the Holy Spirit) is the vine, and we are the branches that are connected to Him. The sap and the life-flow from the main vine goes into the branches. The ultimate purpose of abiding in the vine is to bear much fruit. The Holy Spirit is called the Comforter and the Teacher. He will console us and instruct us so that we can change - first of all to become Christ-like, and secondly to become ministers who represent Him to others.

As we continue abiding in Him, we will naturally produce fruit. The fruit of God includes all aspects and blessings of His kingdom. The fruit includes: souls saved, darkness removed, prisons demolished, freedom gained, health restored, spiritual gifts released, wisdom imparted, character and personalities changed, dignity given, righteous living, financial abundance, angels advancing, morality established, the sovereign rule of Christ being embraced and the kingdom of God expanding. Whenever this fruit is produced in abundance, nations thrive, families prosper and individuals come to purpose and fulfillment. The minister of the gospel must abide in the vine in order to bring forth much fruit. Without the leadership of the Holy Spirit flowing through the minister, they can do nothing, and they will not have any lasting or eternal value coming out of their ministry.

STARTING TO BEAR FRUIT

If you are just starting to minister to others and you are learning to follow the leading of the Holy Spirit, then you are on the right track. As I write this, it is spring here in the Carolinas, and I have enjoyed watching the growth of the bushes and plants around our home. Some are in full leaf, others have buds and flowers, while some in the vegetable garden have already produced fruit. Each stage of development is exciting and beautiful in its own way. That is what happens with a minister-in-training, as they abide in the vine.

When I was just a young teen, I received Jesus as my Savior, and I was immediately called into the ministry. I was determined to be a disciple of Christ and to be fruitful.

I read in the scriptures: *"When you pray, go into your room* [closet]*, close the door and pray to your Father, who is unseen. Then your Father, who sees what is done in secret, will reward you* [openly]*"* (Mt. 6:6).

I did exactly as the scriptures said. I went into my closet, closed the door and sat down on a pile of dirty laundry and began to pray to my Heavenly Father in secret. I prayed and interceded for my friends at school; I asked God to save them.

I was just a new Christian, but I went to the pastor of our church and asked if I could start a youth group. Since there was only one other Christian teen in the church at the time, the pastor and elders agreed to let me begin this ministry, provided an adult church leader could be present at the back of the room during our services. I guess they must have thought, "How much trouble can Peter cause with only one other teen anyway?"

Soon, we were holding Friday night services. I began preaching to a small handful of teens whose parents made them attend. Then the miracles began. Every Friday someone got saved, and within one year, 40 teens were saved from our local high school. The youth group grew to be the most vibrant ministry in the church,at that time. It happened only because I was abiding in the vine.

MORE FRUIT

It is always exciting to see the "Abiding in the Vine" principle working in those we have prayed for. Every year, Joy and I lead a group on a spiritual pilgrimage to Israel. A few months ago, we were there with 30 Christians who were discovering their Jewish roots. Besides the spiritual experiences of visiting the sites, I usually preach at two special meetings on the subject of God's purposes with Israel at the end of the age. During those meetings, we allow time for our guests to receive personal prayer ministry. Most of those who attend receive powerful ministry over their lives. One godly lady received specific healing and commissioning for the work of the ministry.

Since she has been home, she has been abiding in the vine and God has been using her to bring forth much fruit. She phoned me the other day with some amazing stories, the likes of which had never happened to her before. One such story involved a friend who had a series of serious medical traumas. After a scan, the doctors told her that, among other problems, she had black spots on her lungs (an indication of lung cancer) and she also had kidney stones. Appointments were made to see a pulmonary specialist to determine a good course of action for her lungs, and another appointment was made to see a kidney specialist to recommend the necessary medical procedure for the removal of the stones.

The friend, who received a special impartation while with us in Israel, met with this woman for prayer. We did not teach this, but, being led of the Holy Spirit, she wrapped a prayer shawl around her friend and prayed over her passionately. Later, the pulmonary specialist x-rayed her lungs but found no black spots, and the kidney specialist told her that she had no kidney stones. Jesus healed the lady through the prayer ministry of her friend.

Our friend is a humble, gentle soul, and she was so amazed at what had happened that she had to phone us with the story. We talked for about 40 minutes as she shared story after story of what God was doing in her and through her. We give all of the praise and glory to Him.

GOD'S COMMISSIONING FOR YOU

Abiding in the vine starts in the secret place. There in secret, we learn to share the desires of our hearts with the Lord. We study God's word, and He speaks to us in gentle ways. We learn how to listen and recognize His voice, receive confirmations and follow through with risk-taking obedience. Our faith grows and develops like the leaves, buds and flowers on the spring bushes around my home. Get ready for abundance, for kingdom fruit will follow in the time of harvest.

Suddenly, as the Lord leads you, the abiding in the vine process will go public. It will move from the closet to the marketplace. You will be called to minister to others as the opportunity presents itself. As the Holy Spirit leads and empowers, you will minister God's kindness to people. As His grace flows, you will see miracles, experience healings and watch as lives are set free and people are put on track with God. At this level of public ministry, you must learn to hear God's voice on the fly. As you pray, speak His word and minister, He will lead you and you will learn to make adjustments as you go. Be humble and teachable, for God gives grace to the humble, but He resists the proud.

Go slow, but move forward in faith. Most importantly - go with God! You can do nothing without Him, but with Him, nothing shall be impossible. As you minister to others, you will find your own calling; your identiy and your destiny in Christ will begin to emerge. Once you discover who you are, you will know what you are called to do and what direction you should focus your attention on.

Chapter Twenty-six

LION AND THE LAMB MINISTRIES

FURTHER PREPARATION FOR MINISTRY

Ministering to people means that a disciple becomes a channel for God's grace. Disciples abide in the vine, and the life of God wells up within them and flows out through them. Then the light of God shines forth to help and strengthen others. The ministry is what disciples are trained for, but many have not yet answered the call. They are not familiar with a ministry lifestyle, and some think it is just for pastors and hired church staff. All believers are called, however, to do the work of the ministry.

As a disciple takes steps to serve the Lord, they find themselves in the school of the Holy Spirit. The more they press in, the steeper their learning curve will be. Those who follow the Lord will discover that everything in life becomes refocused. Soon, they begin saying and doing things that are beyond their own capability; they do things that were previously unfamiliar. People around them will begin to reap the benefits.

This is very exciting for the budding disciple; it is an adventurous step of faith and that is usually a bit scary. Moving in the power of the Holy Spirit is a step into the supernatural. It is not a place of superficial activity or casual thinking. The Lord will begin to train a disciple in the ministries of the Lion and the Lamb. This work will stretch a disciple and turn them inside-out until the roar of the Lion and the compassion of the Lamb come forth.

TWO KINDS OF AUTHORITY

These ministry dynamics describe two of the names of the Lord Jesus. He is both the Lion and the Lamb. We read of these names in the following verses.

"'See, the Lion of the tribe of Judah, the Root of David, has triumphed. He is able to open the scroll and its seven seals.' Then I saw a Lamb looking as if it had been slain, standing in the center of the throne" (Rev. 5:5-6).

The scroll in the book of Revelation contains the prophetic words of God for the end of the age. Only Jesus has the authority to open the scroll and release the end-time plans of God. The message of the scroll is two-fold: it calls for the destruction of the devil, as well as for the fullness of God's blessings to fall on Israel and the church.

THE LION ANOINTING

The Lion anointing is bold and aggressive. Jesus, the Lion of Judah, will chase down and destroy the enemy. His holy indignation erupts from the throne room with unequalled power. His coming is like a pent-up flood that is suddenly released; it brings the wrath of God. The Lion delivers justice and vengeance against all that is lawless and wicked. He is the champion of heaven, defending the weak and avenging the abused. The Lion rips and devours the works of the devil; He demolishes spiritual prisons and sets captives free. The Lion punishes the vile and finalizes God's retribution on wicked men and women. He rules with a rod of iron, halts the activities of arrogant rebels and destroys those who insist on worshipping wickedness.

THE LAMB ANOINTING

The Lamb authority is equally powerful but with a different approach. The Lamb brings the unbeatable intensity of God's amazing love. He was slain on the cross, not because He was overpowered by the devil, but because He chose to lay His life down for others. This is the sacrificial power of agape love and it is almost irresistible. The Lion does not look for a right response when issuing judgment; He administers the wrath of God to wicked people. The Lamb, however, pursues a right response from people. He has the supernatural ability to lead people away from rebellion, and He can separate people from unrelenting judgment. The kindness of the Lamb leads a person to repentance. He comes with love, kindness, compassion, goodness, mercy, patience and gentleness. Jesus the Lamb can soften the hardest heart and turn a rebel into a prince.

THE LION AND THE LAMB TOGETHER

The book of Revelation shows the work of both the Lion and the Lamb. The Lion shakes and destroys all that is not of God and the Lamb rescues all who will respond to His amazing love. The first judgments that fall on the earth during the great tribulation come as the four apocalyptic horses break forth. As the seals are broken off of the scroll, horses and their riders begin to release God's wrath on the earth. That is the work of the Lion of Judah.

The Lamb of God who takes away the sin of the world is also present. He insists on showering people with mercy and compassion even during the great tribulation. Alongside of the horses of judgment come the oil and the wine (see Revelation 6:6). The oil represents the Holy Spirit of grace, and the wine represents the shed blood of the Lamb. Together, they speak of the mercy ministry of Christ (see the story of the Good Samaritan; he ministered the oil and the wine). Because of the compassion and love of the Lamb, the greatest revivals in all of history will come during the great tribulation (see my book *Unexpected Fire* for details). Even as wrath and judgment are falling, Jesus continues to call people out of darkness and into light. No one can hide from the power of the Lion unless they stand behind the love of the Lamb. The Lion and the Lamb ministries come at the same time.

THE LAMB MINISTRY

The Lamb is the champion of love. He comes to redeem the weak, the fallen, the frustrated, and the rebellious. He comes for the forsaken, the rejected, the abused, and the reprobate. The Lamb died for the whole world, but His work did not stop at the cross. In the power of the Holy Spirit the Lamb continues to minister through the saints. When the Lamb ministry is in us, we comfort the wounded, defend the weak, restore the fallen, inspire the hopeless, heal the sick, receive the rejected, embrace the lonely, forgive the sinner, lift the humble, encourage the fainthearted, heal the broken-hearted, and help direct pilgrims to their destiny. The powerful work of the Lamb is far-reaching. None can avoid His coming and if people pray or prophesy in agreement with His love, the Lamb ministry anointing will come with greater intensity.

MINISTER BOTH AT THE SAME TIME

The work of the Lion and the Lamb is available for every disciple. The Lord wants to destroy any work of darkness in a believer and bring forth the new, spiritual man. Disciples are in a constant state of change because of the ministry of the Lion and the Lamb that is at work within them. This is the refining work of the Lord in a believer's life and it is continuous. The Lion will continue to sanctify and destroy any secret vestige of darkness that lingers in a believer. The Lamb will continually change our character until we shine with all of the fruit of the Holy Spirit.

As you minister to others, you must allow both the Lion and the Lamb to work in you and through you at the same time. This is an important lesson to learn if you are going to be an effective minister. You must hate the works of darkness (Lion work) but be full of love and compassion for people (Lamb work). Both indignation (against the devil) and tenderness (toward people) are functioning at the same time.

As my wife and I minister in different churches around the country, we find different emotions rising within us. One minute we are weeping over the wounded as we pour dignity and grace into them; a moment later we are destroying strongholds of demonic darkness and breaking generational curses with great indignation. It is not difficult to do both within the same minute if you embrace the ministries of Jesus. He brings many spiritual weapons to the battle ground. Both the Lion and the Lamb ministries are absolutely essential in the work of resucing people.

I WANT TO MURDER SOMEONE

I remember ministering at one church where God was releasing incredible healing and deliverance to hundreds of people. My wife and I were going from one person to another as they stood before us in a long line. Every person was finding God's grace and power at some supernatural level. Suddenly, one middle-aged man, who looked like a body builder, grabbed my arm and pulled me toward himself. With sheer desperation in his voice, he whispered in my ear, "Help me pastor, I want to murder someone and I cannot stop myself!"

I looked into his eyes with determination and said, "Tell me about your father."

Like one caught off guard, he glared at me and replied, "I don't have a father."

"Yes, you do." I responded, "Even if you don't know who he is."

He began to cry. I led the man through a series of prayers. We thanked God for his father and for the moment that he was conceived in his mother's womb. He could not stop weeping. He repented for his bitterness and for the rebellion that he had embraced because of the many wounds and frustrations in his life. He forgave those who had hurt and abused him. He rededicated his life to Christ, renounced witchcraft, anger, murder and rejection. Then we broke generational curses off of his life. We rebuked the orphan spirit and broke off the spirit of abandonment, rejection, murder and rebellion. By this time the man was lying on the ground and God was setting him free from powerful strongholds of darkness.

I could not help but love this man. I knelt beside him as the Holy Spirit continued to wash him and operate on him. I spoke God's love, approbation, value, dignity, favor, blessings and purpose into his life. What was happening to him was more powerful than what could come from any medical operation. Dr. Jesus, who is both the Lion and the Lamb, was operating. The Lion was tearing up the enemy while the Lamb was ministering the healing graces. In just a few minutes, amazing change had come to this man's world. Such is the power of the Lion and the Lamb.

Everything he will need did not come that day, but truck loads of good did come to him as the Lion roared and the Lamb loved. Later, in confidence, I told his pastor what the man had whispered in my ear so he would be prepared for any follow-up.

A year later, I returned to that church and prayed for him again. What a different man he had become. He had grown tremendously and the process of sanctification was working in him. Such amazing change had come, and I give all the praise and glory to Jesus; He is the undefeated Lion and the sanctifying Lamb.

I COME EXPECTING CHANGE

The man we just described has a wonderful testimony of restoration and healing. We see these kinds of results repeated thousands of times every year. The Lion and Lamb ministry is supernatural but not unusual. As we travel, we expect results like this, and I think they happen every time we pray with a group of people. I love to preach God's word because faith is released and signs and wonders follow. Change comes when we pray for people. My wife Joy and I minister with great expectations, and we always see God's supernatural power moving among us.

When I step into a room of worshippers, I love to look around and see the people worshipping the Lord. I look at one person and feel the Lion rising in my soul on their behalf. I look at another and sense the Lamb shining forth toward them. I love people and, as I look at them, I know what God wants to do for many of them even before we preach or pray. During the meeting, I am constantly listening and speaking to the Lord so that I might know how to work with Him.

As a minister, I am abiding in the vine and God's power is flowing through me. I work for Him, and when I lay my hands on people, I know that God will lay His hands on them. I love the Lion and the Lamb anointing. Together with these anointings, I come to break prison walls, find the wounded and oppressed, carry them out of the prisons, demolish the prisons by breaking curses, heal the sick and broken-hearted, restore hope, release faith, impart dignity and set people on the path to purpose and destiny.

GET READY FOR MORE

The first dynamic for the minister is to walk with God in the secret place of fellowship and prayer. The second dynamic for the minister is to embrace the Lion and the Lamb in their own life and to embrace the Lion anointing and the Lamb anointing in the work of the ministry.

We still have 8 other ministry dynamics to share with you, and we will do so in the next few chapters. Would you pray a prayer in response to what you have received from the Holy Spirit so far?

Jesus said to His disciples, *"Take my yoke upon you and learn from me, for I am gentle and humble in heart, and you will find rest for your souls. For my yoke is easy and my burden is light"*
(Mt. 11:29-30).

In response to these verses, pray this prayer:

"O, Lord I come to you in the name of Jesus, who is both the Lion of Judah and the Lamb of God. I dedicate my life to you for the work of the ministry.   I choose to be yoked together with Christ in the work of the ministry. Father, let the power of the Lion work in my life to remove that which needs to go, and let me roar as the Lion flows through me to break strongholds of darkness in others.

Lord, I also ask for the work of the Lamb of God in my life. Make me more compassionate and loving. Let me sacrifice where it is appropriate. Let the grace of God soften my heart and help me pull the sinner, the wounded and the oppressed from the brink of hell and from their spiritual prisons. I will not strive, but rest in your grace and power, and I will find peace in the anointing that you give me. Today, I open my life to you for the ministries of the Lion and the Lamb to be formed and released in me. I count you faithful, and I give all of the praise and the glory to you. I pray these things with thanksgiving in my heart, in the powerful name of Jesus. Amen."

Chapter Twenty-seven

CHARACTER OF CHRIST FOR MINISTRY

THE JESUS MINISTRY

*T*he third ministry dynamic that must be activated in the life of a minister is the fruit of the Holy Spirit. The fruit of the Holy Spirit is the character of Christ.

Before discussing our work in the ministry, it will serve us well to look deeper into the life and ministry of Jesus. If someone were to ask you what Jesus is like, you could quote them the verses in the Bible that teach about the fruit of the Spirit, and you would be giving them a correct answer.

Scripture says, "The fruit of the Spirit is love, joy, peace, patience, kindness, goodness, faithfulness, gentleness, and self-control" (Gal. 5:22).

This is how Jesus was and how He is now. In earthly terms, these qualities describe His personality. This is also the personality of God Almighty, for Jesus is the express image of the Father. He told

His disciples that if they see Him, they also see the Father who is in heaven. Jesus and the Father do not have a good-cop, bad-cop routine; both are love, joy and peace personified.

If we could turn back time and you could meet Jesus on the shores of the Sea of Galilee just as He was 2,000 years ago, you would discover that He was a super-fabulous man. He is the same yesterday, today and forever. He is patient, good, kind, gentle, self-controlled, faith-filled and faithful. He is absolutely overflowing with love, joy and peace. He has much more of these characteristics than any other person that you have met. If you have an appreciation for virtue and goodness, then you will be drawn and attracted to Him. You will admire Him so much that you will wish you could be just like Him.

As you continue to study the character of Jesus, another surprising dynamic will come to you. You will begin to believe that you can be like Him, and you will begin to change into His image. The more you spend time with Jesus, the more you will become like Him.

If you saw Jesus ministering, whether He was preaching to a multitude, healing a blind man or dismissing the sins of an adulteress, you would love and admire Him more than anyone you have ever admired before.

If you followed Him and watched Him long enough, you would eventually see Him speaking with stern indignation to some people. That holy anger, however, would only be directed at wickedness and injustice.

He would rebuke hypocrites - those who walk in the opposite lifestyle to what they preach (this does not include those who slip or fall; He loves them).

He would also warn child abusers that great punishment was coming. He will not tolerate those who hurt or abuse children, unless they turn from their hideous ways.

He would also rebuke legalistic leaders who show no mercy or compassion to others. He does not like hypocrites, child abusers or leaders who are legalistic and controlling.

Most people fail and falter through life, but they still want what is good. Although some are bent on wickedness, most are not. They admire goodness and wish there was more of it in the world. Jesus looks beyond the shame and weakness of fallen and wounded men and women. He sees the treasure inside of them that was made in the image of God. He comes to those people with a compelling opportunity. He knows that with His power these people are capable of living godly lives. He loves them, is drawn to them, and He desires to minister to them. Jesus does not need to put on an act of kindness to embrace those who stand before Him, even if they are really messed up. Kindness is who He is, and love and grace just naturally flow out of Him.

Seeing Jesus will inspire us. Hearing Him speak will bring hope to us even if we are depressed or demonized. Watching Him minister to others will make us fall in love with Him. Having a personal encounter with Jesus will open closed doors inside of us so that we can find healing. What He can do because of his great power is fantastic, but it is who He is that wins our hearts. When we begin to respond to Him, we will find ourselves dedicating our lives and worshipping Him. It is then that everything about us begins to change. Old things pass away and all becomes new.

GIVING WHAT JESUS GIVES

Those who minister must have a heaven-sent Jesus anointing on their lives. Human kindness is a good quality, but it will not bring real change in those who receive it. We need the Jesus anointing. Functioning with the fruit of the Holy Spirit is not just being nice; it is the power and personality of God flowing through us. That is why it is called the fruit of the Spirit; it is the product (the fruit) of God's Spirit in us.

I fail to appreciate ministers who are harsh with people. If we are called to break curses and set captives free, it should be done in the love of God. That love is not simply a pious feeling inside of us; it is seen and felt by those around us. Others should experience the tender love of God flowing through us. We must hate the sin but be gentle and compassionate with people. When I minister to people, I want the fruit of the Spirit in me. I want people to see Jesus. I want to give what Jesus gives. Usually, a tear or two will fill my eyes when I am ministering to a group of people, especially if some of those people have deep wounds. I cannot help but feel great compassion for them, and I am overwhelmed when I recognize the healing power of the Holy Spirit flowing through me and into them. I leave those times of ministry so full of God's manifest presence that I feel as though I am bursting with grace. Those times are the most rewarding times in my life, and they are not rare or unusual. Ministering like this is a weekly experience for my wife and me.

THE FRUIT OF THE SPIRIT

It is not wrong to try to imitate the fruit of the Spirit. After all, these are virtuous qualities. The real fruit of the Spirit, however, is supernatural. It is more powerful than human kindness; it is the God-life flowing in us. The fruit of the Spirit is a gift from God that is imparted to us as we walk with God and obey Him.

Jesus said, *"And anyone who does not carry his cross and follow me cannot be my disciple"* (Lk. 14:27).

Jesus is not talking about being a believer in Christianity; He is talking about being a disciple. You can believe in God, be a Christian and go to heaven when you die without becoming a disciple, but that is not God's intention for you. Believing in Jesus and calling out to Him will result in His grace falling on you. You will be saved from Hell, but that does not mean that you have become a disciple. A disciple is one who has come under the discipline of Christ. Disciples become God's friend, and they partner with Him in the work of the ministry. You cannot be a disciple unless you pick up your cross and follow Christ.

Picking up your cross is embracing a death to your own carnal nature. That means denying your natural impulses and rights and letting them die. It means listening to what the Holy Spirit says to you and obeying Him.

One person said, "The cross is where your will and God's will cross. Then you lay down your will and choose His."

There is a natural conflict between the ways of the spiritual man and the ways of the carnal or earthly man. Both are inside of us once we become Christians, but our destiny depends on our choice. We must choose to follow the direction of the spiritual man and reject the carnal man. This is not an easy matter; denial means death to the carnal man.

Jim Elliot, the famous missionary to South America, wrote, "He is no fool who gives up what he cannot keep, to gain what he cannot lose."

This is how Christ is formed in you, and it is one of the basic requirements for ministry. As you follow the Lord by choosing to deny yourself and obey Him, He will put more of Himself inside of you. That is how you change. You cannot create the fruit of the Spirit. You can, however, obey the Lord in every detail of life, and He will produce His fruit in you. In other words, the fruit of the Spirit is given as you walk with God; you catch the qualities of Christ by impartation. An anointing will come and your character will change as you walk in obedience to the cross.

Others will see the changes in your life before you do. They will start to notice that you are kinder and more loving and that you have more patience, peace and joy in your life. They will like you more than they did before. The more you walk with God, the happier you should be. If you are a disciple but you are not growing in righteousness, patience, peace, love and joy, then I think you have been listening to the voice of religious duty and legalism rather than the voice of the Holy Spirit. Christians should not be crabby people. The kingdom of God at work in you will naturally produce righteousness, peace and joy (see Romans 14:17).

The more of Christ that is formed in you, the more you will recognize Him in your life, and you will not be comfortable with anything less. You will see and feel the following qualities inside of you, and they will affect the way you look at life and the way you love and appreciate people. It will be hard for you not to forgive people. It will be difficult for you to watch evil such as horror movies. It will be difficult for you to see fallen people as being evil. The following is what you will see as you pick up your cross and follow Christ:

1. You will see a love that cares and shows compassion to almost all people. You will look beyond their faults and see their needs. You will want to give of yourself to help them.

2. You will see a joy that is bubbling up deep inside of you. You will be thankful and even love the way God has made you. You will be thrilled to know Jesus personally and you will be constantly excited about your friendship with the Holy Spirit.

3. You will see a peace inside of you that is larger and more powerful than any trouble that conspires against you. It is rooted in the realization that God Almighty is watching over you. You have faith so that you can naturally rest in His love and care.

4. You will see patience at work in you. It will give you the ability to be calm in the middle of a storm. It will allow you to release every matter into God's hands. After you have done all that He tells you to do, you will be able to wait on Him for the results.

5. You will see kindness flowing through you. It will begin to work in the attitude and the way you think about other people. Vengeance, retribution or harm coming to others will feel like it is hurting you. You will want to ease their pain in any way you can.

6. You will see goodness in your life, and you will see some good in most people even when it is buried deep beneath a pile of negative baggage. You will love to see wholeness and goodness restored to people.

7. You will see faithfulness at work in you. You will embrace it and inspire it in others. You will speak its praises to all who are floundering. You will preach its merits and welcome its rewards.

8. You will see <u>gentleness</u> being formed in you. A new sensitivity will empower you to open closed doors in people's lives and touch them where they are hurting. This will produce a realistic but powerful encouragement enabling you to reach the unreachable.

9. You will see <u>self-control</u> in your life. It will not be difficult to resist temptation. Discipline will be a privilege and an honor that you embrace for yourself. It will inspire others to follow.

If you have peace, you will impart it to others when you minister. If you have faith, you will impart it to others when you minister. If you have kindness, you will impart it to others when you minister.

You cannot give what you do not have, but if you walk with God, He will change you to be more like Christ. Then you will give life when you minister to others. As we admire Christ and receive an impartation of life from Him so, likewise, others will admire us. We can impart life to them not by what we do alone, but by the character of Christ that is inside of us.

DO YOU WANT IT?

The fruit of the Spirit is the foundation for ministry. These are the qualities we desire to see in others, and we can inspire others when these qualities are in our lives. You cannot give what you do not have. A true minister of Christ is not made in the halls of academic learning but in the intimate place of fellowship with the Holy Spirit. What you are is what you will give to others. What you have is contagious. It has been said that you can preach measles, but if you have mumps, that is what people will catch, regardless of what you preach.

A minister should do what Christ did. You should have what

Christ has and give what He gave. The miracles of heaven flow through the character of Christ as well as through the power gifts. Our goal is to do more than heal broken bodies. We are called to heal broken hearts and set the captives free. How can we do that without love?

We are called to release the year of God's favor and pronounce blessings over people's lives. It is time to bring the full gospel to those we minister to. That cannot be done without the fruit of the Holy Spirit flowing in us and through us.

In our next chapter we will discuss the 4th dynamic of ministry preparation. We will look at the powerful gifts of the Holy Spirit and how we can exercise them as we pray and minister over people. This takes us from piety to purpose, a path that many good Christians have been too fearful to walk down. Get ready to step out of the boat.

Chapter Twenty-eight

POWER GIFTS FOR MINISRTY

JESUS POWER

*I*t is easy and safe to minister to people if the minister gives kindness and encouragement, but that would not have helped Lazarus or his sisters. Lazarus was Jesus' friend, and he died from a disease. He became sick, and his sisters sent word for Jesus to come quickly. They had seen Him heal the sick, and their hopes were riding on His prompt and timely visit.

Jesus delayed His coming, and by the time He arrived, Lazarus was dead. Mary and Martha had their brother wrapped in grave clothes and laid in a tomb. In Israel, even to this day, all who die are buried within 24 hours. All hope for this life went into the tomb along with the body, and the sisters and their friends were grieving when Jesus arrived.

Jesus knew that an imminent resurrection was coming. All power in heaven and earth has been given unto Him, and He loves to release miracles to those who walk with Him.

Jesus said, *"I am the Resurrection and the Life. He who believes in me will live, even though he dies"* (Jn. 11:25).

God breaks the natural laws and performs miracles, even miracles of this magnitude. Recently, Joy and I met a Mormon family at a friend's home. Soon we began discussing the power of God and His ability to make miracles happen. The Mormon man explained his understanding of God's power. He told us that God did not have supernatural power to overrule the natural laws, but because He is more knowledgeable than us, He is able to manipulate the situation. He explained that God's higher understanding of physics and biology gave Him a power that seemed miraculous, but really, it was just advanced science. This is a form of humanism that purports that we will become like God as we receive a higher form of education.

Immediately, I renounced this erroneous doctrine, declaring that God is not a super-educated human. He is God and not subject to the natural laws. A miracle is the power to change the rules and nothing is impossible for God.

The Mormon was humanizing God and deifying man. This is a doctrine of devils; subtle and evil in its intent, it denies the true power of God. Scripture instructs us to stay away from people who embrace that erroneous teaching.

"People will be lovers of themselves ... having a form of godliness but denying its power. Have nothing to do with them"

(2 Tim. 3:2,5).

Jesus did not use a respirator or any scientific knowledge or device when He brought Lazarus back to life. In fact, He was standing at a distance from the dead body when He simply spoke the word, and the man's life returned.

Jesus performs miracles today, and He uses His disciples to speak the word and partner with Him. Jesus brings supernatural power, but His ministers must do their part. In the Lazarus story, Jesus gave two separate instructions.

He said, *"Take away the stone"* (Jn. 11:39).

And, *"Take off the grave clothes and let him go"* (Jn. 11:44).

Although Jesus is the healer, He did not do everything. It was people obeying the Lord, who removed the stone and later removed the grave clothes. Miracles come not when we follow a procedure, but when we listen and obey the Holy Spirit. If God uses you to raise someone from the dead, as Jesus did with Lazarus, then you can believe Him for anything!

ANOTHER LAZARUS

I remember the time I was preaching in Bujumbura, Burundi, in Africa. About 5,000 people were sitting under a tin roof held up by wooden poles. I spoke through an interpreter and found out later that the interpreter was a medical doctor. He asked me to visit his hospital the next day to pray for the patients.

I was blessed to go from bed to bed with the doctor praying for people with malaria, bullet wounds, and many serious diseases. We visited about one hundred patients in this primitive setting. He introduced me to each of them and we ministered God's love and power to them.

During the tour he showed me the baby delivery room. A simple table with stainless steel stirrups stood in the center of the room. Then he told me an amazing story. He said that he delivered a baby here about a year ago. The baby was born dead and no matter what they did, they could not revive him. The nurse laid the dead child on the table, and the doctor called the coroner to come and remove the child's dead body.

An hour later, the cleaning lady came in to clean up the mess. When she saw the baby, she screamed out in despair and began praying passionately. She cried to God for a miracle, and she would not stop. She marched around the compound yelling into the heavens. I was told that people could hear her all over the neighborhood. After an extended session of fervent prayer, she returned to the delivery room and laid her hands on the dead baby and commanded life to come into the child in the name of Jesus. Immediately the baby came back to life and began crying.

The doctor looked at me and said, "The child now lives up in those hills." He pointed to the horizon and continued, "We called him Lazarus."

RESURRECTION HERE IN THE USA

A few years ago, I was preaching on "Breaking Generational Curses," at a conference in Charlotte, NC. We were using St. Giles Presbyterian Church for our meetings, and the place was packed. After the preaching we invited those who wanted prayer to the front. Hundreds of people responded, and we began ministering to them, one at a time. I encouraged those who wanted to learn to gather around and participate with Joy and me as we broke curses, cast out demons and released God's healing power into those who had come up to the front for prayer. Soon the floor was covered with bodies. The Holy Spirit was pouring His love upon these people and there was no shortage of miracles happening in the room. People were crying, some were shaking and screaming as demons came out of them.

At midnight, the meeting was still in full swing, and I was on my knees ministering to someone when I felt a hand touch my shoulder. I turned to see my good friend Marvin Rollins standing before me looking deathly pale. He was covered in beads of perspiration as he said, "Peter, help me; I am very sick."

A spirit of death was at work in him, and he was experiencing a heart attack. Immediately, I led him to the edge of the stage and sat him down. A crowd gathered around us, and in the crowd was a nurse who worked with cardiac patients. I began wiping the sweat from Marvin's face with one hand, as I held his back with the other. I began praying for him as he continued to suffer a massive cardiac arrest. His heart stopped pumping and the blood drained from his face. His head fell back in my arms and his mouth opened wide. He died in my arms with his eyes open. They turned a pale blue color and lost their sparkle as Marvin's life left him. It was as if the lights went out. He lay like a limp rag in my arms as the cardiac nurse searched for his vital signs. They were not to be found.

In an instant, I began rebuking the spirit of death. With a loud voice, I commanded life to come back into Marvin's body and suddenly, he gasped and returned to life. Marvin Rollins had been raised from the dead in my arms.

He sat there on the stage for the next few hours as I went to pray for other people, and every time I looked back at him, he looked better. People stayed with him quietly praying, and he did not want anyone to call for an ambulance. At three o`clock in the morning, he was still there when we finished praying for people.

The next morning, Marvin Rollins returned for the 9:00 AM session. He was there all day and all the next day as well. He still had not gone to the hospital. On the second day, I met with him for lunch. Both he and the cardiac nurse told me that he had died, but now he was feeling great. I asked him to get checked by a doctor when he returned home and to let me know the outcome. Two weeks later, Marvin called to tell me that the doctor had given him a clean bill of health. He also told me that the doctor said that his high blood pressure was completely gone. Furthermore, Marvin said that he was healed of chronic back problems as well.

We give all of the honor and praise to Jesus; He preformed the miracle of resurrection. We did our part to listen and obey the Holy Spirit. Spiritually speaking, we rolled the stone away and took off his grave clothes, but God performed the miracle.

THE NINE GIFTS

Every one of the nine gifts of the Holy Spirit is just as miraculous as raising someone from the dead. Each is an exercise of God's supernatural power. If you are a minister of the gospel, you should experience supernatural signs and wonders. It is not that we see a miracle every time we pray; even Jesus faced limitations. He did not do many miracles in His own hometown because of familiarity and a lack of faith among the people.

The scriptures tell us, *"There are different kinds of gifts, but the same Spirit. ... Now to each one the manifestation of the Spirit is given for the common good. To one there is given through the Spirit the message of wisdom, to another the message of knowledge by means of the same Spirit, to another faith by the same Spirit, to another gifts of healing by that one Spirit, to another miraculous powers, to another prophecy, to another distinguishing between spirits, to another speaking in different kinds of tongues, and to still another the interpretation of tongues"* (1 Cor. 12:4,7-10).

These nine gifts are supernatural works of the Holy Spirit that operate in and through a person as they minister to others on behalf of heaven. It must be understood that these are not just natural talents or abilities: they are supernatural. In other words, they are not functioning unless the Spirit of God is doing the work. The Holy Spirit releases a power of God that cannot be manufactured by earthly intelligence or skill.

Here is a very brief description of these gifts:

1. The word of knowledge is an ability to know something that one would have no way of knowing unless God reveals it to them.

2. The word of wisdom is the ability to know what to do, which way to go, or how to handle a difficult situation because God gives direction. This is not derived by logic or human reasoning.

3. The supernatural gift of faith is the ability to believe when there is no natural reason to believe. It comes when God speaks. It is not the man-manufactured power of positive thinking. A good idea that is not based on a word from God is presumption, not faith.

4.   <u>Gifts of healings</u> are miracles that fix bodies, souls, relation-
      ships, and anything that is broken or dysfunctional. Doc-
      tors prescribe medicines and procedures to work with
      your body to help it heal. That is also healing, but
      the Bible reference to gifts of healing is a supernatu-
      ral act of God that would not happen by natural means.

5.   <u>Miraculous powers</u> will release miracles other than healings.
      These might include changing the weather or walking on water.

6.   <u>Prophecy</u> is hearing and speaking a word from God. It will
      bring supernatural encouragement, instruction, or direction
      from the Lord.

7.   <u>Distinguishing of spirits</u> is the supernatural ability to identify
      specific spirits. A person will know what spirit is at work
      in a certain situation. The gifted person has a word from
      God that enables them to recognize the Spirit of God, a hu-
      man spirit, demons or angels. With this gift, a person may
      know the exact name of an evil spirit that is in someone.

8.   <u>Speaking in different kinds of tongues</u> is the supernatural
      ability to speak in another language. It may be a known
      earthly language that a person has never spoken before
      or a spiritual prayer language understood only by God.

9.   <u>The interpretation of tongues</u> is a supernatural ability to
      understand the spiritual prayer language that, otherwise, only
      God would know.

MINISTERING THE GIFTS

As we minister to people, we look to God for the release of His power. The needs of people are extensive and God has a solution for each of them. It takes spontaneous faith, hearing from God and bold declarations to release the gifts of the Holy Spirit. It is safe but does not require faith to pray things like, "God if it is your will to heal this person, please do it; we know You are able."

There is no risk or faith in a prayer like that, and I do not remember any such prayer resulting in a miracle. It is always God's will to heal and bless, but sometimes there are reasons why the healing may not come. Our place is to find the keys of the kingdom, open the prisons, eliminate the blockages, meet God's conditions, lead a person to the place of healing and miracles and agree with heaven's blessings and assignments for them.

A gifted minister will discern the spirits, pray in the Spirit, receive supernatural knowledge, give the wisdom that comes from above, speak a miracle into existence and prophesy the purposes of God over the one being ministered to. God is at work in us and He longs to use us through the ministry of the laying on of hands and the release of faith. As we walk close to God, He will teach us His ways and perform His great works through us.

Breaking generational curses is only one of the many activities of heaven that we are called to administer. Like a wise master builder, we are given many tools. Each is powerful, but they operate only as the Spirit of God works in us. Every minister functions with a mixture of God and the natural man in them. The more that God leads, the greater the results will be. By God's grace, the Holy Spirit is teaching us and training us to be power-packing ministers of the gospel.

The holy scriptures encourage us to *"eagerly desire the greater gifts"*
(1 Cor. 12:31).

There is no competition between the fruit of the Spirit and the gifts of the Spirit. The fruit speaks of the power of God's character at work in us, and the gifts speak of the power of miracles at work in us. Both are needed to complete the work of the ministry. We should earnestly desire the character of Christ. We should also, earnestly desire the power gifts for the release of miracles. Both the fruit and the gifts point to God's love for people, the release of God's glory, and the expansion of His kingdom.

Chapter Twenty-nine

BREAKING CURSES

OUR FOCUS

We are putting the ministry of breaking curses in the wider context of Christian ministry. In this chapter we focus on the actual breaking of curses. Joy and I will often see the immediate effects of breaking curses as we pray for people. The changes are more dynamic and more noticeable than with any other kind of ministry that we do.

Besides the obvious changes that transpire during the immediate moments following our prayer for people, it is the long term results that excite us most. From Miami to Seattle and Indiana to Texas, we receive the same message when we return to a church where we have ministered before. Someone will inevitably approach us at a follow-up meeting to tell us of a powerful testimony in their lives. It is normal and common for us to discover that physical healings have happened after we broke curses and prayed for people. Families came together, children were saved, addictions ceased, ministry gifts were released and people were set free.

I believe that unresolved curses are the main problem that hinders breakthroughs in the lives of Christians.   Once the curses are removed, other ministry dynamics will flow more readily.

A BREAKTHROUGH IN TEXAS

A couple of years ago, I was ministering at a church in Texas. The pastor asked if I would accompany him to a home to pray for a family.   The oldest child had Asperger's syndrome, a medical disease which is a type of autism.

Upon entering the home, I felt the presence of an oppressive, tormenting spirit. The parents were wonderful people, but they were completely exhausted and presently unable to cope with the situation in the home. Both parents were highly skilled nurses who were well educated and effective workers in their profession. Despite their knowledge, patience, and skill in the workplace, they were at a loss to know what to do on the home front. They had tried everything they could possibly think of, and nothing was working. All of their love and parental discipline had failed to produce the results they were looking for. The children were out of control due to the frustration, anger and demands of the autistic child. The state authorities had threatened to take the child from the home and put her in an institution where she would be drugged and medically confined. With heavy doses of drugs they would render her passive and manageable.

During our time of ministry, we could not even get the children to come to us so that we might lay our hands on them. They were running all over the house trying to play, but they were arguing and fighting constantly. The parents were constantly breaking away from our ministry session to deal with another explosive situation. After bringing a limited measure of peace, they would return to the living room where we were talking.

For about 45 minutes, I listened to their stories and told them about breaking generational curses. Then we prayed. I laid my hands on the parents and broke curses off of them. I also broke the curses off of the children even though they were in the other room. Then we took authority over the demon spirits that had filled the house with torment, disease, rebellion and hopelessness. My own spirit was vexed and on edge but I continued to press forward with the ministry. By the time I left, many curses were broken and the situation had improved greatly. I asked God to send His angels and to complete the work He had started.

I met with them about 1 year ago while doing another ministry event at their church. I also met with them again just two days ago. It is now more than two years since the time we prayed for them in their home. The report I received a year ago and the one I heard just this week were the same.

Let me tell you their story. I will call them Tom and Linda, although that is not their real names. Tom and Linda told me that everything changed dramatically in their home from the very moment we ministered there. Both of these parents have been committed Christians for more than 15 years, yet this was the breakthrough night for their family. Since then, they have known peace in their home. The children are behaving, and God is blessing them abundantly. The medical condition of the Asperger's child is still there, but she is able to receive instruction now, and she has found her place in the family. The children play together, and smiles are on the faces of the parents. Linda said that she knew that night would be a turn-around night for their family, and indeed, dramatic and positive change came. Now the children are lovely - they run to hug us when they see us! In the last few months, we have had family visits with them. What a great time we have had.

The reason we were together a couple of days ago was to see if we should include their story in this book. I interviewed them and discovered more of Linda's amazing story. Here is the short, testimony version:

LINDA'S TESTIMONY

As far as Linda knows, she is the first Christian in her family lineage. She told me that her grandparents were nasty people; hateful and uncaring. Her father was an alcoholic. He was also hateful and verbally abusive to everyone in the family.

Linda's mother worked for the Mafia and seemed to be afraid of everything. As a child, Linda remembers her mother crying constantly and warning her to be careful or the Mafia would hurt them. To put it in a few words, Linda's mother was a tormented woman.

Linda grew up under the power of a violent, controlling spirit of rejection, abuse and fear. She blocked out most of her childhood and became totally detached from reality. At age 11 she would walk the streets of New York City alone at night because she could not sleep. She felt safer on the streets than in her own bedroom. She was diagnosed as having multiple personalities and she spent more than 3 years in mental institutions during her late teens. At that time, she was told that she would be confined to the institution for the rest of her life.

She hated herself and she hated life. She began practicing self-mutilation, cutting herself with knives. She was what those in the medical world call, "a cutter."

Linda first heard about God when she was 21 years old, and a year later, she heard about Jesus and salvation. She would not let anyone touch her or even get near to pray for her, but she dedicated her life to Christ when she was alone in her apartment. At that time she was so dysfunctional that people had to tell her how to shop, clean her house, bathe, cook and even how to order food at a fast food restaurant.

Amazing as it sounds, Linda was able to begin her formal education and by the time she was 26 she had become an excellent nurse. She was so skillful and capable in her profession that she became a supervisor of a 105 bed hospital in Texas.

During the years that followed, Linda was a productive member of the work force but was in a constant battle against demonic oppression. She was still suffering under the power of dark curses. Many people may be successful in the secular world and still carry a lot of heavy ancestral baggage. Years before I met this family, the Holy Spirit led Linda to a couple who had learned about curses and deliverance from Derek Prince, my grandfather. Her new found friends began ministering to her, and Linda grew spiritually. For the next 13 years, they walked with her and saw her constant progress of freedom.

Today, Linda is in her late 40's and is such a solid Christian that you would never guess that she could have had such a past. She is a great wife to Tom, an amazing mother to her children, and a fabulous worker in the church. Both Linda and Tom now serve as nurses in Charlotte, North Carolina, not too far from where we live. They are finding their God-given destiny, and both believe that their 3 girls, including the one with Aspergers, will grow up to be powerful women of God.

Linda is a radiant woman of God. She is refreshing and fun to be around. All who meet her love her. Her story is a testimony to the power of breaking generational curses. Millions of people around the world have dreadful background stories, similar to Linda's. Most of them live and die in torment because the ancestral curses and judgment are never broken off of them. Many of them are Christians, but they still live in fear. Some cannot function properly because of the strongholds of interfering demons in their lives. They have received salvation, and they will not go to hell when they die, but they suffer under the pressures of debilitating curses.

GIVING AND RECIEVING MINISTRY

As Joy and I minister, we follow the leading and prompting of the Holy Spirit. That means we use a full array of spiritual tools to apply God's grace as needed. More often than not, I will break curses off of a person during the early stages of ministry. I have learned that other blessings come with greater release once the judgments are removed.

I look for a point of contact with the person I am praying with so that our spirits come into agreement with God. I look for legal permission, and sometimes I have to draw it out because a person is not always willing to trust. I often lead a person through a prayer of dedication, repentance, forgiveness, or thanksgiving before trying to to minister deliverance, healing or breaking off of curses.

Sometimes we give approbation and honor to a person first, because they are so wounded and hurt that everything inside of them has closed up. Compassion, acceptance and love will open the doors of the heart so that faith may follow. Without the release of faith, nothing will happen.

ESTABLISH A BIBLICAL FOUNDATION

We prefer to preach before we minister the breaking of generational curses because many Christians do not understand that a Christian can still be under a curse or judgment. Somehow, the fact that we are all suffering under Adam's generational curse does not come into their theological reasoning. Everyone is getting older, and unless Jesus comes soon, we will all die. That is a part of the Adamic curse, and if we were free from it, we would not suffer any ill health. Even Christians suffer from the Adamic curse, and the cross of Christ has not removed this from us yet. One day, the work of the cross will be completed in us, and even the Adamic curse will be gone.

The Bible teaches us that Jesus became a curse for us when He died on the cross. He legally took our generational curses and gave us the blessings that were promised to Abraham (see Galatians 3:13-14). Our place is to understand the work of the cross, meet its conditions, and apply its work to our lives.

CUTTING AND PROCLAIMING WITH PASSION

Sometimes, I raise my voice when I break curses but not because I am a showman. I do not believe that volume is power, but passion and fervency are important.

I am reminded of the story in the Bible where Elijah met with King Jehoash. Elijah was a prophet, and he told the king to strike his arrows on the ground and he would see his enemies defeated. The king casually tapped the arrows on the ground 3 times and Elijah became angry with him.

Elisha said, *"You should have struck the ground five or six times; then you would have defeated Aram and completely destroyed it. But now you will defeat it only three times"* (2 Kgs. 13:19).

Often I break curses with a loud voice, but not because I plan to; in fact, sometimes I try not to be too demonstrative. The passion, however, rises within me, and I find myself yelling when I break curses.

I call upon the Lord, take a spiritual stand with the one I am praying for, and verbally break the curse. I cut off ungodly ropes, chains and vines that connect them to their ancestors' sins, then untangle them from wrongful soul ties. I remove judgments that have come down upon them from both sides of their family lineage and symbolically tear up the legal documents written against them. Then I lead them out of prisons and strongholds. In the power of the Holy Spirit, I destroy spiritual prisons that they have been trapped in. I do not pronounce all of these things over every person, every time, but use this kind of language to affect the curse-breaking work of the cross over people.

Usually and almost immediately, a person is set free, and the change is visible. People are instantly filled with emotions; they often cry, fall to the ground, become flush in the face, sigh deeply, swoon, shake, or begin to pray and thank God.

After this initial step of breaking curses, we continue the ministry.

We bring deliverance, healing, prophecy, ministry commissioning, or some other release or blessing that the Holy Spirit instructs us to bring.

REPEATING THE PROCESS

Like with other aspects of sanctification and ministry, it is common to repeat a process to bring about a deeper work. It is not always necessary to break more curses later, but God works with us one step at a time. Sometimes there are layers of baggage that need to be removed and some levels of freedom come only after others are properly received. As people live in their new found freedom, they mature and grow in Christ. A disciple will rise to a new level of destiny, and when that happens, more stones must be removed from the road.

I am not surprised to find out that people need more ministry later. I am always deeply moved, however, when I see how much good God accomplishes in a person's life in just a few moments of faith-filled prayer and ministry. God is good!

YOU CAN MINISTER

God is looking for more partners, and while some will have a more powerful anointing, all disciples should minister in the power of the Holy Spirit. If you will walk closely with the Lord and allow Him to train you, He will use you to break curses off of people's lives. I recommend that you find a capable minister of the gospel, and have them pray over you for ministry impartation. Learn how they minister and receive what God has shown them. Then step out in faith and do the work of the ministry as the Holy Spirit leads you. The

Lord will show you things that no one else can teach you. God is looking for people to partner with Him. Are you ready?

Chapter Thirty

THE DELIVERANCE MINISTRY

DEMONS AND CURSES

Casting out demons is the sixth stage in our teaching on ministry dynamics. We have already written about the relationship between curses and demons, but to bring it back into our thinking, here are a few important truths:

1. Curses are spiritual judgments.

2. Demons cannot attack or live inside whomever they please; they must have a legal right and an open door to interfere with people.

3. Once a judgment has been passed, that person rightfully deserves to be punished.

4. Demons get involved if they have legal right. Then they participate by seeing that the penalty is fulfilled. They hinder, torment, hurt, kill, and destroy as much as they can.

5. Demons cannot possess a Christian, for that would require ownership of a Christian's life. They can, however, live inside and trouble a Christian, and that
can be quite invasive if they have legal access.

Many Christians suffer because of demon harassment. There
are two kinds of demonic troubles. One is an attack from without
and the other comes when a demon lives inside of someone. Believers have power to resist demons who attack them from without and they have authority to cast them out when they live
inside. This chapter contains a short study of demonology. Casting out demons should be a part of the ministry of every minister
of the gospel.

A LOST MINISTRY

Most churches today do not practice the ministry of deliverance,
even though Jesus did. Perhaps they do not know how to cast out
demons, or they may be afraid because they lack understanding.
Perhaps some believe that this is not an important part of the ministry. Some may think that while sinners can have demons, that
when a person comes to Christ, all demons are immediately cut off
or cast out. Therefore, deliverance is not necessary for Christians.

Further reasoning suggests that there is no point in casting demons out of heathen sinners, for the demons would only return later. If you should not cast demons out of unrepentant sinners and
Christians can't have demons, then there is simply no reason for
the deliverance ministry at all. This kind of reasoning has left most
churches devoid of the deliverance ministry. So many Christians are,
therefore, harassed or suffering because of the demons that oppress
them from without or from within.

JESUS CAST OUT DEMONS

Although many good Christians do not agree with the deliverance ministry, it is, nevertheless, an essential part of the work of Christ and a vital ministry today. Just before Jesus died, He taught that the ministry of deliverance would be a normal experience for His followers.

He said, *"And these signs will accompany those who believe: In my name they will drive out demons"* (Mk. 16:17).

Why would that be recorded in the last chapter of Mark if deliverance was unimportant? Furthermore, before Jesus came, there was no deliverance ministry. At least 1/3 of Christ's ministry was casting out demons. He drove out evil spirits everywhere He went, and this ministry continued throughout the book of the Acts of the Apostles. It is available to all believers today.

One of my favorite Bible stories is recorded in Mark chapter one. When we go to Israel, we always take our travelling companions to the archeological site of the synagogue at Capernaum. Although the structures have changed, this was one of the places where Jesus cast an evil spirit out of a man. We read that Jesus went to Capernaum and entered the synagogue and began to teach.

The Bible says, *"Just then a man in their synagogue who was possessed by an evil spirit cried out, 'What do you want with us, Jesus of Nazareth? Have you come to destroy us? I know who you are - the Holy One of God' 'Be quiet!' said Jesus sternly. 'Come out of him!'* ***The evil spirit shook the man violently and came out of him with a shriek.*** *The people were all so amazed that they asked each other,*

'What is this? A new teaching – *and with authority! He even gives orders to evil spirits and they obey him.' News about him spread quickly over the whole region of Galilee"* (Mk. 1:23-28 - emphasis mine)

Here are a few interesting facts:

1. A Jewish, demon possessed man was present in the church meeting.

2. The demon in the man was afraid of Jesus.

3. The demon cried out as Jesus was preaching.

4. Jesus told him to be quiet and to come out of the man.

5. The man fell down, shook and screamed as the demon left him.

6. The Jews had never seen anything like this before. This was a new teaching.

7. The news of the demonic deliverance quickly spread throughout the region.

There is no record of a demon being cast out of a man in the Old Testament, but Jesus came to destroy the works of the devil, and one way He did that was casting out demons. He ministered deliverance to devout, church (Synagogue) attending, Bible-believing Jews.

In His own words, Jesus described His ministry of casting out demons and breaking curses.

He said, *"The Spirit of the Lord is on me, because he has anointed me to preach good news to the poor. He has sent me to proclaim freedom for the prisoners and recovery of sight for the blind, to release the oppressed, to proclaim the year of the Lord's favor"* (Lk. 4:18-19).

A WITCH IS SET FREE

I was just 17 years old when the Lord began to teach me how to cast out demons. Although I was raised in a Bible-believing church, I had never heard a message on deliverance. My family and I were scheduled to visit my grandfather, Derek Prince, in Florida, but just before the visit, I had a powerful experience.

Grandpa had been in Africa and England while I was growing up, so I did not know what his ministry was all about. I was scheduled to preach at our Sunday night church service in Toronto, Canada. Once a month, the youth of the church led the Sunday night meeting, and I was the youth leader. A few nights before the meeting, I had a dream.

In the dream, I was walking along a hallway towards a large hall where a powerful church meeting was in progress. Suddenly, a dozen creatures that looked like monkeys with cat's faces were all around me. They were poking at me and trying to pinch me. I was pushing them away. I escaped their harassment as I entered the doors of the great meeting hall. Thousands of people were in front of me worshipping God, but a couple of the tormenting demons had managed to come into the meeting room with me. I quickly opened the door, looked at the evil spirits and said, "Get out, in the name of Jesus!"

They did not budge. I repeated the command three times, each time with more authority and finally, they left. I closed the door and woke up. That was my introduction to the subject, my first lesson on deliverance in the school of the Holy Spirit. That Sunday night, I preached about demons and the authority that God gives us over them.

MINISTERING WITH DEREK AND LYDIA

A week later, I was in Florida visiting Grandpa Derek and Grandma Lydia Prince. We went to a church meeting, and that is where I first discovered that my grandfather had a powerful ministry of deliverance. At the end of the meeting, my cousin, Stephen Hedges, and I were busy casting out demons. To use a metaphor, I had been thrown into the deep end of the pool.

The next day, Stephen and I traveled north to Georgia to set up Grandpa's book table at the Tennessee/Georgia camp meetings. Powerful Bible teachers came from different parts of the country, and some came from other nations. Bob Mumford, Charles Simpson, Corrie Ten Boom and, of course, Derek Prince were just a few of the many leaders who were gathering for the event.

Stephen and I had finished setting things up and we stood in the hot Georgia sun watching as hundreds of people drove onto the campground. That's when I met a young lady named Vonda. She came over to talk with us. Vonda told us that she had come to give her testimony. She said she had been a witch and was painted black three times in the caves of Tennessee. Vonda used to carry a human skull in her purse. She said she had been delivered from demons but I, who had very little experience in these matters, felt that Vonda had not yet been set free from all her demons. I said, "Vonda, I think you still have some demons inside of you."

On the outside she was a beautiful looking person, but her spirit was full of darkness. The Holy Spirit gift of discernment was at work in me and although I had little training, the Lord had put me on a fast track for learning. From that moment on, Vonda met with me, followed me and confided in me. Within a day, she admitted that she was full of demons and unable to attend the meetings. She was full of fear and the demons would not let her go.

The speakers at the meetings began announcing the need for special prayer. They said that powerful forces of witchcraft were at work on the campground. Symbols of witches' hats, pentagrams, broken crosses and other touch point markers were being chalked on sidewalks and on the sides of buildings.

Of course, it was Vonda's work. She talked with me every day, and I did my best to encourage her to go to the meetings or to let me set up a meeting for deliverance with Grandpa Derek and Lydia. She could not or would not comply, but then on Wednesday night something unusual happened.

It was reported at the Thursday morning meeting: A lady chaperone had been asleep in the girls' dorm room where Vonda was staying. She woke up in the middle of the night and saw an evil spirit standing at the foot of Vonda's bed. Later, she described the demon as a man with long straight hair that hung halfway down his back. He was wearing a robe, the kind that you would have to pull over your head to put on.

The counselor sat up as the demon looked toward her. Then the counselor pointed her finger at the spirit and yelled, "In the name of Jesus, get the hell out of here!"

The demon shook violently and suddenly disappeared. Vonda looked toward the counselor then rolled over and went to sleep but the counselor stayed awake praying in tongues for the rest of the night.

The next day, Vonda met with me for a long talk. After the morning meeting, which she did not attend, we walked and talked for well over an hour. I told her that she could be free of these demons if she would obey the Lord. It was very hot in the Georgia sun, and I remember sitting down on the grass by the lake. After a while we stopped talking and things got quiet. I laid back on the ground and put a towel that I had brought along, over my face.

Suddenly, a creepy, eerie feeling came over me. I pulled the towel away from my face and there was Vonda sitting beside me. With both hands, she was holding a sharp pointed stick over my stomach. When she saw my eyes, she immediately tossed the stick to one side and said, "I was just going to kill you."

I leaned back, covered my face with the towel and told her that she really needed to get help, now!

Later that afternoon, she did. She met with several of the Bible teachers, including Derek and Lydia. They prayed over her for three hours. She bit my grandfather's arm and they saw little results by the end of the deliverance session. During the ministry, Grandma Lydia asked Vonda to reveal more; she accused her of holding back important information. It was then that Vonda said that she had tried to kill a boy down by the lake earlier that day. When asked what the boy's name was, she replied, "Peter Wyns." Needless to say, my grandmother was mortified.

More than a thousand people came to the evening meeting, and as I entered, Grandma Lydia met me at the door. She grabbed my arm and pulled me to one side. "Peter," she said, "Keep away from that girl. She has so many demons that even your grandfather could not help her."

I went into the meeting, and Grandpa Derek preached a powerful message on "Being Set Free from Demons." Following the message, he gave instruction for ministry. He led us through prayers of repentance, rededication, forgiving others and renouncing witchcraft. Then, all over the room, people began praying for one another. Demons were coming out, en masse. I walked down to the front of the meeting room to see whom the Lord would have me pray for. I noticed little children talking with old men's voices. I heard the demons in one child say, "I am not leaving. This is my home and I am staying here."

The person praying rebuked the demons and they began coming out with much crying and screaming. All over the room people were vomiting, shaking and writhing on the floor as they were being set free.

I walked to the front of the stage, and there on the first row was Vonda. She looked like a terrorized child as she sat with her knees drawn up into her chest. She was staring straight ahead and to my surprise, her eyes were glowing yellow. I asked, "Vonda, do you want to be delivered?"

She gave no response but just stared straight ahead as if she was in some kind of trance. The room was so noisy and I thought that maybe she didn't hear me, so I leaned toward her and yelled, "Vonda, do you want to be delivered?"

Immediately, she flew out from her chair yelling, "Nooooooo!"

She came at me, snapping her teeth, clawing and scratching as she advanced. I was quickly backing up and deflecting her blows when Grandma Lydia grabbed my shoulder and pulled me away. With a finger pointed in my face, she said, "Peter, I told you to stay away from that girl."

About ten men descended on Vonda and held her to the ground as they began rebuking the evil spirits that were manifesting in her. I turned and looked up toward the stage and there was my grandfather sitting on a chair, looking at me and laughing. He was thrilled to see his grandson being trained in the ministry of Jesus.

Later in the week, a bonfire was lit for people to burn anything that was connected with witchcraft, just as they did in Bible days (Acts 19:19). Each individual told a testimony of their deliverance from demons. Then they threw tarot cards, snake jewelry, dragon amulets, rabbit's foot charms, inappropriate books and magazines, and anything they had with them that was connected with witchcraft, into the flames.

Vonda stood forward with a dress draped over her arms. She said, "This is the dress I used to worship Satan in."

She threw it on the fire with great cheers and rejoicing coming from the crowds. That week, she and hundreds of other people were set free from the tormenting power of evil spirits.

JESUS WE KNOW AND PAUL WE HAVE HEARD ABOUT

As the early church was formed, the apostles went all over the

the known world casting out demons.

"Philip went down to a city in Samaria and proclaimed the Christ there. [Samaria is in the heartland of Israel] ... **With shrieks, evil spirits came out of many, and many paralytics and cripples were healed.** *So there was great joy in that city"* (Acts 8:5,7-8 - emphasis mine).

Besides Philip, Paul was also very active in the deliverance ministry. Seven sons of a chief priest, named Sceva, were not living in the anointing of God's Holy Spirit, but tried to deliver a man from demons. A demon in the man yelled out, *"Jesus I know, and I know about Paul, but who are you?" Then the man who had the evil spirit jumped on them and overpowered them all. He gave them such a beating that they ran out of the house naked and bleeding"* (Acts 19:15-16).

The deliverance ministry is not learning a program, saying some powerful words, or adopting a pattern for setting people free. It is a life flow of God's power and authority moving in and through a minister. The sons of Sceva saw what the apostles were doing and they thought they could imitate them. Soon after, they were having a very rough experience with a violent demon. They thought they could cast out a demon without God's help.

The demons in the man knew who Jesus was, and they had heard about Paul. He had cast out so many demons that they talked about him until he became a household name among them. The demons in your area should know you and be afraid of you.

A FEW SUGGESTIONS

Those who desire to be used of God should minister deliverance to those who are demonized. If you need training, I suggest that you find a godly mentor whom you trust, and partner with them in the ministry. Derek Prince has a couple of good books on deliverance that give good instruction on the basics of deliverance. You may order them through Derek Prince Ministries.

When my wife and I minister deliverance, we do the following:

1.   We ask the Lord for His guidance and power to flow in us and through us.

2.   We always give thanks to God and acknowledge His Lordship in our lives.

3.   We lead a person who is receiving deliverance through prayers of salvation, repentance, forgiveness for others and rededication.

4.   We lead them through the renouncing of witchcraft and other evil activities.

5.   We break generational curses.

6.   We listen to the Holy Spirit throughout the ministry session as the Lord releases the gift of discernment in us. As we detect the presence of different demons, we rebuke them, cut them off, and command them to leave. It does not matter what the demons say or do; in Jesus' name we cast them out by commanding them to leave.

7.   We do not have long conversations with demons. They are

liars and like spoiled children, they love attention. Talking at length with demons is consulting with a familiar spirit - a practice forbidden by the Lord.

8.   We always have parents, or someone acting in the place of a parent, present when ministering to little children.

9.   After commanding demons to leave, we do all that the Lord tells us to do, but we refuse to have extensive deliverance sessions. The examples of deliverance given in the scriptures take no more than one hour. If God is not delivering a person from the demons, there are other steps that must be taken. The person may not be co-operating, or a key revelation is needed to unlock the prison door. We ask God for revelation, and if none comes, we leave the matter with Him.

10. Instruction should be given to help one keep their deliverance.

11. We follow all of the steps of ministry that we give in this book because deliverance is only one aspect of a person's ministry needs.

DO NOT BE AFRAID OF DEMONS

The more you minister deliverance, the less you will be afraid of demons. It is a good thing when demons cease to be a sensation to you. If you walk with God in the ministry, you will have authority over every evil spirit. Then they will become afraid of you. At first, it is normal to have a fear of the unknown and most of us are unfamiliar with the spirit world. I recommend, however, that you have only as much interaction with demons and witchcraft as you must. If you are a minister, you will have to deal with them, and casting them out is a privilege.

I encourage you not to have a deliverance ministry; just be a person who ministers deliverance. In other words, let your ministry focus be directed mainly on the good graces of Christ. I encourage you not to study witchcraft, even for ministry purposes. Your place is to resist, renounce, rebuke and remove any demonic attacks on your own life and to minister deliverance to those who come before you.

The ministry of deliverance will increase in the future. Like counseling or praying for the needy, deliverance will become a normal church activity in the days ahead. The spiritual tide is intensifying in the world, and battle lines are being sharpened. The spiritual darkness on the planet is already overwhelming, and it will become much worse. As we approach the end of the age and the great tribulation, God's people will rise up with amazing authority. As I write this book, I call out to God's people everywhere: "Get ready! You have a great and wonderful work to do! Pray and ask the Lord to teach and train you. Ask Him to use you in this powerful ministry of setting captives free."

Demons will be afraid; the finger of the Lord Jesus is pointing at them. God is moving on the earth with great power, the gifts of the Holy Spirit are increasing in the church, the people of God are responding to the call of heaven, the kingdom of God is growing rapidly on the planet and the King of kings is preparing for His return.

Chapter Thirty-one

HEALING THE BROKEN-HEARTED

HANDICAPPED PEOPLE

The seventh area of ministry that we focus on is healing the brokenhearted. Wounds or broken hearts can be much more painful or debilitating than broken bones or other physical ailments. Physically speaking, people may become handicapped due to traumas like a car accident, a stroke, a heart attack, an amputated limb or cancer. They may lose their energy, be unable to function normally, or be totally bed-ridden. Traumatic wounds to the heart can cause similar handicaps in someone's life.

More than half of the people we minister to have deep spiritual scars that, to a lesser or greater degree, hinder their vision for the future, their spiritual mobility, their ability to work with others, and their progress in the Lord. These people are handicapped.

Many live in turmoil and fear, and due to their inner pain, they have become numb or apathetic about life. They are dissolutioned, depressed, and often aimless. They may have little or no confidence, will tend to cast off restraint, become addicts, fall into temptation, or live a shallow life of loneliness and emptiness. They just exist from day to day, attending a pattern of maintenance rather than purpose.

Others may look at these downcast people and say, "What's wrong with that person? What happened to them? They just need to get over it."

This is not as easy as some would like to think. Our inability to forgive relational abuse, to release those who have hurt us, or to deal with hardship and pain will render us spiritually crippled. Whether the trauma is caused by others or by our own wrong choices or just because life has been unfair, the residual effects are the same. Unresolved spiritual issues and a lack of inner healing will leave us in a mess.

I encourage you to look over the following checklist to see if you carry the signs of a wounded spirit or a broken heart. A wounded heart stems from: sexual, verbal or physical abuse; severe rejection; abandonment; traumas; curses and judgments; continuous disappointment; unfulfilled expectations; unrelenting criticism; legalism; prolonged or unbearable hardships; being controlled by others; undesired isolation; guilt or shame due to sin; loneliness; self-hatred or hopelessness. A person with a broken heart has little joy, peace or faith, and they often lack the righteousness that comes from Christ alone.

They may serve others and outwardly be responsible people, but inside, a wounded person feels like a shattered glass plate. Living in this malaise will result in unbearable frustration, a deep seeded anger, and a massive debilitating sense of apathy.

DEPRESSION

It has been said that 'depression is not about pain but the absence of it'. To avoid the pain, a person may become detached from others, from the world around them, and even from themselves. They become spiritually numb. This can lead to self-hatred, disengagement with life, and even suicide. Evil spirits have a hay-day tormenting and aggravating those who are wounded or brokenhearted.

Even when these wounded people try not to dwell or think of life's disappointments, they are still numb. They walk around with a sense of disapproval on their lives. Many good Christians come to us for prayer because they have no joy and little peace. They love God and live right, but they know that something is deeply wrong. Often they are stoic, emotionless people who feel empty, trapped and forsaken. They may have a great family, a good church and no financial needs, yet they have no happiness. They need to be fixed, but they cannot find the answer. They are suffering from a wounded spirit.

New relationships, different activities, and motivational directives can help heal a wounded spirit to some degree, but complete healing can only come from the power of Christ. Only after they are healed can they discover their full destiny and purpose.

THE BANE OF CAIN

It is easy for us to criticize Adam's son, Cain. After all, he murdered his brother, Abel. God, nevertheless, still attended Cain. He relieved a measure of his judgment and pain, and it seems likely that Cain made it to heaven at the end of his life. His story of the first family is instructive for us today. Let's dig a bit deeper.

"The Lord looked with favor on Abel and his offering, but on Cain and his offering he did not look with favor. So Cain was very angry, and his face was downcast" (Gen. 4:5).

It is inferred that God told both Cain and Able that a lamb must be sacrificed. The lamb was the symbolic type of Christ. Cain ignored the directive and offered some of his homegrown vegetables instead. God was not pleased with Cain's offering, but He was with Abel's. Cain became angry and jealous because his brother found favor with God and he did not.

His own sin caused his rejection, and a chain reaction was set in motion. God told Cain to repent and do what was right, or things would get much worse. So many people are given this word of warning but often ignore it. Unfortunately, most problems become compounded when an individual fails to deal with it early in life. Problems in childhood can fester through the teen years and become a crippling wound in adulthood. It is like cancer; it can start small but mushroom into a larger tumor. In Cain's case, frustration turned to anger and anger turned to murder; Cain killed his brother. After that, things got much worse for Cain. It seemed that he had dug a hole that he could never get out of.

"The Lord said, 'What have you done? Listen! Your brother's blood cries out to me from the ground. [God is the judge and avenger of the innocent] ***Now you are under a curse*** *... When you work the ground, it will no longer yield its crops for you. You will be a restless wanderer on the earth.' Cain said to the Lord, 'My punishment is more than I can bear. Today you are driving me from the land, and I will be hidden from your presence; I will be a restless wanderer on the earth, and whoever finds me will kill me'"*
(Gen. 4:10-12 - emphasis mine).

Cain was cursed for shedding the blood of an innocent man. God judged Cain because he committed murder and that brought a five-fold punishment to him.

1. He was removed from his country.

2. He would not prosper economically (poor crops).

3. He would not be able to find God's presence.

4. He would be a restless wanderer.

5. People would try to kill him.

Cain was in a desperate situation, and it all began because he had a wounded spirit. Besides the pain of debilitating curses, he also feared for his life. This can happen with people like child abusers. When they are imprisoned, they fear for their lives because other inmates will try to kill them.

Cain cried out to God for mercy and God heard his cry. He put a mark on Cain so that he would be protected from those who wanted to kill him. Even in Cain's terrible situation, a measure of God's mercy was extended to him; he received a kind of protective custody.

MORE GRACE TODAY

Today, the power of the cross can remove the worst curses. It is not as though the removal of a curse is automatic for Christians, but when we meet God's conditions curses can be broken.

Healing a broken heart is just as important as breaking curses. No matter what has caused the wound, it must be healed. If it is not healed it will lead to other problems. Look at the following three-step pattern.

1. Cain did not give what the Lord asked and his offering was rejected by God.

2. Cain took on himself a victim mentality, and that always fosters a wounded spirit.

3. God spoke to Cain before he committed his curse-causing sin. Listen to the warning the Lord gave him.

"Why are you angry? Why is your face downcast? If you do what is right, will you not be accepted? But if you do not do what is right, sin is crouching at your door; it desires to have you, but you must master it" (Gen. 4:6-7).

Essentially, God tells us to get our wounds healed before worse things happen. You cannot afford to live with unforgiveness, resentment, abuse or unresolved disappointment. Sin and demons are crouching at the door of a wounded heart, and they lead people to enormous trouble. Whether it is a crippling dysfunction or a temptation leading to a curse-causing sin, a wounded heart must be healed. This is a very serious matter and only Jesus is able to heal a broken heart.

HEALING THE BROKENHEARTED

Luke 4:18 is a scripture that we looked at earlier. It is a quote from Isaiah, and it speaks of healing the brokenhearted. Notice that healing the brokenhearted is connected with the ministry of deliverance and breaking curses. It is setting people free from dark prisons.

"The Spirit of the Sovereign Lord is on me, because the Lord has anointed me to preach good news to the poor. He has sent me to bind up the brokenhearted, to proclaim freedom for the captives and release from darkness for the prisoners" (Isa. 61:1)

The Lord will work through those who minister to bind up or bandage the brokenhearted. This is what my wife and I do when we minister healing to a person with a wounded spirit. First of all, we minister the gifts of the Holy Spirit, rededication and repentance, forgiving others, the breaking of curses and deliverance. Then, as the Holy Spirit leads, we begin to bind up the brokenhearted.

As we begin this ministry, most people will begin to cry. Some will sob and others will weep profusely. We know that it is the love and kindness of the Lord that opens the soul and tenderizes the toughest chambers of the inner man. We lay our hands on the person who is receiving ministry, and we speak the following things over them:

1. In the name of Jesus, we pull the arrows and knives out of their backs. This includes removing judgmental words, curses, accusations, abuses, abandonments, betrayals, unbearable burdens, guilt, shame and all kinds of poisonous wounds.

2. We take the unbearable burdens and by faith we give them all to God.

3. We verbally open up all of the doors inside of their hearts, including doors that were slammed shut at childhood. In the spirit, we open the secret closets, basement doors, and cupboards of all

sizes. This is a moment of great vulnerability and it may be painful for some.

4. Then we ask the Lord to wash all of the rooms inside of them. Spiritually speaking, we wash their feet. We welcome the wind of the Holy Spirit and the river of God to blow through and flush the deep places in the person's life. Darkness cannot stay as the love of the Lord moves within them. It is displaced by the powerful presence of God.

5. Then we ask the Lord to pour in the healing oil of the Holy Spirit and to bind up or bandage the brokenhearted.

6. By this time, a person may be bent over or be lying on the floor. We instruct them not to get up until God tells them to get up. God is operating on them and they should not get up from the operating table until the operation is complete.

7. We will often kneel beside them and continue to speak the love of God over them. The Lord will cut away layers and layers of scar tissue and wounds. He will mend, heal and refresh. Often, before He is finished, He will speak to them or show Himself to them. This brings a change of atmosphere and attitude to the one being healed. They will never forget this powerful healing encounter. They will never be the same again.

This is not the end of what God plans for them. It is, however, a new beginning. There are still three other dynamics of the ministry that we extend to those we pray for. We will do as much as we can in the time we have, and God knows what can be accomplished during this spiritual visitation. He loves people, and we love people as well.

We pray that all who read this book will move in the power of God's grace and see fabulous change come to all they minister to.

Those who minister in this capacity will receive special blessings from the Lord. They will be drawn into an inner circle with Him. They will become partners with heaven and co-workers with God. Their personal lives will shoot forward, and they will start to know the permanent presence of the Lord. Those who minister healing will find that their walk and partnership with God will move to a much higher level.

Chapter Thirty-two

HEALING THE SICK

JESUS FACED SKEPTCISM

The eighth dynamic for ministry is physical healings. Every Bible student knows that Jesus went everywhere healing the sick. In some places, every sick person was healed, and in others, such as his home town or at the pool of Bethesda, only a few were healed because of skepticism. The people did not have enough faith.

The results of a physical healing can be seen, and that puts it into a different category from other miracles. The outcome tells us if a person is cured or not; then judgments are made. Some believers will judge the person being prayed for; others will judge the minister. When we pray for physical healing, unbelievers might make a judgment regarding the reality and existence of God.

Sometimes physical healings happen gradually. Healing may come in stages, and then it is not so easy to judge. This happened when Jesus prayed for a blind man twice. After the first prayer, the man began to see, but his eyesight was blurred. After the second prayer he could see perfectly. Even in this case, the entire miracle did not take long.

Jesus faced a judgmental wall of unbelief when he was preaching around the Sea of Galilee. He had already preformed many notable miracles, and scores of Pharisees and teachers of the Jewish Law came from every village around the Galilee, as well as from Judea and Jerusalem.

The Bible says, *"And the power of the Lord was present for Him to heal the sick"* (Lk. 5:17).

It was there that Jesus was teaching in a house, and some men brought their friend for healing. They were carrying the paralytic on a cloth stretcher but could not get to Jesus because of the crowd. Finally, they took him up on the roof, removed some tiles and lowered the sick man into the room, right in front of Jesus.

"When Jesus saw their faith, he said, 'Friend, your sins are forgiven.' The Pharisees and the teachers of the law began thinking to themselves, 'Who is this fellow who speaks blasphemy? Who can forgive sins but God alone?' Jesus knew what they were thinking and asked, 'Why are you thinking these things in your hearts? Which is easier: to say, 'Your sins are forgiven,' or to say, 'Get up and walk?' But that you may know that the Son of man has authority on earth to forgive sins....' He said to the paralyzed man, 'I tell you, get up, take your mat and go home.' Immediately he stood up in front of them, took what he had been lying on and went home praising God. Everyone was amazed and gave praise to God. They were filled with awe and said, 'We have seen remarkable things today'"
(Lk. 5:20-26).

A CROWD GATHERS

This happens today. Wherever miracles abound, people travel from across the globe to see them. It happened in Toronto in the 1990's, then in Brownsville and now, even while I am writing this book, hundreds of thousands of people are flocking to Lakeland, Florida to see miracles.

At this time, it seems that the entire church is trying to judge the situation. Some judge the miracles to be true and the event to be godly. Others take the opposite posture, condemning the event as fraudulent or even demonic.

There is always a mixture when any minister speaks or prays. We see the person, and hopefully, we see the Lord as well. I do not focus on the style, the inconsistencies, or the minister's faults, but thank God for every bit of grace and power that comes from heaven. I cry out, "Let us see more miracles, Lord!"

We should not be surprised at the skepticism or the unbelief that we see, for even Jesus, the greatest of miracle workers, faced such opposition from the Pharisees and teachers of the law.

I ask all ministers, "What would you do if the Lord performed great miracles through you?"

You would become famous. You might not do everything right, and you would not please everyone in the body of Christ. It is important to judge every situation in order to approve those things that are from God, but let us err on the side of graciousness and faith rather than legalism and negative judgments.

TAKE THE RISKY ROAD

Expect miracles of physical healing to come more often. You will not experience them unless you step out in faith and pray for people. Perhaps you are afraid to pray in case nothing happens. Then you will be judged as lacking God's anointing and power. For a minister who represents God, that can be embarrassing. Due to a fear of failure, some ministers take the safe road. Rather than rebuke the sickness and command it to go, they pray, "Lord, if it is your will, please heal this person."

Jesus instructed His disciples to pray for the sick, therefore, it is the minister's place to pray with faith and expectancy, and it is God's business to do the healing. For the minister, this is an act of humility. It is done in the face of judgment because everyone present will see the results of your prayers. It is a time to die to ourselves and trust God again. Miracles will come if we continue to obey the Lord.

AN INCREASE OF MIRACLES

Jesus healed the blind, lame, diseased, epileptic, leper, paralytic, a woman with an issue of blood, and many other people who suffered from various ailments.

He told His disciples, *"I tell you the truth, anyone who has faith in me will do what I have been doing. He will do even greater things than these, because I am going to my Father"* (Jn. 14:12).

A flow of healing miracles began to emerge in the ministry of the disciples. After Jesus rose from the dead, they even did things that seemed greater than what Jesus did. Notice the following verses:

*"The apostles performed many miraculous signs and won-
ders among the people. ... Crowds gathered also from towns
around Jerusalem, bringing their sick and those tormented
by evil spirits, and all of them were healed"* (Acts 5:12,16).

*"As a result, people brought the sick into the streets and
laid them on beds and mats so that at least Peter's shadow might fall on some of them as he passed by"* (Acts 5:15).

*"God did extraordinary miracles through Paul, so that even
handkerchiefs and aprons that had touched him were taken to the
sick, and their illnesses were cured and the evil spirits left them"*
(Acts 19:11-12).

As with Jesus, on some occasions, the apostles saw every sick
person, healed. People were healed as they were touched by Peter's
shadow. Some were healed as handkerchiefs or aprons, that Paul
had touched, were laid on them. These were called extraordinary
miracles. They happened in the early church, and we will see them
happen at the end of the age. Jesus told us that greater miracles
would be coming. Get ready. Step out in faith!

CANCER HEALED

We have seen so many miracles of physical healings, and we are
continually hearing of more. When we return to a church after a
previous ministry time, we will often have someone approach us to
give us a report of a miracle that happened after our first time of
prayer with them.

In the early days of our ministry in Canada we saw many miracles. On one occasion, a 25-year-old friend in the church named Bob

(not his real name) found out that he had cancer. This was discovered while I was three thousand miles away, ministering at another church. By the time we arrived home Bob had received an emergency operation; the doctors cut off his leg.

Three months later, they x-rayed his lungs and discovered many black spots. His body was filled with cancer. They cut open his back, scraped out his lungs, and in essence, they sent him home to die. The doctors told the family that he would most likely die within six months.

Some members of the church met with us to pray for him. About fifty people gathered around Bob and his wife and fervently worshipped the Lord for almost an hour. Our worship team led us and we sang songs that only focused on exalting the Lord. Then all of us faced Bob and began to pray extemporaneously. Some broke curses, others pleaded with the Lord, some rebuked the sickness, some prophesied and others spoke the word of healing over him.

In the days that followed, Bob refused chemotherapy. He changed his diet and took a natural holistic approach to medicine. Later, when Bob went to the doctor they could find no trace of cancer in his body. I am not advocating one type of medicine over another, but what happened to Bob was a miracle.

Bob was miraculously healed. More than twenty years have passed since the day we prayed over him, and Bob is still in good health. He has no signs of reoccurring cancer in his body. We praise God for all that He has done.

HE WAS BRAIN DEAD

My wife Joy and I led "Intercessors for Canada" (a national prayer movement) for many years. During that time, the Lord gave Joy many prayer initiatives that we inspired Canadians to participate in. One such initiative was prayer driving.

We gathered with members of several different churches, filling many cars with prayer warriors. Each car was given an envelope with different prayer instructions. A car load of people would drive to City Hall, and as they did they would pray for the mayor and city workers. Then they would drive to the police station and pray for the officers. They would go to the high school, the mall, the business district, and the hospital. Specific prayers were lifted spontaneously for each venue along the prayer driving route.

I was driving a van with seven people in it. We had picked up Sue (not her real name) on route. She remained quiet until we arrived in front of the hospital. Suddenly, Sue spoke up. She told us that last night, her teenaged cousin had been in a terrible car accident. He was still alive but was being sustained only by life support systems. The brain monitor showed no brainwaves, and the doctors told Sue's aunt that her son was brain dead. The doctors had recommended that the aunt give them permission to pull the plug in the morning and let him die.

Sue asked if we would pray that the Lord would comfort her aunt and give her the courage to let the doctors pull the plug in the morning. We began to pray, but one brother was not happy with the request. He began to pray for a complete healing. Soon everyone in the van was united with him in fervent prayer.

The next day, Sue phoned me. She was crying. The doctors had removed all of the life support systems from her cousin. Her tears were not caused by grief but happiness. Her cousin was alive without the assistance of the machines. God had healed a man who was brain dead.

Sue's aunt and cousin were not believers, and they lived in another city, far from where we were, but God performed a miracle. God healed the cousin because seven people in a van prayed the prayer of faith. We give God all of the glory!

HEALING HANDS

Healing the sick is one of the nine gifts of the Holy Spirit (see 1 Corinthians 12). The gifts of healing are given to God's people so that all may be blessed by them. Mark chapter 16, verse 18 tells us that healing the sick can be accomplished by all who believe. Specifically, church elders have been given an anointing to heal the sick.

We read, *"Is any one of you sick? He should call the elders of the church to pray over him and anoint him with oil in the name of the Lord. And the prayer offered in faith will make the sick person well; the Lord will raise him up"* *(Jas. 5:14-15).*

Like Peter, who stepped out of the boat and walked on water, all of God's people must step out of their comfort zone (the boat) and walk in faith. Those who dare to partner with God will see His power. Miracles may come gradually or suddenly, but miracles will follow those who believe.

When my wife and I pray for physical healing, this is what we do:

1.   We ask the Lord for guidance and thank Him for His faithfulness.

2.   We cover the bases for repentance, forgiveness and rededication.

3.   We break generational and self-imposed curses.

4.   We renounce, rebuke and cast out demons.

5.   We speak healing over broken and wounded hearts.

6.   We lay our hands on the sick person and pray the prayers of faith.

7.   We ask the Lord to heal all who are sick.

8.   We speak healing into the person's body. At this point of ministry, we do not ask. Instead, we speak boldly and command healing to come. The Lord gives His disciples this authority.

9.   We encourage the person to remain in the presence of the Lord as He operates on them.

10. We praise the Lord and give Him glory and thanks for all that He has done.

THE PRACTICE OF HEALING

Believers should have a practice of healing not unlike a doctor's practice. It should be a normal, even a daily, focus. All disciples are commissioned by God to minister to those in need. They are called to heal the sick and cast out demons. I recommend that every person who reads this book attend a church or participate in a ministry that believes in the supernatural power of miracles. Each of us should be joined with the family of faith. We should be connected to friends who expect to see God's power.

Pray to the Lord in the secret place. Then ask the Lord to open doors of opportunity to pray over people. Pray for powerful miracles of healing. Then get ready; obey the Holy Spirit when He inspires you to step out and minister to people. The book of Acts (the Acts of the Apostles) could be called the Actions of the Apostles. May the Lord Jesus move all of us from the place of thinking to the place of doing. Once you cross over into a life of action, every part of your Christian experience will become real. As you go, God will go with you.

Let me pray over you. If you are sitting, will you open your hand and place it face up, on your lap? Now, with a heart full of faith, will you read out loud the following words as I speak them over you?

"Lord, I ask that all who are reading this book would be empowered by your Holy Spirit. I ask that even now they would experience an increase of faith and courage. I ask that the power of God would flow through their hands so that extraordinary miracles, signs and wonders would follow. I ask that doors of opportunity would open before them that they might be able ministers of Your glorious gospel. I pray this for God's glory, in Jesus' name. Amen!"

Chapter Thirty-three

RESTORING DIGNITY

A CAVERN OR A FLOWERBED

The ninth dynamic for ministry is giving people honor and dignity. Some people have never known the tender love, approbation, and acknowledgment of fathers, mothers, grandparents, aunts, uncles, teachers or pastors. It has been said that it takes a village to raise a child, but some children have not had so much as a caring father. No one with authority in their lives has ever told them that they were wonderfully made or that they are wonderful. The lack of words like these, and the absence of heartfelt love and acceptance has left a gaping hole inside of them, and the hole is totally empty.

Neglecting to give approbation to your child is a type of verbal abuse. It will produce a deep darkness inside of them. The darkness will develop a life of its own. It will eat away at them and grow more cavernous with each passing season. Neglected children feel like aimless wanderers abandoned in a desert. They have been set adrift on a lonely sea of sand. Each day, they bear the scorching heat, the howling wind, and the dryness of an empty life. Many feel that their life is a kind of punishment; they feel worthless, directionless, rejected, and forsaken.

It is God's design for the acceptance hole in every person to be filled with love from one's parents. Love should then be added from family members, church leaders and a community of caring people. When a child is embraced, the hole is not a hole at all; it is a fertile flowerbed filled with learning, laughter and love. Then it is natural for God's love to come and fill the soul. When those who carry authority in a child's life affirm them, the door is open wide for God's amazing love to rush in.

When the foundation of human love and approbation is missing, a soul is scarred and wounded. They will inevitably have a closed spirit. They will find it difficult to trust and love other people, even though that is what they desire more than anything else. Trust and love involves vulnerability, but that is an opportunity for pain. It can open the door for more rejection, loneliness and the terror of increased emptiness.

If a person has been physically, sexually, or verbally abused in any way, the door to their heart will be shut even tighter. It will be fastened down with heavier bolts. It is hard for that soul to hear God's voice.

WONDERFULLY MADE

At a young age, children should know what the Bible has to say about them. They should learn the truth.

They should be able to say, *"For you created my inmost being; you knit me together in my mother's womb. I praise you because I am fearfully and wonderfully made; your works are wonderful, I know that full well. My frame was not hidden from you when I was made in the secret place…. your eyes saw my unformed body. All the days or-dained for me were written in your book before one of them came to be. How precious to me are your thoughts, O God!"* (Ps. 139:13-15,16-17).

Every child, regardless of ethnicity, culture or religion, is made in the image of God. They are fearfully and wonderfully designed by the Lord. No one is an accident or a mistake. On the contrary, they have been made with more potential than any other created be-ing. Every person has a call of greatness on their lives, and it is their God-given destiny to discover that greatness. A minister of the gospel is called to bind up the brokenhearted and reconcile people to God. This is bringing people to dignity so they may discover their destiny.

God's word teaches us that we have been created for dignity and nobility. We are priests and kings before the Lord.

We read, *"you also, like living stones, are being built into a spirit-ual house to be a holy priesthood"* (1 Pe. 2:5).

And, *"[Jesus] has freed us from our sins by his blood, and has made us to be a kingdom and priests"* (Rev. 1:5-6).

And, *"Blessed and holy are those who have part in the first resur-rection … they will be priests of God and of Christ and will reign with him for a thousand years"* (Rev. 20:6).

Those who believe in Jesus are called sons and daughters of the Living God. He is the King of kings, and that makes His children princes and princesses. We are part of a royal family destined to rule and reign with Christ.

DIGNITY IS ESSENTIAL

Dignity and nobility are essential requirements for human fulfillment and completion. Anything less than nobility leaves a soul de-
praved and lacking. Dignity is the inalienable privilege and right of
every human being, but it will be realized only by those who walk
with God. There are only two kinds of people who will possess dignity: those who know God and walk with Him, and those who do not
know Him but want to. They will spend their lives searching for Him.

People from both camps may need the help of a minister. An
anointed minister can speak God's love and release dignity. Even
when the parental foundation of human approbation is missing, God will often circumnavigate the dark hole. With the help
of ministers, He will open locked doors and fill the empty heart
with His acceptance and love. There are millions of needy people
who have come to Christ and His team for approbation and love.

FROM CURSES TO DIGNITY

I am reminded of a young man named Todd (not his real name)
who came into our lives when I was twenty-five years old. He
showed up with his family at the church I was pastoring. He was
seventeen years of age and six foot, six inches tall, but he had a
serious inferiority complex. When I shook his hand he turned his
head to one side because he could not look at me. His greeting was
muffled and almost non-existent. He was a believer and was raised

in a Christian family, but he had a hole inside of him that was larger than his lanky body.

After attending our church for several weeks, Todd met with me. His heart and soul were so tightly shut that he could hardly talk. He liked the church, and he and his family agreed that he needed to move away from home and get a job in town. After some prayer, Joy and I invited him to live in our home so we could help him become a better disciple of Christ.

Todd had poor hygiene, no communication skills and very little self-worth. We accepted him, befriended him, and even our young children extended the love of God to him. We treated him as part of our family. We went on many walks together, and I asked him many questions, but it was like pulling a dead tree up out of a river with a thin rope; the progress was slow and difficult.

In time, Todd told me about his life at home. His father was a very angry man, and the entire family was frightened of him. They lived on a dirt road in the country. If a car drove past too quickly it would stir up a cloud of dust. His dad would run to the window waving his fist in the air. He would yell and scream as he glared out through the window, even though the car was long gone and it was impossible for the driver to hear him. This story was just one of several that I managed to pry out of Todd's painful memory.

One day, Todd told me how he reacted to his father's anger. Rather than witness his father's violent behavior, every day after school, Todd would retreat to his bedroom. He spent most of his time lying on his bed, listening to rock music through headphones. He told me that he refused to become like his father, so he alienated himself from him.

Todd did not escape his father as he thought he had; he only inter-
nalized his father's anger. Instead of volcanic anger, he developed
a frozen anger, and it was bubbling up inside of him with nowhere
to go. He felt so worthless and dejected that he was depressed and
had no motivation for life.

   Soon, he did not want to go to church, but I insisted that if he
lived in our home he would attend. One Sunday morning, after fin-
ishing my sermon preparations, I discovered that Todd was still in
bed. Joy told me that he was not sick but he refused to rise and get
ready for church. I went into his room and told him he had to get
up and come with us. He refused, so I ripped the covers off of Him.
He just curled up into a fetal position, so I lifted the mattress and
turned it upside down. He still refused to budge, so I went to the
kitchen and brought in a glass of water. I told him that I would pour
the water on him, and if that didn't work, I would return with a full
bucket of water. As I started to pour the water over him, he bolted
to his feet and got ready for church. Of course, God met him there.

   Little by little, Todd gained bits and pieces of his dignity. He began
to talk freely and his spirit opened up to receive more of God's love.
He gained some confidence and became a very likable person but
he was not yet free from his ancestral baggage. As a minister and a
friend, I wish I knew then what I know now about breaking curses.
I am sure that his progress would have come much more quickly
and some awful traumas could have been avoided.

   There were many curses on Todd's family. I am not sure of their
roots, but he inherited them. One day while visiting his home, Todd
had a terrible motorcycle accident. He rode the bike out on the
dirt road, lost control, and hit a pedestrian. The man he hit was severely hurt and had to have his spleen removed. Todd was sued for

hundreds of thousands of dollars. A pattern of trauma followed him for years. In time, he married, but soon after, he contracted cancer, and later, his first born child died of cancer while she was still a young girl.

Todd suffered so much pain and, even today, I am amazed when I think of the healing that came to such a wounded man. It was a long process, but with lots of ministry, love and approbation and the eventual breaking of generational curses, Todd was healed of a wounded spirit and a broken heart. In time, he was set free from his spiritual prisons as well.

Like in the case of Lot, God began to restore life for all of the years of loss that he suffered. Today, he carries the dignity and grace of a prince. When I last saw him, he was a leader in the church and an example of kindness and compassion. All who know him love him.

WHAT WE DO

Often, my wife and I minister to a long line of people who have responded to an altar call following a time of preaching. We also pray for individuals by special request, however, we find that ministry is more effective after we preach. Increased understanding, faith and the power of God are present when we preach, and that opens hearts that might otherwise remain closed.

As we stand before a person for ministry, we have an immediate sense of their needs and the condition of their lives. Taking hold of their hands, asking for their names and hearing a one-word prayer request becomes a moment of connection that the Holy Spirit uses to release a huge amount of information to us. Usually we know of sins, curses, wounds, deceptions and demonic strongholds that are inside or hanging over the person who is standing before us. We know these things by the Spirit even though the person requesting prayer has not told us any details.

No matter how bad the situation is, it does not matter to us; we have come in the name of the Lord to bring good news. We plan to bring godly change. Inevitably, we have a deep love for the person in front of us, and the more pain we feel, the more compassion and care we have for them.

A pure heart is especially wonderful and easy to minister to, while a twisted heart demands a much slower approach. A wounded person will receive healing quickly, but sometimes we face willful rebellion, secret deception, and dark perversions. Those spirits are filthy, and I feel like I need a shower after praying for some people. Even then, we seek God's grace and ask for his mercy. We do not uncover a person's sins. We are there to bring people to dignity not more shame.

I lead many people through prayers of rededication. Even when I know that some are cynical and a few are not serious, I have faith that God will show up because of the words they are speaking. I expect great things to happen in those who have come, especially when they have come with a genuine hunger for God. We find that so many people have little or no dignity. This must be restored if they are to find stability, wholeness, and the purpose of God for their lives.

Sometimes we begin ministering dignity before we do anything else. Other times, the Lord leads us to speak dignity into a person's life at the conclusion of our ministry time with them. Almost always, we see a well of tears erupt from the depths of a wounded soul as we restore dignity to them. If these doors of dignity are not cracked open, a person may have insufficient faith to move forward or to receive any healing or purpose in their lives.

We will often do the following:

1. We thank God for the day they were conceived in their mother's womb.

2. We thank God for making them just the way they are.

3. We thank God for their journey and His faithfulness in their lives.

4. We thank God for protecting them and watching over them along the way.

5. Often, we detect that the person before us has been a Christian for many years, so we speak honor and blessings over them for their outstanding walk of service.

6. We break curses and renounce the spirit of depression, heaviness and self-rejection.

7. We lead them through a pray of forgiveness toward those who have abandoned, neglected or abused them.

8. We pull arrows of judgments and abuse out of their backs.

9. As if we are removing a coat off of their backs, we take off a garment of shame, guilt and failure, and we put on them the

spiritual garments of nobility and honor.

10.   Sometimes I take them by the hand and lead them out of the
        spiritual prison they have been trapped in.

11.   We speak acceptance, approbation and approval into their
        lives. We tell them they are beautiful, wonderful and extraordi-
        nary. These are the things their father should have spoken over
        them. Now their Heavenly Father is speaking these things to
        them, through us.

12.   We bless them with the goodness and the kindness of the Lord.
        In just a few moments, we try to pour a whole bucket of
        God's love upon them.

13.   We remove the old assignments off of them and speak God's
        favor into their lives.

14.   We anoint them with the oil of gladness and confidence in the
        Lord.

15.   Sometimes we hug them, and then we ask someone to stay
        with them and pray gently over them as they soak in the love
        of the Lord.

PHYSICAL CHANGE

A powerful physical change usually comes as we pray and speak
these blessings over people. At first they are broken by the sheer
magnitude of God's love. Before now, most have felt undeserving
of His grace, and when it comes upon them, it comes like the waters
from a bursting dam. They are emotionally overwhelmed. Tears of

joy begin to flow, and healing comes to the inner man. This may continue for an hour, during which time they may be lying on the floor while we are off praying for someone else. The Holy Spirit is doing the work. Soon, a very real heaviness lifts off of their shoulders. Shame and unbearable guilt is taken from them, and they come out of a spiritual prison and into the bright light of God's glorious day. Sometimes they begin to laugh because they have never felt such lightness and freedom since they were young children. It all happens in a few minutes and we are amazed at the awesome power of God's love and grace, once again.

Chapter Thirty-four

CONNECTING WITH DESTINY

THE HIGH CALLING

We have come to our final ministry dynamic: leading people to destiny. Christianity is not a long list of rules that must be obeyed. It is not about evil things we cannot do, but about a life with God that leads to extraordinary things we can do. Ministers of the gospel must do more than warn about worldliness, separation from sin, and making wrong choices. Their focus should not be set on the negative but on the positive. They must show the pathway to life, impart the anointing of God, and help equip people for purpose. A minister must bring good news, which is Christ in us, the hope of glory. The goal of Christianity is leaving an old life of ruin to discover an amazing new life of blessings.

Paul said it like this: *"I press on to take hold of that for which Christ Jesus took hold of me ... one thing I do: Forgetting what is behind and straining toward what is ahead, I press on toward the goal to win the prize for which God has called me heavenward in Christ Jesus"* (Php. 3:12,13-14).

Every person has a heavenly assignment designed just for them. That is what we press towards. Finding who we are and what we were made for is a person's most important journey.

THE PROPHETIC TEMPLATE

Any person who creates a website works with a template. A template is a network of empty spaces that must be filled in. One box is for your company name, another for a photo, one for a description of your company and another for the services you offer.

Every created thing in the universe has a prophetic template. Angels, animals, planets, stars, and trees have a design that was given to them at creation. They have a prophetic template that will be filled in and completed. Human beings possess the greatest of all prophetic templates because they alone have been made in the image of God.

A person's prophetic template is their real identity. No one knows who you are. You do not know, your parents do not know, the person you are married to does not know; only God knows your true identity. Most people embrace an identity that is not who they are. It is usually an identity that is far inferior to their prophetic template. Walking down the path of intimacy with God and living in extreme faith is the only way to discover who you are.

FINDING YOUR NAMES

Jesus has many names, such as Lion of Judah, Lamb of God, Savior, Bright and Morning Star, and Messiah, to name only a few. Each of his names describe an aspect of His character and reveal some of the things He does. He even has a secret name that only He and the Father can know.

You also have many names; they describe who you are and what you are supposed to do. Your names describe your prophetic template. A study of scripture reveals the importance of names. Both Jesus and John (the Baptist) were given heaven-designed names. Their parents had to name them appropriately, for their names were announced by angels. Many Bible characters had their names changed because they had to receive their real identity. Names were changed from Abram to Abraham, Jacob to Israel, Simon to Peter, Saul to Paul and Joseph to Barnabas. Each new name was part of the individual's true identity.

The book of Revelation tells us that, one day, all those who walk with God will be given the name of their Heavenly Father, the name of the Lord Jesus, the name of the city of God, and a secret name that no one else can know. Between now and the receiving of those names, there are many God-inspired, personal names that each of us should discover. That is how we find our identity.

Parents, ourselves, friends, and even enemies, may give us names that are not part of our prophetic template. People have received derogatory names, empty names, nick-names, and some have even been named after false gods. Those names should be discarded and the names that God has assigned us should be discovered and adopted. Finding our prophetic template and finding all of our names, is a life-long pursuit.

Here are five things that will help us discover our prophetic names. I have included a Bible character as an example of each of them.

1.   The Lord gives us a new name when we walk as an intimate

friend with Him (Simon changed to Peter).

2. The Lord gives us a new name when we wrestle with God until He blesses us (Jacob changed to Israel).

3. We can receive a new name by being excellent in our service and gifting (Joseph changed to Barnabas).

4. The Lord gives us a new name when we are overcomers (new names given in the book of Revelation to those who overcome).

5. We can receive a new name through the hearing of faith (Mary received the name of her Son, Jesus, from an angel).

MINISTERING NAMES AND DIGNITY

God can reveal our names and our identity directly or indirectly. We may hear the on-going, upward-call through dreams, scriptures, an audible voice, an inner voice, or through a prophet, to name only a few of His channels.

As we hear our names, we discover our identity, and that is who we really are. Only then can we find our destiny and discover what we are supposed to do. I have many names that God has given to me, and each of them gives me direction, strength and dignity.

The minister of the gospel may be used by God to give a person a part of their prophetic template or some of their prophetic names. In India, I was led by God to change a person's name from that of a false god to John. Joy and I have spoken prophetic names over hundreds of people as part of our ministry to them.

WHAT WE DO

The ministry over a person is not complete until that person begins to embrace their destiny. I am not suggesting that all of this
can be accomplished at one time. Sanctification is a life-long experience and requires constant pursuit; nevertheless, an abundance
of spiritual things may happen in just a few moments of prayer and
ministry.

After ministering some or all of the nine dynamics that we have
described in this book, we finish our ministry time by helping
connect people with their destiny. This can only be done with the
anointing of the Holy Spirit. This is not an automatic procedure but
a release of God's timing and will in a person's life. The minister
must be led by the Holy Spirit and resist saying things that sound
good but are really not from God. Given these prerequisites, we
follow through with prayers, proclamations and prophetic words.

This is how we minister to people:

1. We pour dignity and honor into their lives.

2. We sweep the highway clean for new beginnings.

3. We put the train that has been derailed back on the tracks of
    God's destiny and purpose.

4. We speak an opening of the heavens, doors of opportunity and
    the purposes of God.

5. We speak prophetic names to them, but only as the Lord proph-
    esies through us.

6.   We speak directional words for the work of the ministry. We commission them to specific ministry assignments, but only as God releases those words to us.

7.   We release gifts of the Holy Spirit to them, including a release of the Spirit of revelation, the prophetic gift and powerful inter-cessory prayer to flow through them.

8.   We speak an opening to their spiritual ears and eyes.

9.   We tell them who they are and some of the things God has for their future.

10.   We give specific instructions that will help them walk in step with the word of God they have received.

11.   We speak financial abundance, relational blessings, health and long-life over them.

12.   We speak the wonderful year of God's favor over them.

We do not minister this prophetic anointing lightly or casually but in the fear of God. Wrong words can create unrealistic assumptions and lead a person astray. Like any aspect of ministry it must be exercised with bold faith in obedience to the Holy Spirit. Some blessings from God will not come unless someone prophesies. This is a very important part of the ministry.

A MINISTRY TRAINING WEEK

I recall the young Baptist brother who came to us for ministry and training. The prophetic words we spoke over him released him into the call of God for his life. We were conducting what we call a "Ministry Training Week." During the week, we preach several key messages each day. On two of the evenings we pray and minister over people following the preaching of the word. One of those sessions is for the breaking of generational curses and deliverance, and the other night is dedicated to commissioning people into the ministry.

The young brother whom I will call John (not his real name) was not in full-time ministry but desired to be. I did not know him or what he was seeking, but after praying for his spiritual freedom, I prophesied over him saying that he would be entering into a full-time ministry position. Within a week after arriving home, to his surprise, he was hired by his local church to the position of assistant pastor.

Next year, he returned to another "Ministry Training Week." Again, I prayed over him without any knowledge of his situation. To my surprise, I prophesied that the apostolic ministry was coming upon him. It was a shock to him, but when he arrived home his Baptist pastor released him and commissioned him as an apostle. This was unheard of for most Southern Baptist Churches.

He was still a paid staff member of the church but was released to discover and develop his apostolic gift. The prophetic commissioning he was released to through me was confirmed and further released through his home church.

After our ministry with him, God used John and his wife in the ministry. They began to break curses off of hundreds of Baptists who travelled across the country to their home church to get help. Baptist pastors who found a road block when ministering to people, were recommending John, a fellow Baptist pastor, who God was using with this special anointing. We prayed for John, but he prayed for hundreds of other people. They are people that we will probably never come in contact with.

As you help others find their destiny, God will help you find your own. May your journey be blessed as you find your names and complete your prophetic template. When you minister to others, give them vision. Ask the Lord to help them discover who they are and what they are called to do. Some levels of healing will only come as people find their destiny.

Chapter Thirty-five

YOUR CHANGING MINISTRY

THE PURPOSE OF MINISTRY

I trust, by now, that you are discovering the reason for your ministry. I call all ministers, pastors, evangelists and Christian workers to take hold of change. Our goal as ministers is to bring people to Jesus, and if someone has already come to Christ, our goal is to help them find their godly blessings and purpose.

We have studied the scripture in Luke 4:18-19. These verses describe this positive ministry approach. They give us a description of Jesus' ministry and a description of the ministry of those who would be His disciples.

We read, *"The Spirit of the Lord is on me, because he has anointed me to preach good news to the poor. He has sent me to proclaim freedom for the prisoners and recovery of sight for the blind, to release the oppressed, to proclaim the year of the Lord's favor"* (Lk. 4:18-19).

Jesus tells us the following details about His ministry:

1. Jesus and His ministers are anointed by the Holy Spirit **to preach good news to the poor.** (Good news is not guilt, manipulation, legalism or bad news; it brings a hope for what may seem impossible.)

2. Jesus and His ministers **have been sent from heaven** to bring blessings to people. That means it's God's plan to bless people.

3. Jesus and His ministers have been sent **to proclaim or speak freedom** over those who are trapped or imprisoned. There are many kinds of prisons that people are in, but Jesus announces freedom.

4. Jesus and His ministers have been sent **to open people's eyes** because they cannot see God's blessings or the path that they must take to enter into His purposes.

5. Jesus and His ministers have been sent **to release the oppressed.** First, He proclaims freedom. Then He opens the prison doors and sets people free from their bondages, their dungeons, their addictions and their demonic chains.

6. Jesus and His ministers have been sent **to proclaim or announce the year of God's favor.** He speaks success and blessings over those who have known failure and suffering. These blessings and favors are not just momentary; this is an announcement for positive change for an entire year. At the end of the year, the Lord will speak another year of His blessings and favor.

Jesus did not come as a cosmic policeman, a condemning despot, or a legalistic judge. He came as the reconciler of all who have missed the target and failed. He is the undisputed champion of way-ward people, the Savior of the world. He and His ministers reconcile people back to God. Besides bringing people to God, He reconciles people back to God's blessings.

If you are a minister you should take people by the hand and bring them to God's blessings. If they will not come, then bring God's blessings to them. If the connection between God's blessings and people is made, repentance and sanctification will follow. The kind-ness of God leads a man to repentance. Here is God's message to humanity.

*"All this is from God, who reconciled us to himself through Christ and gave us the ministry of reconciliation: that God was reconcil-ing the world to himself in Christ, **not counting men's sins against them.** And he has committed to us the message of reconciliation. We are therefore Christ's ambassadors, as though God were making his appeal through us. We implore you on Christ's behalf: Be rec-onciled to God. God made him who had no sin to be sin for us, so that in him we might become the righteousness of God"*
(2 Cor. 5:18-21 - emphasis mine).

Here is an essential revelation for ministers of the gospel. Average grace can come from any nice person, even if they are not Chris-tians. Ministers of Christ, however, extend a level of grace that is unreasonable. It reaches far beyond justice and human compassion; it is called agape love. This kind of ministry is painful for ministers because it leads them to embrace people who are extremely undeserv-ing. Some of these people are rebellious and unresponsive, and that makes the minister want to turn away. This is an opportunity for the awesome power of God's love to work. God's love believes all things, hopes all things, and endures all things; love never fails. This is the purpose of Christian ministry.

As your ministry changes, the lives of people who come before you will change radically. It is time to prepare the way of the Lord and prepare the way for people. They come together in the ministry of reconciliation.

PREPARING THE WAY FOR THE PEOPLE

Isaiah prophesied about this powerful ministry almost 2,700 years ago. The ministry description that he gave covers the dynamics that we have mentioned in this book. It is the upward call for all ministers of the gospel.

He said, *"Go through, Go through the gates! Prepare the way for the people; Build up, Build up the highway! Take out the stones. Raise a banner for the peoples!"* (Isa. 62:10, NKJV)

The chapters surrounding Isaiah 62 are about the glory of God coming on the Jewish people and on the people of the world who will embrace the Lord. They are about spiritual battles, promises being fulfilled, and the amazing plans of God being released on the earth. In the middle of this end-time prophecy comes powerful instruction for ministers.

1.   Ministers must go through the gates.

This requires a minister to overcome personal difficulties so that they can press through into God and receive His anointing and power. Disciples must deny themselves, renounce sin, completely dedicate their lives to serve Him, and walk in submission to the Holy Spirit so that He might teach them. They leave the status quo to walk with God. Salvation is free, but discipleship and godly purpose that leads one to destiny will cost everything. Whatever it costs, Isaiah says, "Press through the gates." The gates are doorways of destiny, designed by God for every person. Our task is to find them and go through them. Whatever it takes, do not turn back or quit. All rejection, church politics, personal failures, persecution, or demonic attacks are designed by the devil to make a minister quit. If you will go through your God given gates, God will continue to work in you and through you. Going through is a military term. It is time to fight. It is time to press through.

2. The next focus is to prepare the way for the people.

Our ministry is not about the minister, but about God's love for people. The first followers of Christ were called, "The People of the Way." They had found a new and living way into the holiest place, into God's throne room, into the presence of God. It is no longer the task of one High Priest to go through the curtain once a year to come into the presence of God. Now all who meet God's conditions can find the way and come into God's holy presence through the body and blood of Christ. The minister's task is to prepare the way for the people, to help them find their way and press through into God's presence to receive the goodness of God.

3. This requires building up the highway.

Although God calls everyone to Himself, many have no highway connecting them to God, and they cannot find or reach Him. Ministers are ambassadors for God, and their task is to build highways. Ministers are engineers and construction workers. They have been given building permits to build highways, and they have Holy Spirit training and special equipment to build the roads. They are reconcilers, bringing people and God together by the roads they build. This involves giving weary travelers identity, hope, vision, and dignity. It involves giving godly counsel and direction, and releasing God's manifold blessings over the lives of people. This is the highway that leads to deep inner healing, financial blessings and destiny.

4. As the highway is being built, the minister removes the stones that block the traveler from moving forward.

Ministers are not only builders, they are demolition experts. This means they break curses, pry open prison doors, destroy strongholds, remove judgments, smash addictions, minister deliverance, renounce sickness, and remove evil soul ties and wrong relationships. Removing the stones from the highway may also include displacing any form of false teaching which may be doctrines of demons or removing any ungodly or humanistic worldviews. Unless the demolition work is done, the traveler will have huge roadblocks that will hinder their progress. These roadblocks will hold them back from some of the blessings of God that otherwise would come to them.

5. Raising a banner for the people

This has a twofold application. First of all, this is a military flag. The banner goes before the armies of God as they take the land. The people rally around the flag and know that they are victorious as long as their banner is flying. Ministers release God's victorious glory as they blow the trumpet and sound the charge. They lead the people through the gates, along the kingdom highway, to the Source of all that is wonderful. They direct people into the blessings and purposes of God. The way a leader lives is also important; a godly example is a flag flown high for others to see. It encourages others to fight for what is right. The banner must be raised.

Secondly, the banner is a testimony of God's love and grace; it bears the Lord's insignia. The banner declares that our God reigns. Claiming the land for Christ, we take our stand and plant the flag. We declare that families, communities, nations, and the whole world belong to God! His ministers are overcomers; they claim victory for the people of God.

A MINISTER'S PRAYER OF DEDICATION

All believers should become disciples and all disciples should become ministers. Your destiny is to be a minister of the gospel. You may not be a paid staff member of a church, but you are called to a life of ministry.

I encourage all believers, disciples and ministers, paid or unpaid, to pray with me. I ask you to boldly knock on heaven's doors; to ask, seek, proclaim and prophesy the following prayer. Speak it forth with passion and proclaim it with a loud voice:

"Heavenly Father, I come to you in the name of Jesus, my Lord. He alone is the Messiah, the Christ, the ultimate Anointed One. Thank you, Jesus, for all you have done in my life and for all that you are doing with me, and thank you for all you will do in and through me in the future. I rededicate my life to you and ask you to forgive me of all of my sins.

My life is dedicated to the Lord Jesus, and I will have no God but the true and living God in my life. I worship you. Where you send me, I will go. What you tell me to do, I will do.

Lord, I ask now that your powerful anointing would come upon your servant for the work of the ministry. I ask you to show me my place as I partner with you in the ministry. I ask for wisdom, for the gifts of the Holy Spirit and for miraculous signs and wonders to accompany the ministry that I am called to. In the name of Jesus, I proclaim open doors of opportunity so that I may walk in your plan and purpose for my life.

I declare and prophesy the word of the Lord in faith. I go through the gates of my destiny. I prepare the way for the people. I build up the highway of grace and provision for your people. I remove the hindering stones that block the spiritual journeys of your people. I raise your banner high for the nations to see.

I am a minister of the gospel, and I step forward as an ambassador of the Lord. By God's grace I am ready to bring blessings. The Spirit of the Lord is upon me. He has anointed me and I come to bring godly change to the lives of people from this day forward. This is the word of the Lord, and I speak it forth, in Jesus' name. Amen!"

All that you need has been given to you in the seed that God put within you when you were saved. As the seed grows, all of His grace will be discovered, one piece at a time. He will teach you how to work with His people. He will sanctify and separate you for service. He will train you by using many people, events and spiritual encounters. He will orchestrate life for you. He will equip you with weapons of authority and power as you step out in faith. He will bless you by opening the windows of heaven over you and by opening the doors of purpose before you. Whatever He leads you to do, whether small or large, do it as unto the Lord, with all of your might.

It is time. Go forth in the name of the Lord your God and the Lord will go with you. The Kingdom of God is righteousness, peace and joy. So as you walk with God and bless people, be sure that you embrace peace and revel in the joy of the Lord. Let the adventure begin!

Fighting Death

Dr. Peter Wyns

If you are facing a dark battle for life or staring at hopeless impossibilities, this story is for you. From a certain death tragedy comes unbelievable recovery. From hopeless diagnosis comes a report so incredible that everyone fighting for life should read it. Too many give up without fighting, often because they lack the knowledge of how to win. Against all odds, Clarice Holden, armed with faith, fought a battle and saved the life of her husband. She would not go into the night quietly. Neither should you.

Great Reward Publishing
PO Box 36324
Rock Hill, SC 29732

Great Reward Publishing

Christians for Messiah Ministries
www.peterwyns.org
www.unexpectedfire.com
e-mail: ReachUs@peterwyns.com

Unexpected Fire

Dr. Peter Wyns

Finally it is here, a teaching on the book of Revelation that makes sense from start to finish. For students of end-time studies, this book will bring a truck load of new understanding. It challenges popular beliefs with amazing details backed up by hundreds of scriptures. This thrilling study will inspire and embolden every believer who is longing to see the church's finest hour. You will not want to put this book down until you pass it on as a precious treasure to someone else.

Great Reward Publishing
PO Box 36324
Rock Hill, SC 29732

Great Reward Publishing

Christians for Messiah Ministries
www.peterwyns.org
www.unexpectedfire.com
e-mail: ReachUs@peterwyns.com

Chronicles of Righteousness Vol. 1

Dr. Peter Wyns

In 2005, Dr. Peter Wyns began producing a new series of special teaching letters called Instructions in Righteousness. Right from the very start, reports and testimonies came to us with words of thanksgiving and gratitude. We have compiled the first 50 teachings of Instructions in Righteousness in this beautiful special edition book. This book is designed with a genuine bonded leather cover and gold edging. It is a Special Limited Edition with only 500 copies printed.

Great Reward Publishing
PO Box 36324
Rock Hill, SC 29732

Great Reward Publishing

Christians for Messiah Ministries
www.peterwyns.org
www.unexpectedfire.com
e-mail: ReachUs@peterwyns.com